The Art of
Cooking for Two

Coralie Castle   Astrid Newton

Illustrations by Sara Raffetto

101 Productions
San Francisco

Third Printing, November, 1977

Copyright © 1976 Coralie Castle and Astrid Newton
Drawings copyright © 1976 Sara Raffetto

Printed in the United States of America
All rights reserved

Published by 101 Productions
834 Mission Street, San Francisco, California 94103

Distributed to the book trade in the United States by
Charles Scribner's Sons, New York

Library of Congress Cataloging in Publication Data

Castle, Coralie.
    The art of cooking for two.

    Includes index.
    1. Cookery.   I. Newton, Astrid, joint author.
II. Title.
TX652.C38   641.5'61   76-6892
ISBN O-912238-77-1
ISBN O-912238-76-3 pbk.

Contents

Preface

This book is designed for both the beginning and the experienced cook who must deal with the problem of cooking for just two persons. We have tried to concentrate on low-cost food items, to stress the importance of avoiding waste and to instill a concern for healthful eating by eliminating, wherever possible, convenience and processed foods which contain preservatives and chemical additives.

For the beginning cook we have included general cooking hints, basic recipes and serving suggestions, plus all of the essential information for making a wide variety of dishes. For the experienced cook we have endeavored to introduce enough new ideas to make cooking for two both interesting and challenging. Assuming that in many cases, both members of a household of two are working full time, we have given many recipes which can be prepared in advance such as soups, stews and casseroles, plus quick one-pot meals and some dishes of four servings, which may be reheated for a second meal. There are also ideas for using leftovers, to help overcome one of the greatest problems of cooking for two—spoilage and waste.

Many cookbooks for two attempt to solve the problem of waste, and that of time, by utilizing packaged and convenience foods. Unlike these books we emphasize the use of natural ingredients and eschew the use of chemically treated foods. The time that would be saved by using convenience foods is more than compensated for, we believe, by flavorful dishes, healthy, nutritious eating, and less expense.

Foods for breakfast, lunch and dinner, plus snacks, are included here with a de-emphasis on those courses that play a limited role in dining *à deux*—appetizers and desserts. We hope that mastering the art of cooking for two will be an imaginative and rewarding experience for our readers.

—Coralie Castle and
Astrid Newton
March 23, 1976

Appetizers
and Snacks

Appetizers and Snacks

HORS D'OEUVRE SUGGESTIONS

The following are suggestions for easy-to-prepare hors d'oeuvre. Expand these ideas, or create your own with what you have on hand.

• In 1/2 tablespoon butter, butter steam 1/2 cup diagonally cut celery. When just tender crisp, blend in 1/4 teaspoon anchovy paste and 2 teaspoons minced fresh tarragon. Serve with toothpicks in warmed small bowl.

• Combine equal amounts of liverwurst and soft butter with chopped black olives to taste. Spread on crackers.

• Marinate drained green olives 1 hour in garlic olive oil.

• Wrap cleaned raw shrimp (tails remaining) diagonally in 1 wonton skin. Deep fry in hot oil until golden and serve with soy sauce seasoned with sherry, sugar, minced garlic and minced ginger root to taste.

• Wrap water chestnuts, pitted prunes, halved raw chicken livers, pitted dates, raw shrimp, pitted ripe olives stuffed with sharp cheddar cheese, small mushroom caps or fresh figs in bacon cooked just to soften. Secure with toothpick and broil until bacon is crisp.

• Cut tortillas into bite-size pieces and crisp in oven. Cover liberally with grated sharp cheddar cheese and return to oven to melt cheese. Serve plain or with avocado dip.

• Sandwich Gorgonzola cheese between walnut halves.

• Stuff small celery stalks with Roquefort mixed to taste with brandy.

• Serve cubes of cooked ham with Aioli Sauce dip.

• Skewer cherry tomatoes and cooked sweetbreads. Baste with melted butter and broil.

• Marinate thinly sliced jicama or sunchokes in fresh lime juice and chill. Serve with toothpicks.

• Sprinkle thinly sliced young kohlrabi with lemon juice and Herb Salt. Chill.

• Fill raw mushroom caps brushed with fresh lemon juice with cream cheese softened with mayonnaise. Top with caviar and freshly grated lemon peel.

• Butter steam in Tamari soy sauce, minced ginger root and garlic and sherry, sliced giblets from chicken and season with Herb Salt. Serve with toothpicks.

• Marinate cubes of cream cheese in soy sauce and sprinkle with toasted sesame seeds. Serve as spread for crackers.

• Marinate raw cleaned shrimp in soy sauce, lemon juice, minced garlic, honey and minced ginger root. Broil and dip in toasted sesame seeds. Or dip in sesame seeds before broiling.

• Serve raw vegetables such as cauliflowerets, carrots, etc. with a dip of mayonnaise seasoned to taste with curry powder.

• Serve smoked oysters, sardines or anchovy fillets on crackers.

• Skewer apple chunks rubbed with lemon juice and cubes of any complementary cheese.

• Remove pulp from cherry tomatoes and stuff with sauerkraut or with any of the cream cheese ball or spread mixtures which follow. Sprinkle with paprika. Chill.

• Soften cream cheese with a little mayonnaise and soy sauce. Shape into balls and roll in grated unsweetened coconut.

• Soften cream cheese with a a little cream and mix with finely flaked tuna fish and finely minced celery. Shape into balls and roll in minced fresh parsley.

• Soften cream cheese with mayonnaise and mix in finely minced cooked shrimp and anchovy paste. Shape into balls and roll in minced chives.

FIRST COURSE SUGGESTIONS

The following are suggestions for at-the-table appetizers. Refer to the soup and salad chapters for additional first-course ideas.

• Fill avocado or papaya halves, pineapple wedges or cooked artichoke bottoms with Shrimp Salad. Garnish as for salad.
• Wrap melon wedges or fresh figs with prosciutto.
• Marinate cooked meat, finely slivered, in Vinaigrette Dressing and chill. Serve on lettuce leaves.
• Serve slices of lox and cream cheese on pumpernickel bread.
• Make several slices almost all the way through in small, ripe, cored tomatoes. Tuck between each slice a slice of hard-cooked egg. Top with mayonnaise and sprinkle with minced fresh parsley. Serve on butter lettuce leaf.
• Marinate sliced fresh mushrooms in Vinegar and Oil Dressing with minced fresh herbs, salt, white pepper and cayenne pepper to taste. Serve on small butter lettuce leaf.
• Serve raw oysters or clams, halved if large, sprinkled with fresh lemon or lime juice. Serve with Tabasco sauce or Chili Sauce on the side.
• Sauté shrimp or prawns in butter, minced garlic and white wine to taste. Serve sprinkled with minced fresh parsley.

GRILLED SANDWICH SUGGESTIONS

Butter outside of bread slices, place filling on unbuttered side, close and broil or grill, turning once, until golden on both sides.

• Rye bread, freshly ground lean beef mixed with grated onion, minced garlic, salt and pepper to taste, with or without thin slice of mild cheese.
• Rye or whole-wheat bread, Creamy Tuna Fish Spread or Shrimp Salad.
• Firm white, rye or whole-grain bread, minced raw mushrooms, salt, pepper, paprika, garlic powder and oregano to taste; mayonnaise to bind.
• Firm white, rye or whole-grain bread, mustard, thin slice ham, cheese and ripe tomato.
• Whole-grain bread, mango chutney, cheddar cheese slice.
• Rye bread, peanut butter, crisply cooked, finely minced slab bacon.
• Rye bread, mustard, liverwurst, thin slice Monterey Jack cheese.
• Whole-grain bread, sliced mushrooms lightly sautéed in butter, avocado slices, alfalfa sprouts.

CROQUE MONSIEUR

Spread lightly with:
Dijon-style mustard
2 thin slices firm white bread
Top with:
2 thin slices cooked ham or turkey
Cover each with:
2 thin slices firm white bread
Spread outside of bread with:
softened butter
Coat each side of sandwich evenly with:
2 to 3 tablespoons grated Gruyère cheese
In skillet melt over low heat:
1 tablespoon butter
Carefully place coated sandwich in butter and cook slowly to brown. Turn and brown other side, adding more butter if needed. Keep warm. Repeat with second sandwich.

Appetizers and Snacks

OPEN FACE SANDWICH SUGGESTIONS—COLD

Lightly butter bread, if desired, and layer ingredients in order given.

- Whole-wheat toast, mayonnaise, lettuce, Shrimp Salad with ripe tomato and avocado cubes, alfalfa sprouts, minced parsley.
- Rye or whole-grain toast, curry mayonnaise, thinly sliced turkey or chicken, thinly sliced radishes, minced green onion, salt, white pepper, paprika.
- Firm white or whole-grain toast, herb mayonnaise, shredded lettuce, thinly sliced turkey or chicken, avocado rings brushed with fresh lemon juice, Herb Salt, white pepper, paprika.
- Rye toast, mustard-mayonnaise, thin slice of ham, thin slice of Comté cheese, ripe tomato slice, minced fresh parsley.

- Whole-grain bread or toast, mayonnaise, lettuce leaf, slice of cooked tongue, slice of ripe tomato, crumbled crisp bacon.
- Rye or whole-grain bread or toast, mayonnaise, lettuce leaf, slice of chicken or turkey, slice of tomato, crumbled Gorgonzola cheese.
- Rye or pumpernickel bread, cream cheese, minced dill pickles or black olives.

OPEN FACE SANDWICHES—HOT

Toast bread on one side under broiler. Lightly butter untoasted side, if desired, layer ingredients in order given and bake in 475° oven or broil under medium-low heat.

- Whole-grain toast, cream cheese, chopped mango chutney, tuna salad, sprinkling of curry powder, fresh orange sections, small cubes of cream cheese. Bake or broil and garnish with grated lemon peel.
- Rye or whole-grain toast, herb mayonnaise, tomato slice, freshly scrambled eggs, grated cheddar or Monterey Jack cheese. Broil just to melt cheese. Sprinkle with minced fresh parsley, chervil, chives or watercress and paprika.

- Rye toast, German or Dijon-style mustard, liverwurst, sautéed onion rings, paprika. Bake or broil and garnish with minced fresh parsley.
- Toast rubbed with cut garlic clove, slice of Gouda cheese, tomato slice, minced basil or thyme.
- Toast, minced raw mushrooms, grated cheddar or Monterey Jack cheese, green bell pepper ring.
- English muffin, lean ground beef mixed with grated onion, minced garlic, grated cheddar or Monterey Jack cheese, Chili Sauce, salt and pepper. Broil until almost cooked to taste. Top with ripe tomato slice and thin slice of Teleme, cheddar or Monterey Jack cheese. Broil to melt cheese.
- English muffin, tomato slice, bay shrimp mixed with minced green bell pepper and green onion, cheddar cheese slice.

FILLING SUGGESTIONS FOR PITA (ARAB) BREAD, HEATED TORTILLAS, HALVED AND HEATED ROLLS

• Lamb and Veal Meatballs or tiny Shish Kebabs, minced fresh mint, minced garlic, chopped ripe tomatoes, minced hot chili peppers, yoghurt, shredded lettuce, diced avocado brushed with fresh lemon juice.

• Thinly sliced ripe tomato, bean or alfalfa sprouts, thinly sliced ham, chicken or turkey, avocado slices brushed with fresh lemon juice, sunflower seeds, cubes of cream cheese.

• Chile Con Carne, chopped ripe tomatoes, pine nuts, shredded lettuce or spinach leaves, grated cheddar or Monterey Jack cheese, yoghurt.

• Shredded cooked pork, finely julienne-cut bamboo shoots and water chestnuts, lightly scrambled eggs, shredded Napa cabbage, Tamari soy sauce.

• Lamb Kebabs and selection of: garbanzo beans and minced onion marinated in vinegar, oil and pepper; cooked artichoke hearts, cut up; halved black olives; minced peeled and seeded ripe tomato, cucumber, green bell pepper, zucchini and parsley in any combination; yoghurt seasoned to taste with minced garlic, minced fresh mint and fresh lemon juice; minced canned or fresh hot peppers; Armenian string cheese or grated Monterey Jack cheese.

• Shredded lettuce, chopped hard-cooked egg, diced avocado tossed with fresh lemon juice, crumbled blue cheese.

• Thinly sliced roast beef, mango chutney, minced onion, sour cream or yoghurt, sliced cucumbers, thinly sliced red or green bell peppers.

TACOS

Combine and set aside for filling:
1/2 cup hot cooked rice
1/2 cup grated Monterey Jack or cheddar cheese
1 tablespoon pumpkin or sunflower seeds
Cook quickly to soften and lightly brown in:
1 teaspoon butter or corn oil
1 corn or flour tortilla
Remove to plate and repeat with 2 or 3 more tortillas, adding butter or oil as needed. Quickly fill each softened tortilla with:
reserved filling
Fold in half and bake in 350° oven to melt cheese and crisp the tacos.

Appetizers and Snacks

MUSHROOM SANDWICH SPREAD

Sauté 2 to 3 minutes in:
1 to 2 tablespoons safflower oil
3/4 cup sliced fresh mushrooms
3 tablespoons minced celery
Combine in bowl with:
3 tablespoons chopped red bell
   pepper
2 tablespoons chopped green
   onion and some tops
2 tablespoons chopped fresh
   herbs of choice
1 tablespoon fresh lemon juice
3 tablespoons mayonnaise
salt and pepper to taste
Chill and serve as a dip or spread
for crackers, a sandwich spread
or as an appetizer salad on lettuce
leaves.
Makes approximately 3/4 cup

BACON OR HAM SANDWICH SPREAD

Combine and mix well:
1/4 cup finely diced slab bacon,
   sautéed until crisp and
   drained, or
1/4 cup finely diced cooked ham
3 tablespoons minced celery
2 green onions and some tops,
   chopped
2 tablespoons minced green or
   red bell pepper
1/4 apple, finely diced
1 small carrot, grated
2 tablespoons chopped fresh
   herbs of choice
1 tablespoon fresh lemon juice
3 tablespoons mayonnaise
salt and pepper to taste
Chill and serve as a dip or spread
for crackers, as a sandwich spread
or on lettuce leaves as a salad.
Makes 3/4 to 1 cup

OLIVE-EGG SALAD SPREAD

Combine well:
3 tablespoons plain yoghurt
1 tablespoon fresh lemon juice or
   cider vinegar
Mixing well, toss with:
2 hard-cooked eggs, finely
   chopped
1/4 cup minced black olives
1 small garlic clove, minced
1 tablespoon each chopped fresh
   parsley and fresh chives
salt, pepper and paprika to taste
Serve on:
toast or whole-grain crackers
Garnish with:
tomato slices
Makes approximately 2/3 cup

CREAMY TUNA FISH SPREAD

Combine:
2/3 cup drained canned tuna fish
1 hard-cooked egg yolk, crumbled
1 hard-cooked egg white, minced
1/4 cup plain yoghurt
2 tablespoons minced celery
2 teaspoons each minced onion
  and chives
1 teaspoon fresh lemon juice
Herb Salt and white pepper to
  taste
Serve as spread for crackers or
bread or as an appetizer salad on
lettuce.
Makes approximately 1 cup

PEANUT BUTTER WITH HONEY

Grind shelled raw peanuts in
mortar and pestle or in blender
or food mill, leaving some of peanuts in chunks. Add salt to taste,
a little peanut oil if needed to
moisten and enough honey to
make creamy consistency. Jar
and store refrigerated. Serve on
toast or crackers.

BROWN RICE PATTIES

A tasty crunchy snack that's
especially good for traveling.
Make a large batch to take on
your next camping or hiking trip.

Combine:
1-1/2 cups cold cooked brown
  rice
3 tablespoons sesame seeds
2 tablespoons whole-wheat flour
1/2 teaspoon each salt and
  Tamari soy sauce
Knead with one hand until rice
sticks together. Form into 6
2-1/2-inch patties and fry (do
not use cast-iron skillet) 10 minutes per side or until very
brown in:
1 tablespoon hot corn oil
Patties should be crispy and
almost burned. Good warm,
better cold.
Makes 6 patties

NUTRITIOUS DRIED-FRUIT-AND-NUT SNACK

Combine equal parts assorted
dried fruits and assorted shelled
fresh nuts and/or seeds. Experiment with raisins, prunes, apricots, dates, figs, apples, peanuts,
whole filberts, whole blanched
almonds, cashews, pine nuts,
Brazil nuts, sunflower seeds,
pumpkin seeds. Great as a
between-meal snack for people
on the go, for hurried lunches,
for backpackers.

CRUNCHY BROWN RICE SNACK

In heavy non cast-iron skillet
toast without oil until browned,
stirring frequently, 2 cups raw
brown rice. Combine with 1/4
cup Sesame Salt or to taste. Store
refrigerated in airtight container.
When traveling, store in glass jar or
plastic bag. Eat by the spoonful.

Soups

SOUP

The soup section is divided into two categories—simple soups to serve for lunch or as a first course and main meal soups. We suggest making main meal soups in larger quantities; it takes little additional work to make a two-day meal and flavor is improved upon reheating.

STOCKS

Stocks are the medium by which nutrients, otherwise inaccessible or overlooked, can be conserved and recycled in a variety of ways, thus enriching your eating experience. These nutrients are in all foods—bones, scraps, carcasses, gravies, unserved portions, vegetable scrapings and trimmings, water in which vegetables have been cooked, leftovers in the refrigerator. They need only to be put into a pot, covered with water and simmered, covered, 2 to 3 hours with the addition of herbs and seasonings. For complementary com-

bination suggestions, see individual recipes for making stocks with fresh bones. A pair of pigs' feet, blanched and rinsed, will add nourishment, flavor and gelatin. Chicken, beef and vegetable stocks are the most versatile ones, but do not overlook lamb and pork bones from roasts, chops and other cuts, as these stocks have an especially distinctive flavor.

Stock can be carefully strained to make a clear broth, or the pulp can be pushed through the strainer resulting in a thicker stock. After straining, jar, cool, cover and refrigerate up to 10 days. The fat that rises to the surface keeps the stock fresh. If not using within that length of time, bring back to boil and re-jar. If freezing, allow at least 1 inch of air space for expansion. Defrost, bring to boil and re-jar before using, as freezing changes the consistency of the stock. Refrigerate so that fat congeals. Before using, discard fat with the exception of chicken fat; if it is a golden yellow, it is pure enough to use for frying.

Heat stock and adjust seasonings to taste. For extra flavor, simmer with chopped tomatoes or tomato paste, celery leaves, parsley leaves and stems, mushroom stems, watercress, herbs, leftover vegetables. For concentrated stock, boil down to reduce to desired strength.

Bones may also be cooked without vegetables and seasonings and the stock can then be flavored when used as a stock for making gravies or cream sauces, when cooking vegetables, legumes and grains, for poaching eggs, and as a base for soups and stews.

FROZEN STOCK CUBE CONCENTRATE

Simmer 2-1/4 cups stock seasoned with salt and Tamari soy sauce until very salty 45 minutes or until cooked down to 1 cup. Spoon 2 tablespoons into each of 8 individual ice tray holders, freeze, wrap and use as directed in recipes.

Soups

CHICKEN STOCK

Bring to boil:
3 pounds chicken backs, necks
    and wing tips, cut up
2 quarts cold water
Skim off any scum that rises to
surface, lower heat, cover and
simmer 1-1/2 hours. Add and
bring back to simmer:
2 carrots, chopped
1 onion, chopped
1 turnip or parsnip, chopped
1 celery stalk and leaves, chopped
1 leek and some tender green,
    chopped
1 garlic clove, crushed
1 bay leaf
8 parsley sprigs
1 sprig each thyme and savory
6 to 8 peppercorns, lightly
    crushed
1/2 teaspoon each turmeric
    and Herb Salt
Simmer 1-1/2 hours. Strain and
jar as directed.

TURKEY STOCK

Substitute for chicken bones
equivalent in turkey bones. The
above seasonings complement
any other poultry such as duck
and Cornish hens. These bones
can be used in combination with
chicken or turkey bones.

PORK STOCK

Substitute pork bones for the
chicken bones, fresh sage for turmeric and add 1 large oregano
sprig.

BEEF STOCK

Bring to boil:
2 pounds meaty beef bones,
    cut up
1 pair pigs' feet (optional)
1 pound marrow bones, sawed
    into 3-inch pieces
2 quarts water
Skim off any scum that rises to
surface, lower heat, cover and
simmer 1-1/2 hours. Add and
bring back to simmer:
2 carrots, chopped
2 turnips or parsnips, chopped
1 celery stalk and leaves,
    chopped
1 onion, stuck with 2 cloves

1 leek and some tender green,
    chopped
1/4 cup chopped bell pepper
2 garlic cloves, bruised
8 parsley sprigs
2 thyme or lemon thyme sprigs
2 oregano or marjoram sprigs
2 bay leaves
10 peppercorns, lightly crushed
1-1/2 teaspoons salt
Bring back to simmer and cook
1-1/2 hours. Strain and jar as
directed.

Note: For spicier stock, add with
vegetables 2 tomatoes, cut up,
and 2 to 3 dried red chili peppers,
seeded and crushed.

LAMB STOCK

Substitute lamb blocks or other
lamb bones for beef, increasing
the amount to 3 pounds; omit
pigs' feet and marrow bones. Add
1 to 2 rosemary sprigs with
vegetables.

VEAL STOCK

Blanch and rinse:
1 pound each meaty veal
    knuckle bones and shinbones,
    cut up
1 pair pigs' feet
Place in soup pot and add:
2 quarts water
1 large carrot, chopped
1 turnip or parsnip, chopped
1 onion, chopped
1 large celery stalk and leaves,
    chopped
2 leeks and some tender green,
    chopped
1 onion, chopped
8 parsley sprigs
1 thyme or lemon thyme sprig
1 bay leaf
1 teaspoon salt
8 white peppercorns, lightly
    crushed
1/2 teaspoon turmeric
Bring to boil, skim off any scum
that rises to surface, lower heat,
cover and simmer 3 hours. Strain
and jar as directed.

FISH COURT BOUILLON

Bring to boil:
1 quart water
3/4 cup dry white wine
1 pound fish heads, bones and
    trimmings
1/2 cup each sliced celery and
    leaves, onions and carrots
6 parsley sprigs
3 thyme sprigs
3 tarragon leaves, or
1 bay leaf
8 peppercorns, lightly crushed
1 garlic clove, bruised
1/2 teaspoon salt
Cover, lower heat and simmer
no longer than 30 minutes. Strain,
jar and cool. Refrigerate up to
2 days or freeze up to 2 weeks.
Use for poaching fish or as part
of liquid when making cream
sauces for fish or for crêpes to be
filled with seafood filling.

VEGETABLE STOCK

In saucepan bring to boil:
1 quart water and/or water in
    which vegetables have been
    cooked
3 cups chopped vegetables such
    as carrots, turnips, rutabagas,
    celery, Swiss chard, tomatoes,
    etc.
1 cup chopped fresh parsley
    and/or watercress
2 sprigs oregano, marjoram or
    other herbs of choice
2 garlic cloves, bruised
1 to 2 teaspoons Tamari soy sauce
1/4 teaspoon salt
2 peppercorns, lightly crushed
Lower heat, cover and simmer
2 hours. Adjust seasonings to
taste. Strain, pushing as much
pulp through strainer as possible.
Jar and refrigerate. As there is
no fat to seal and keep the stock
fresh, use within 3 days. If not
using within that time, bring
back to boil and rejar. Tomato
juice may be substituted for
part of the water.

Soups

DASHI

Bring to boil:
2 cups water
1 2-inch by 2-inch piece kombu
(dried sheet kelp), broken up
1/2 cup katsuobushi (dried
bonito shavings)
1/8 teaspoon salt
Cook rapidly 3 minutes. Strain
and reserve kelp and bonito
refrigerated for making 2 more
cups dashi. When using second
time, increase boiling time to
5 minutes.

QUICK SERVING
SUGGESTIONS FOR STOCKS

• Bring 2 cups pork or chicken
stock or dashi to gentle boil.
Gradually stir in with fork 1 egg
beaten with 1/2 teaspoon fresh
lemon juice or Tamari soy sauce.
Cook until egg is just beginning
to set and serve with minced
parsley, chives or chervil.
• Bring 2 cups poultry stock to
boil and cook in it 2 tablespoons
fresh peas or asparagus tips until
just tender. Add 2 tablespoons
minced cooked chicken, ham or
turkey. Reheat and sprinkle with
grated Parmesan, Monterey Jack,
Edam or Gruyère cheese.
• Bring 2 cups poultry stock to
boil and add 2 teaspoons dry
sherry. Cut in rings or dice 1/2
avocado and sprinkle with 1/2
teaspoon fresh lemon juice. Add
avocado to stock just before
serving. Garnish with watercress
leaves. Avocado is especially
good with turkey stock.
• Bring 2 cups poultry stock to
boil and gradually stir in with
fork 1 egg beaten with 1/2 teaspoon lemon juice and 1 tablespoon grated Parmesan cheese.
Stir slowly to make large strands.
Serve with extra grated Parmesan cheese.
• Heat together 3 cups lamb or
chicken stock and 1-1/2 cups
chopped cooked leftover vegetables, pasta or grains. Place in
each of 2 bowls 2 teaspoons
crumbled Gorgonzola cheese.
Pour hot soup over and serve as
luncheon meal with garnish of
minced fresh parsley and diced
ripe tomatoes.

• Heat 2 cups poultry stock with
cooked sliced giblets, mushrooms, shredded crêpes, sorrel,
spinach or Swiss chard. Garnish
with minced fresh parsley.
• Heat 2 cups dashi. Gradually
stir 1/4 cup heated dashi into
1 to 1-1/2 tablespoons miso.
Return to remaining heated soup
and blend well. Adjust with salt
and Tamari soy sauce.
• Top any rich heated stock with
dollops of sour cream, Aioli
Sauce or plain yoghurt.

FARINA OR CORNMEAL
SOUP DUMPLINGS

Combine:
1 egg, lightly beaten
1/4 teaspoon salt
6 tablespoons farina or yellow
cornmeal
1/8 teaspoon freshly grated nutmeg (optional), or
crumbled dried or minced fresh
herbs to taste (optional)
Drop by spoonfuls into boiling
soup or stock. Simmer for 10
minutes.

LIGHT SORREL BROTH
(Appetizer)

Simmer 10 minutes in:
2 cups rich chicken stock
1 cup firmly packed finely
    shredded sorrel
1/4 cup finely shredded iceberg
    lettuce
1 teaspoon grated onion
    (optional)
Beat:
1 egg
Whisk into egg:
1/4 cup hot soup or heated
    half-and-half
Gradually beat egg mixture
into remaining soup and reheat.
Do not boil. Adjust seasonings
with salt and pepper and
sprinkle with:
minced fresh chervil or parsley
Herb Croutons

Variation: Add when reheating,
1 tablespoon dry sherry or dry
vermouth.

CREAMY CHEDDAR
CHEESE SOUP
(Appetizer)

Sauté until transparent in:
1 tablespoon butter
1/2 to 2/3 cup finely minced
    onion
2 tablespoons finely minced
    celery
Remove skillet from heat and
sprinkle over onion:
1 tablespoon unbleached white
    flour
Stir well and return to heat.
Stirring constantly, gradually
blend in:
1-1/2 cups milk
Add and simmer gently 2 to 3
minutes until thickened:
2/3 cup firmly packed grated
    cheddar cheese
1/2 teaspoon Herb Salt
dash of sweet Hungarian paprika
Garnish with:
2 tablespoons minced fresh
    parsley

CARROT-ORANGE SOUP
(Appetizer)

In saucepan sauté 5 minutes in:
1 tablespoon butter
2 medium-size carrots, sliced
    (approximately 1-2/3 cups)
1/4 cup minced onion
Add and cook 20 minutes or until
carrots are soft:
1 cup chicken or vegetable stock
1/2 teaspoon Herb Salt
1 bay leaf
Mash carrots with potato masher
and add:
1/2 cup fresh orange juice
Reheat and season with:
1/8 teaspoon ground ginger,
    freshly grated nutmeg or
    freshly ground cardamom
salt and pepper to taste
Garnish with:
mint sprigs

Soups

CREAM OF PUMPKIN SOUP
(Appetizer)

Sauté in:
1 tablespoon butter
1 tablespoon grated onion
Sprinkle over and stir until foamy:
1 tablespoon unbleached white
    flour
Remove from heat and add:
1 cup Pumpkin Purée*
1-1/4 cups chicken stock
1/2 teaspoon salt
1/4 teaspoon ground ginger
1/8 teaspoon each freshly grated
    nutmeg and white pepper
Return to heat and cook, stirring
with wire whisk, until thickened
and smooth. Stir in:
1/4 cup each half-and-half and
    heavy cream
Heat through but do not boil.
Adjust seasonings and garnish
with:
parsley sprigs
lemon or orange peel curl

To serve cold, cool before adding
heavy cream. Chill thoroughly,
adjust seasonings and serve in
chilled bowls.
*If using canned pumpkin purée,
use other 1 cup of small can
in Moist Pumpkin Bread.

TOMATO-WATERCRESS SOUP
(Appetizer)

Cover and steam 10 minutes in:
2 tablespoons butter
1/4 cup chopped white of leek
1/3 cup chopped onion
Add and boil gently 10 minutes:
1 4- to 5-ounce unpeeled new
    white potato, sliced
1 small garlic clove, minced
3/4 cup chicken stock
2 large ripe tomatoes, peeled
    and chopped

Add, cover and cook until vegetables are very soft:
1 cup firmly packed chopped
    watercress leaves and tender
    stems
1 tablespoon chopped fresh
    parsley
1/4 teaspoon each salt and
    white pepper
1/8 teaspoon mild honey or
    raw natural sugar
Pass through food mill or purée
in blender and then sieve.
Add and simmer without boiling
until just heated through:
1/2 cup heavy cream
chicken stock if too thick
1/2 cup chopped watercress
    leaves
Adjust seasonings and serve hot
garnished with:
finely diced, peeled and seeded
    ripe tomato
watercress sprigs
To serve cold, cool, chill thoroughly, adjust seasonings and
serve in chilled bowls with
garnishes.

Main Meal Soups

AVOCADO MUSHROOM SOUP

Good served as main meal soup with Tacos.

Sauté 3 minutes in:
3 tablespoons butter
1/4 cup minced onion
2 tablespoons each minced celery stalk and tender leaves
1 small garlic clove, minced
Add and sauté 2 minutes:
2/3 to 1 cup sliced fresh mushrooms

Sprinkle while sautéing with:
1/2 teaspoon crumbled dried oregano
1/4 teaspoon seeded and crushed dried red chili pepper
1/8 teaspoon salt
Blend in and cook and stir 3 minutes:
2-1/2 tablespoons unbleached white flour
Gradually add:
1 cup half-and-half
2 cups rich chicken stock

Cook and stir over medium heat until well blended and slightly thickened. Cube:
1 large avocado
Toss avocado cubes well with:
2 teaspoons fresh lemon juice
Remove 2/3 of the avocado cubes and mash. Add mashed avocado to soup and reheat without boiling. Adjust seasonings and garnish with:
remaining avocado cubes
minced fresh parsley or coriander
Serve immediately with Tacos.

Soups

VEGETABLE CREAM OF MUSHROOM SOUP
(Main Meal)

In large saucepan, sauté
5 minutes in:
2 tablespoons butter
2 cups sliced fresh mushrooms
   (approximately 1/2 pound)
Remove mushrooms with slotted
spatula and set aside. Adding
additional butter to pan if
needed, sauté 5 minutes:
1 small carrot, grated
1 celery stalk and tender leaves,
   finely chopped
4 green onions and some tops,
   chopped
Add:
2-1/2 cups milk
1 cube frozen stock concentrate,
   or
1 teaspoon Tamari soy sauce
1/2 teaspoon Herb Salt
1/4 teaspoon white pepper
1-1/2 teaspoons each minced
   fresh basil and oregano
2 tablespoons grated Parmesan
   cheese
Bring slowly to boil, lower heat
and bind with mixture of:
1 egg yolk, beaten
1 tablespoon soy flour, sifted
3 tablespoons hot milk from
   saucepan

Add and heat through:
reserved mushrooms
Blend in:
1/2 cup plain yoghurt or sour
   cream
Serve as a main meal soup with
fresh bread or rolls and tomato
slices, and pass a bowl of chopped
fresh parsley or chives.

SPICY THICK LENTIL SOUP WITH CLOVES
(Main Meal)

The cloves lend an unusual,
delightful spicy flavor to this
thick, dark red soup.

In large saucepan, sauté 5 minutes in:
2 tablespoons olive oil or butter
1 medium-size onion, diced
1/2 cup each diced carrots and
   celeriac
1 garlic clove, minced
1 tablespoon minced red or green
   bell pepper
Stir in:
3 to 4 cups heated beef stock
3/4 cup brown lentils
1/4 cup Tomato Paste
Add bouquet garni of:
2 to 3 whole cloves
1 bay leaf
2 parsley sprigs
1 large thyme sprig

Bring to gentle boil, cover, lower
heat and simmer 1 hour. Add and
simmer 15 minutes:
1 cup diced potatoes, sprinkled
   with
salt, pepper and sweet Hungarian
   paprika
Just before serving, remove
bouquet garni and add:
2 tablespoons red wine
Adjust seasonings and sprinkle
with:
minced fresh chives

CREAM OF VEGETABLE SOUP FROM LEFTOVERS
(Main Meal)

Purée in blender:
1 cup cooked and chopped
   vegetables
1/4 cup chicken or veal stock
Combine and heat without
boiling with:
1 cup Béchamel Sauce made with
   chicken or veal stock
half-and-half to thin to desired
   consistency
salt and pepper to taste
Aromatic Curry Mixture, Herb
   Salt or freshly grated nutmeg
   to taste
Sprinkle with:
minced fresh parsley
paprika for color

FRENCH ONION SOUP
(Main Meal)

Dry in 200° oven and set aside:
2 to 4 thin slices French bread
In saucepan melt:
3 tablespoons butter
Add:
4 cups coarsely chopped onion
1/4 teaspoon each salt and white
    pepper
Sauté, stirring often, until onions
start to turn golden.
Add:
2 cups each dry white wine and
    beef stock
1 bay leaf
Bring to boil, cover, lower heat
and simmer, stirring occasionally,
15 minutes. Discard bay leaf and
adjust seasonings. Add and stir
until melted:
2 tablespoons grated Gruyère
    cheese
Spoon soup into 2 heated ovenproof crocks or soup dishes (or
one casserole). Place on top of
each reserved slice of bread:
2 to 3 tablespoons grated Gruyère
    cheese
Place bread slices on top of soup
and broil until cheese is melted
and just turning golden.

CREAM OF ONION SOUP
(Main Meal)

Sauté until onions are transparent in:
2 tablespoons butter
1 cup chopped onions
Sprinkle with:
1 tablespoon unbleached white
    flour
Cook and stir 3 minutes and
gradually add, stirring constantly:
2 cups milk
Add, blend well and bring to boil:
1 cube frozen beef stock con-
    centrate, or
1 teaspoon Tamari soy sauce
1 bay leaf
1/2 teaspoon salt
1/4 teaspoon white pepper
1/8 teaspoon sweet Hungarian
    paprika
1/2 cup grated Parmesan cheese
1 small carrot, finely grated (1/3
    to 1/2 cup firmly packed)
Lower heat and stir in:
1/4 cup heavy cream
3 tablespoons dry white wine
2 tablespoons minced fresh
    parsley
Remove from heat, cover and let
stand 5 minutes. Discard bay
leaf and adjust seasonings.

RUSSIAN BRUSSELS
SPROUTS SOUP
(Main Meal)

This is an ideal soup for a cold
evening. The fresh sour cream is
a must to bring out the delicate
flavor of the Brussels sprouts.
Be sure to pass the pepper mill.

Wash and trim:
1 pound young Brussels sprouts
Cut crosswise incision 1/2 inch
deep in bottom of sprouts and
sauté them for 5 minutes in:
2 tablespoons butter
Add:
3 cups lamb or beef stock,
    heated
3 to 4 small potatoes (approxi-
    mately 3/4 pound), cut in
    1/2-inch dice, lightly sprin-
    kled with
salt and pepper
Bring to boil, lower heat, cover
and simmer 20 minutes. Adjust
seasonings with salt and pepper
and garnish with:
minced fresh parsley or dill
dollops of sour cream

Soups

MILK SOUP WITH TINY DUMPLINGS
(Main Meal)

This is an old-country favorite on cool evenings, when nobody feels much like cooking.

Combine and knead with hands to make very stiff dough:

1 egg, beaten
1/8 teaspoon each salt and freshly grated nutmeg
2/3 cup unbleached white flour

With coarse blade of grater, grate half of dough onto lightly floured surface. Wrap and refrigerate or freeze remaining half for later use. Heat to just boiling:

2 to 3 cups milk

Add, stirring constantly:

grated dumpling dough

Cook over low heat 5 to 7 minutes. Before serving, sweeten and season to taste with:

mild honey
crushed cinnamon stick
freshly grated lemon peel

HEARTY BARLEY SOUP
(Main Meal)

This thick, hearty soup has the consistency of a breakfast cereal or rice pudding. On a cold fall or winter day, it is soothing to the hungry stomach. The vinegar adds a special zing.

In a large saucepan, combine:

3 to 4 cups heated beef or chicken stock
3/4 cup hulled barley
2 carrots, sliced
1 white of leek and a little green, sliced
1 onion, chopped
1/4 cup chopped celery and tender leaves
1 ripe tomato, peeled and chopped
1 tablespoon tomato paste
1/2 teaspoon salt
1/4 teaspoon each pepper and sweet Hungarian paprika
1 teaspoon each minced fresh thyme and marjoram

Bring to gentle boil, cover, lower heat and cook 1 hour.
Serve with:

1 tablespoon cider vinegar in each bowl
minced fresh parsley for garnish

OYSTER STEW
(Main Meal)

Combine and scald:

1 cup each milk and half-and-half
1 tablespoon butter
1 teaspoon grated onion
1/2 teaspoon salt
1/8 teaspoon white pepper

Keep milk mixture warm. Frizzle until edges curl in:

2 tablespoons butter, melted until bubbly
1 pint oysters, drained (reserve liquor)

Add oysters to milk mixture. Then add and cook 2 to 3 minutes:

reserved liquor

Adjust seasonings, adding if desired:

1 to 2 teaspoons fresh lemon juice, or
2 to 3 tablespoons dry white wine

Tabasco sauce to taste

Reheat and pour into heated soup bowl. Sprinkle with:

minced fresh parsley
paprika

OXTAIL SOUP
(Main Meal)

Coat with mixture of:
1 tablespoon unbleached white flour
1/4 teaspoon salt
1/8 teaspoon pepper
1 pound oxtails, cut up
Brown on all sides in:
1 tablespoon butter and/or rendered beef fat, or as needed
Remove oxtails with tongs and brown:
1/2 cup chopped onion
1 garlic clove, minced
Return oxtails to skillet and deglaze with:
1/2 cup burgundy or Madeira
Let reduce by half and add:
3 cups beef stock
bouquet garni of:
  1 small celery stalk
  1 small carrot
  2 parsley sprigs
  1 sprig each thyme and oregano
Bring to gentle boil, cover, reduce heat and simmer 1-1/2 hours. Cool, cover and chill. Remove fat from surface and reheat. Discard bouquet garni and add:
1 cup mixed chopped vegetables such as bell pepper, carrot, celery, celeriac, potatoes

Bring back to boil, cover, lower heat and cook until vegetables are tender. Add:
2/3 cup sautéed mushrooms
2/3 cup cooked pasta, lentils or grains
Reheat and adjust seasonings with wine and salt and pepper. Serve in large shallow bowls.

UKRAINIAN BORSTSCH
(Hearty Main Meal)

This recipe doubles well. The attractive beet-red color and slightly tangy flavor of this main meal soup are a delight to guests for a simple, informal meal.

Over high heat, brown a few pieces at a time in:
1 tablespoon rendered beef fat
1/2 pound beef brisket or stew meat, cut in 1-inch pieces
Brown quickly; the frying surface of the skillet may look burned. Deglaze pan with:
3 to 4 cups water
Add and bring to boil:
1 pound beef shanks
Cover, lower heat and simmer, skimming off any scum that rises to surface, for 30 minutes. Then add:

1 cup each sliced potatoes and chopped white cabbage
1/4 pound beets, peeled and sliced (approximately 2/3 cup)
1 medium-size carrot, sliced
2 small celery stalks and tender leaves, chopped
1 to 2 ripe tomatoes, peeled and diced
2 to 3 garlic cloves, minced
1/4 cup Tomato Paste
2 tablespoons cider vinegar or fresh lemon juice
2 bay leaves
1 teaspoon raw natural sugar (optional)
1/2 teaspoon salt
1/4 teaspoon pepper
1 1-inch cube slab bacon (optional)
Bring back to boil, cover, lower heat and simmer for 1 hour. Remove shanks, trim off meat and discard bones. Cut meat into 1-inch pieces and return to soup. Adjust seasonings.
Garnish with:
chopped fresh parsley
Serve with a bowl of sour cream and fresh rye bread.

Salads

TOMATO SALAD WITH YOGHURT

Combine in bowl:
2 to 3 ripe tomatoes, cubed
1/4 cup plain yoghurt
salt and pepper to taste
Chill and garnish with:
parsley or mint sprig
The tomato juices and yoghurt combine to make a smooth sauce. The pepper taste should be distinguishable.

TOMATO WITH OREGANO

An excellent way to perk up flavorless tomatoes.

Place in shallow dish:
3 to 4 tomatoes, cut in wedges
Pour over tomatoes mixture of:
3 tablespoons corn oil
1 tablespoon cider vinegar
1/4 teaspoon salt
1/8 teaspoon each white pepper
    and raw natural sugar
Sprinkle over:
1 teaspoon minced fresh oregano,
    or
1/4 to 1/2 teaspoon crumbled
    dried oregano
Refrigerate, stirring occasionally,
3 to 4 hours.

TOMATO AND GREEN PEPPER SALAD

Combine and toss:
3 to 4 ripe tomatoes, cut in
    wedges
1/2 green bell pepper, cut into
    3/4-inch by 1-inch pieces
1/4 cup chopped celery
2 green onions, cut in 1-inch
    lengths
2 tablespoons chopped fresh
    parsley
1 teaspoon minced fresh basil or
    dill
2 tablespoons olive oil
Herb Salt to taste
Chill 5 to 10 minutes before
serving.

SIMPLE TOMATO SALAD

Toss together:
3 to 4 ripe tomatoes, sliced
1 small onion, sliced
1 to 1-1/2 tablespoons olive oil
Herb Salt to taste
Serve as accompaniment to meat,
fish or fowl dishes, or soufflés.

TOMATO AND BERMUDA ONION SALAD

Combine:
2 tablespoons olive oil
1 tablespoon fresh lemon juice
Toss in:
3 to 4 ripe tomatoes, cut in
    wedges
1/2 medium-size Bermuda onion,
    sliced
salt to taste
Serve in dark or wooden bowl as accompaniment to meat, fowl or fish entrée. French bread is good for dipping in dressing and tomato juices.

RADISH SALAD

Crumble yolk of:
1 hard-cooked egg
Stir in:
2 to 3 tablespoons plain yoghurt
    or sour cream
Combine with:
1 to 1-1/2 cups sliced radishes
sliced white of hard-cooked egg
1 tablespoon minced fresh
    parsley, or
1 teaspoon minced fresh chives
    or dill
salt and pepper to taste
Toss to coat well with dressing and chill. Garnish with:
parsley or dill sprigs

Salads

FRESH BEAN SALAD

Combine:
2 cups steamed or boiled green
    or wax beans
1 medium-size onion, chopped, or
2 to 3 green onions, chopped
2 tablespoons olive oil
1 to 1-1/2 tablespoons cider
    vinegar
1 tablespoon chopped fresh
    parsley
Herb Salt and pepper to taste
Chill at least 1 hour and
garnish with:
parsley sprigs

Variation: Add other herbs to
taste and 1 tomato, peeled and
sliced, and/or 2 to 4 slices of
green or red bell pepper.

QUICK CUCUMBER SALAD

Combine:
1 small cucumber, peeled and
    thinly sliced
1 small onion, cut into rings
2 tablespoons safflower oil
1 to 1-1/2 tablespoons cider
    vinegar
salt and pepper to taste
Let stand 2 to 3 minutes before
serving. Garnish with:
fresh dill sprigs

CUCUMBERS
IN SOUR CREAM

Toss together:
1 cucumber, peeled and very
    thinly sliced
2 to 3 tablespoons sour cream
Mix well until sour cream is
evenly distributed and makes
a smooth dressing. Season with:
Herb Salt and pepper to taste

HEARTS OF PALM SALAD

Slice in half lengthwise:
4 to 6 hearts of palm (1 8-ounce
    can), drained
Place slices on:
small butter lettuce leaves
Combine and pour over slices:
2 tablespoons olive oil
1/2 tablespoon fresh lemon juice
1 teaspoon each finely minced
    celery, green onion and
    pimiento-stuffed olives
dash each angostura aromatic
    bitters (optional), sweet Hun-
    garian paprika, raw natural
    sugar and salt
Garnish with:
minced fresh parsley

Note: Vinaigrette Dressing may
be used in place of dressing.

CARROT AND APPLE SALAD

Combine:
1 carrot, grated
1/2 Golden Delicious apple,
    grated
Sprinkle with:
2 tablespoons fresh lemon juice
salt to taste
Spoon on:
lettuce leaves
Serve with ricotta or cottage
cheese.

Note: Use rest of apple for cheese
and apple dessert or grated on
morning cereal.

SPINACH SALAD

Toss to coat evenly with dressing:
3 cups torn tender spinach
    leaves, washed and patted dry
1 recipe Creamy Lemon-Garlic
    Dressing, or
1/4 cup Mustard French Dressing
Chill. Just before serving, toss in:
1/3 cup Herb Croutons
Sprinkle with:
1 to 2 tablespoons grated
    Gruyère cheese

Variation: Toss with spinach
1/3 cup thinly sliced fresh
mushrooms.

FRESH MUSHROOM SALAD

A simple and refreshing salad, especially attractive when served in a dark bowl. May also be served on lettuce leaves.

Combine and mix well:
1-1/2 cups sliced fresh
     mushrooms
2 tablespoons chopped green
     onions and some tops
1 tablespoon minced fresh
     Italian parsley
2 tablespoons fresh lemon juice
1 tablespoon olive oil
1/8 to 1/4 teaspoon salt
1/8 teaspoon pepper
6 to 8 pitted, halved black olives
     (optional)

Variations: Add 2 tablespoons julienne-cut Fontina cheese, crumbled Gorgonzola or diced Provolone cheese.

BEAN SPROUT SALAD

Combine:
3/4 cup bean sprouts
1/4 cup finely minced Bermuda
     onion
1 ripe tomato, diced
Toss with:
Oriental Salad Dressing

KOREAN SALAD

Blanch 1 minute and drain well:
1 cup bean sprouts, or
1 bunch watercress, tough
     stems removed
Combine with:
1 tablespoon each Tamari soy
     sauce and fresh lemon juice or
     rice wine vinegar
2 tablespoons each minced green
     onion and tops and toasted
     sesame seeds
1/2 teaspoon Oriental sesame oil
Adjust seasonings and chill before serving.

SUNCHOKE SALAD

Scrub well and trim:
6 to 7 sunchokes
Slice thinly and toss in bowl with:
1/4 cup thinly sliced Bermuda
     onion or chopped green
     onions
1/4 cup Vinegar and Oil
     Dressing with finely minced
     garlic and mixed fresh herbs
     to taste
Season with:
salt and pepper
Serve on:
Romaine lettuce leaves

GARBANZO AND MUSHROOM SALAD

Toss together:
1 cup sliced fresh mushrooms
2/3 to 3/4 cup cooked garbanzo
     beans
1/4 cup each diagonally cut
     celery and julienne-cut sweet
     red pepper
2 tablespoons each julienne-cut
     sweet onion and minced fresh
     parsley
beaten mixture of:
     3 tablespoons garlic olive oil
     1-1/2 tablespoons red wine
          vinegar
     1/2 teaspoon Tamari soy sauce
salt, pepper and cayenne pepper
     to taste
Chill and serve on:
butter lettuce leaves

CELERIAC SALAD

Toss and chill:
1 to 1-1/2 cups shredded celeriac
1 tablespoon chopped green
     onion
1-1/2 to 2 tablespoons
     safflower oil
1 tablespoon cider vinegar
1/8 teaspoon powdered fenugreek
salt and white pepper to taste

Salads

FARMER SALAD

Combine in bowl:
1/2 cup grated celeriac
1 medium-size carrot, grated
1/2 Golden Delicious apple, grated
1/4 cup minced white of leek
3 to 4 tablespoons plain yoghurt to make coleslaw consistency
salt or Herb Salt and sweet Hungarian paprika to taste
Garnish with:
minced fresh parsley, or parsley sprigs

WATERCRESS/SORREL SALAD

Toss together:
1-1/2 cups chopped watercress leaves and tender stems
1/2 cup chopped sorrel
1/2 tart apple, diced
3 tablespoons Vinegar and Oil Dressing

BELGIAN ENDIVE SALAD

Combine for dressing:
1/4 cup plain yoghurt
2 teaspoons fresh lemon juice
fresh minced thyme, Herb Salt and pepper to taste
1/4 teaspoon dry mustard (optional)
Halve lengthwise or slice crosswise:
2 Belgian endive
Pour dressing over and serve immediately.

Variation: Add for color fresh herbs such as chopped parsley, chives, dill or chopped green onion, or very finely grated carrot.

Dressing Variation: Combine until smooth 2-1/2 tablespoons olive oil, 1-1/2 tablespoons cider vinegar, 1/4 teaspoon dry mustard, salt and white pepper to taste.

RUSSIAN BEET SALAD

Toss together:
1/2 pound beets, cooked and sliced (approximately 1-1/4 cups)
1/4 cup sliced Spanish onion
2 tablespoons sour cream, mixed well with
1/2 tablespoon cider vinegar
salt and white pepper to taste
Chill before serving and garnish with:
curly light-green lettuce leaves

ORANGE-MINT BEET SALAD

Toss together:
1/2 pound beets, cooked and sliced (approximately 1-1/4 cups)
1/4 cup sliced Spanish onion
1-1/2 tablespoons each safflower or walnut oil and fresh orange juice
2 fresh mint leaves, minced
salt to taste
Garnish with:
mint sprigs
Chill before serving.

ITALIAN FENNEL TOSSED SALAD

A beautiful and colorful salad of delicate greens, red and black. The vegetables should all be finely chopped for even texture.

Combine to make a smooth mixture:
2 tablespoons olive oil
1-1/2 tablespoons fresh lemon
  juice or cider vinegar
salt and pepper to taste
Toss oil mixture with:
1 cup finely chopped Italian
  endive (chicory)
1 large ripe tomato, cut in
  small cubes
1/2 cup finely chopped fennel
  bulb
1/4 cup each minced green
  onions and celery
2 tablespoons finely chopped
  pitted black olives

GRUYÈRE SALAD

Toss lightly:
1 cup finely shredded Gruyère
  cheese
2 tablespoons each minced fresh
  parsley and dry white wine
Let stand 5 minutes. Serve
garnished with:
small butter lettuce leaves
ripe tomato wedges
Serve with whole-grain bread or
crackers and sweet butter.

Note: If serving as appetizer
salad, cut proportions in half.

FENNEL SALAD

Slice into rings to make 1 to
1-1/2 cups:
bulb and stalks of 1/2 medium-
  size fennel
Arrange in bowl and garnish with:
2 radishes, thinly sliced
1 orange or 2 tangerines, peeled
  and sectioned
2 black olives, pitted and halved
2 tablespoons minced onion
torn feathers of fennel
Pour over smooth mixture of:
2 to 3 tablespoons corn oil
1-1/2 tablespoons cider vinegar
1 teaspoon Pernod (optional)
1/2 teaspoon salt
dash of cayenne pepper

SHRIMP SALAD

Marinate 15 minutes in:
2 teaspoons fresh lemon juice
1 cup bay shrimp
Combine with:
1/4 cup finely minced celery
2 tablespoons each finely minced
  green onion and minced fresh
  parsley
6 tablespoons mayonnaise
Herb Salt and white pepper to
  taste
Aromatic Curry Mixture to taste
  (optional)
Place on:
butter lettuce leaves
Garnish with:
chervil or parsley sprigs
sprinkling of paprika
lemon wedges

Salads

OMA'S BAVARIAN POTATO SALAD

Cook 10 to 15 minutes or until tender but still firm in:
water to cover
1 pound unpeeled potatoes
Drain, peel and slice. Set aside and keep warm. Brown in:
1 tablespoon each butter and corn oil
1 tablespoon unbleached white flour
Gradually add:
1/4 cup each water and cider vinegar
2 tablespoons corn oil
Cook and stir, adding:
1 cube frozen chicken stock concentrate, or
1 teaspoon Tamari soy sauce
1/2 teaspoon salt
1/4 teaspoon pepper
Combine and add to slightly thickened sauce:
1/2 apple, very finely chopped
equal amount of finely chopped celeriac
reserved potato slices
Stir gently just to moisten potato slices and adjust seasonings.

Transfer to serving dish and sprinkle with:
sweet Hungarian paprika
Garnish with:
1 hard-cooked egg, grated
1/4 to 1/3 cup chopped fresh parsley
For typical Bavarian dinner, arrange on platter with salad, Wiener Schnitzel and tomato slices. Serve with butter lettuce salad.

HOT POTATO SALAD

Cook 10 to 15 minutes or until tender but still firm in:
water to cover
1 pound unpeeled potatoes
Drain, peel and slice. Set aside and keep warm.
Sauté in large skillet until beginning to brown:
2 to 3 tablespoons minced slab bacon
Add and cook until transparent:
1 onion, finely chopped
Drain off excess drippings and add:
3 tablespoons each water and cider vinegar
2 tablespoons corn oil
1 cube frozen chicken stock concentrate, or
1 teaspoon Tamari soy sauce
1 teaspoon cornstarch, dissolved in
1 tablespoon water
1/2 teaspoon Herb Salt
1/8 teaspoon black pepper
Bring to boil, lower heat and cook and stir until thickened.
Add:
reserved potatoes
Stir gently just to moisten slices evenly. Serve warm.

Note: If boiling potatoes in advance, toss sliced potatoes with freshly made sauce and gently reheat.

Variation: Add 1 cup freshly cooked broken beans when adding sliced potatoes.

Vegetarian Potato Salad: Omit bacon and sauté onion in 2 teaspoons corn oil. Substitute 1 cube frozen vegetable stock concentrate for the chicken stock.

Salads

CHICKEN SALAD
(Serve As a Main Course)

Cook, covered, 20 minutes or
until tender in:
chicken stock to cover
1 whole chicken breast, halved
Cool, reserve stock for another
use, and skin and dice chicken
meat to make approximately
2 cups. Toss with:
1/4 cup diced celery, water chest-
nuts, jicama or sunchokes or
any combination of these
1/4 cup chopped dates (optional)
1-1/2 cups mixed fresh fruits
such as halved seedless grapes,
diced pears, oranges, tanger-
ines, papaya, pineapple, figs,
apples, melons, avocados,
mangoes or peaches
1-1/2 teaspoons fresh lemon juice
2 tablespoons grated fresh or
unsweetened coconut

Chill. One hour before serving,
toss with mixture of:
1 cup plain yoghurt
1-1/2 teaspoons mayonnaise
1/2 tablespoon honey (optional)
salt and white pepper to taste
Serve as main luncheon or supper
dish on:
lettuce leaves

Variations:
Omit coconut and toss in with
   dressing 2 tablespoons broken
   walnuts or toasted almonds
Omit fruits and toss chicken with:
• 1 cup cooked white or brown
rice or bulghur
• 1 cup mixed crisply cooked
vegetables such as carrots, beets,
potatoes, peas, green beans
• 1 cup mixed minced raw vegetables such as onion, green or
red bell pepper, carrots

Substitutions:
• Tarragon Vinegar and Oil
Dressing for yoghurt mixture
• cooked turkey for chicken
• 1 cup diced cooked ham
for 1 cup of the chicken or
turkey

SPANISH ARTICHOKE
AND TUNA SALAD
(Serve As a Main Course)

Beat together to make a
smooth mixture:
3 tablespoons olive oil
1 tablespoon fresh lemon juice
Toss in:
1 7-ounce can tuna fish, drained
and flaked
6 cooked artichoke hearts or
bottoms, halved or quartered
if large
1 large ripe tomato, cut in
wedges
1/4 Spanish onion, sliced in rings
2 teaspoons minced fresh dill
salt and pepper to taste
Serve on:
lettuce leaves

COLORFUL LUNCHEON SALAD

Wash, drain, dry, wrap in towel and refrigerate:
4 large lettuce leaves
To make dressing, combine:
3 tablespoons corn oil
2 tablespoons cider vinegar
Herb Salt and pepper to taste
Combine and toss with dressing:
3 radishes, sliced
1 to 2 ripe tomatoes, sliced
1 3-inch section of cucumber, peeled and sliced
2 green onions and some green, chopped
1 small celery stalk and tender leaves, chopped
1 tablespoon chopped fresh parsley
2 teaspoons chopped fresh chives

Break up 2 of the lettuce leaves and toss into salad. Arrange salad on remaining leaves and garnish with:
2 hard-cooked eggs, each cut into 6 wedges
Serve with cheese and whole-grain bread or crackers.

Variation: Omit dressing and dress with mixture of 2 tablespoons sour cream and 2 teaspoons fresh lemon juice. Toss into salad 1/2 cup julienne-cut salami or cooked ham. Omit hard-cooked egg wedges and garnish with 1 hard-cooked egg, grated.

SOYBEAN SALAD

Marinate for 1 hour in:
1 recipe Oriental Salad Dressing
1 cup cooked soybeans
Combine and toss with:
1 ripe tomato, diced
1/2 cup sliced fresh mushrooms
1/4 cup diced yellow cheese or cooked ham
1/4 cup chopped green onions
Arrange on:
bed of lettuce
Garnish with:
parsley sprigs
halved, pitted black olives
Serve for lunch or light supper with whole-grain bread and sweet butter.

Salads

SALAD DRESSINGS

Some salad dressings may be made in advance and refrigerated, others are better mixed fresh each time a salad is made. Every dressing may be varied with both fresh and/or dried herbs. For a salad for 2 persons allow approximately 3 cups vegetables including lettuce, or approximately 2 cups without lettuce, and 3 to 4 tablespoons dressing. Always add salad dressing to greens and vegetables just before serving.

REFRIGERATING SALAD DRESSINGS

Salad dressings which are made in larger amounts than needed for one salad should be tightly covered and stored in the refrigerator. Let come to room temperature and shake or stir to combine ingredients before tossing into salad.

VINEGAR AND OIL DRESSINGS

Combine:
2/3 cup olive oil
1/4 to 1/3 cup cider vinegar or fresh lemon juice
salt and pepper to taste
Makes approximately 1 cup

Variations:
• Herb: Add 1 tablespoon dried herbs.
• Garlic: Add 1 bruised garlic clove.
• Tarragon: Add 1 teaspoon minced fresh tarragon.
• Pimiento: Add 1 tablespoon chopped pimiento.
• Parmesan: Add 1 to 2 tablespoons freshly grated Parmesan or Romano cheese.

MUSTARD FRENCH DRESSING

Combine and blend well:
1/2 cup walnut oil
2-1/2 to 3 tablespoons wine vinegar
1 teaspoon homemade or German-style mustard
1/2 teaspoon salt
1/4 teaspoon each pepper and mild honey
Makes approximately 3/4 cup

ITALIAN SALAD DRESSING

Combine and blend until smooth:
1/2 cup olive oil
1/4 cup red wine vinegar
2 tablespoons each fresh lemon juice and minced or grated onion
1 tablespoon grated Parmesan cheese
1 small garlic clove, minced
1 teaspoon salt
1-1/2 to 2 teaspoons each minced fresh basil and oregano
1/2 teaspoon each dry mustard, pepper, Tamari soy sauce and honey or raw natural sugar
1/2 to 1 dried red chili pepper, seeded and crushed (optional)
Store refrigerated. Let come to room temperature and blend well before serving.
Makes approximately 1 cup

GORGONZOLA SALAD DRESSING

Combine and blend well until smooth:
2 to 3 tablespoons crumbled
   Gorgonzola cheese
2 tablespoons mayonnaise
1/4 cup buttermilk
Add:
salt and white pepper to taste
1 tablespoon minced fresh
   parsley

CREAMY LEMON-GARLIC DRESSING

Hard boil and shell:
1 egg
Mash half of the yolk and combine it with:
1-1/2 tablespoons fresh lemon
   juice
2 tablespoons corn or olive oil
2 teaspoons minced onion
1 small garlic clove, minced
1/4 teaspoon salt
Stir until creamy, then pour over
and toss with salad vegetables.
Especially good on firm lettuces
such as ruby or red lettuce, iceberg lettuce or fresh spinach.
Garnish with crumbled, grated
or minced remaining hard-cooked
egg yolk and white.

ORIENTAL SALAD DRESSING

Combine and blend until smooth:
1-1/2 tablespoons rice wine
   vinegar
1-1/2 teaspoons each Tamari soy
   sauce and sesame or walnut oil
1/2 teaspoon mild honey
1/4 teaspoon each salt and dry
   mustard
1/4 teaspoon finely minced
   ginger root (optional)
1 teaspoon toasted sesame seeds
   (optional)
Good on bean sprouts or on a
salad of peeled tangerine sections,
sliced Bermuda onions and avocado slices.

MISO DRESSING

Combine and beat until smooth:
2 tablespoons miso
1 teaspoon rice wine vinegar
1/4 teaspoon raw natural sugar
2 tablespoons peanut oil
3 drops Oriental sesame oil
2 tablespoons ice water
Serve immediately on wedges of
chilled iceberg lettuce.

LAST-MINUTE DRESSINGS

YOGHURT SALAD DRESSING

Combine in cup and stir with
small spoon until creamy:
2 tablespoons each plain yoghurt
   and peanut or safflower oil
1 tablespoon cider vinegar
1/4 teaspoon Herb Salt
dash of white pepper
2 tablespoons minced fresh herbs
   or to taste
Pour over and combine with salad
vegetables. Good with lettuces,
cucumbers, tomatoes, celery,
bell peppers.

LEMON OR VINEGAR AND OIL DRESSING

Combine and stir until smooth:
1-1/2 tablespoons fresh lemon
   juice or cider vinegar
2-1/2 tablespoons olive oil
1/4 teaspoon Herb Salt
1/8 teaspoon pepper
Other oils may be substituted and
lemon or vinegar and oil proportions may be varied according to
individual tastes. Good on tossed
salads and delicate lettuces such
as butter lettuce.

For French Dressing: Add 1/4 to
1/2 teaspoon homemade or Dijon-
style mustard.

Salads

FRUIT SALADS

Fruit salads may be served in a variety of ways: with cereals for breakfast, with breads and cheeses for light lunches, as accompaniments to delicately flavored rice dishes, pork, ham or poultry, or as desserts. They are best when made from sun-ripened fruits, cut into slices, cubes, wedges, or made into small balls as with melons. Berries may be left whole. Citrus fruit sections may be peeled and separated into attractive wedges. The possibilities for creating aesthetically pleasing, delectable combinations are infinite.

A combination of no more than 4 fruits will allow individual flavors to remain distinguishable. Try to include at least one fruit of contrasting color. Always chill cut fruit and to avoid discoloration of certain fruits toss with lemon juice. Dessert fruit salads may be tossed with a sweet white wine, fruit liqueurs, bourbon or rum before chilling.

Fruit Combinations:

apples, bananas, mandarin orange
   sections and strawberries
apricots and raspberries
bananas, pears and strawberries
grapes, bananas, strawberries
   and orange sections
grapefruit or tangerine orange
   sections and avocado
mangoes and bananas
mangoes, bananas and blueberries with fresh coconut
nectarines and orange sections
orange sections and bananas
   with figs or mint
papayas and strawberries
peaches and blueberries
pineapple with mint, or strawberries or blueberries
watermelon, blueberries and
   bananas

HONEY DRESSING

Combine to dissolve honey:
**1 tablespoon each boiling water
   and mild honey**
**fresh lemon juice to taste
   (optional)**
Cool and toss with:
**1-1/2 to 2 cups fresh fruit of
   choice**
ground cinnamon to taste

YOGHURT OR SOUR CREAM DRESSING

Combine and blend well:
**1/3 cup plain yoghurt or sour
   cream**
2 tablespoons fresh orange juice
2 teaspoons mild honey
Combine with above the following seasonings to taste:
ground cinnamon
freshly grated nutmeg
ground ginger
grated fresh vanilla bean
minced fresh mint leaves
Toss with:
**1-1/2 to 2 cups fresh fruit of
   choice**

Variation: One tablespoon fresh lemon or lime juice may be substituted for the orange juice. Increase amount of honey to taste.

FRUIT ESCAROLE SALAD

Combine and mix well to make
smooth consistency:
2 tablespoons walnut or
    safflower oil
1 tablespoon cider vinegar
1 tablespoon crumbled Gorgon-
    zola cheese
1/4 teaspoon each salt and
    minced fresh thyme
Place in salad bowl:
2 cups coarsely shredded
    escarole
1/2 cup julienne-cut fresh
    pineapple
2 tablespoons pine nuts
Pour dressing over and toss gently.
Chill before serving.

FRUIT COLESLAW

Toss together:
1 cup shredded cabbage
1 cup mixed fresh fruit such as
    diced pineapple, halved seed-
    less grapes, thinly sliced
    apples, diced orange sections
1 teaspoon grated onion
Stir in mixture of:
2 to 3 tablespoons plain yoghurt
    or mayonnaise
1-1/2 teaspoons fresh lemon or
    lime juice
1/4 teaspoon mild honey
Chill well before serving.

FRUIT SALAD LUNCH

Combine in serving bowl:
3 to 4 butter lettuce leaves, torn
2 cups mixed sliced fresh fruit
    of choice
Toss in:
1 to 2 teaspoons fresh lemon
    juice
2 ounces cream cheese, diced
Serve with whole-grain crackers
or toast.

Variation: Omit cream cheese
and serve with a scoop of cottage
or ricotta cheese.

PERSIMMON SALAD

When persimmons are in season
they are a real treat. This simple
salad brings out their fresh taste.

Place stem side down on flat
surface:
2 ripe persimmons
Cut into top surface of skin
a small cross shape. Gently peel
skin away from pulp a short dis-
tance down the side of the fruit.
Keeping skin intact, loosen
remaining skin from pulp with
a spoon to facilitate eating.
Place each fruit on:
butter lettuce leaf
Combine and spoon over fruit:
2 tablespoons sour cream or
    plain yoghurt
1/2 teaspoon fresh lemon, lime
    or orange juice, or to taste
Top with:
chopped blanched almonds or
    unsalted cashews
Garnish with:
parsley sprigs

Eggs

EGGS

Whenever possible, buy fresh ranch eggs in the country, especially when using for soft-boiled or poached eggs. Store-bought eggs can be used for baking. Recipes in this book call for grade A large eggs. Store eggs in refrigerator pointed end down.

Soft and Hard-Cooked Eggs

To prevent cracking while cooking, it's best to have eggs at room temperature. If this isn't possible, cover cold egg(s) with cold water, bring to boil over moderate heat, cover tightly and remove from heat. Let stand 3 to 5 minutes for soft, 5 to 7 minutes for medium, and 15 minutes for hard. (If using eggs at room temperature, reduce standing time slightly.) Drain and rinse with cold water. For hard-cooked eggs, let stand covered with cold water 1 or 2 minutes before cracking and peeling. Fresh eggs peel less easily than older eggs.

Poached Eggs

Poach eggs in salted water, tomato juice or stock. In shallow saucepan bring liquid to gentle boil. (If using water, add 1/2 teaspoon white vinegar.) With spoon, swirl liquid in round motion to form a whirlpool. Drop egg gently into whirlpool and cook until set. Remove with slotted spoon and place on toast. Poached eggs are also good eaten in the tomato juice or stock in which they were cooked. Garnish with croutons. If using an egg poacher, eggs can be topped before cooking with grated cheese and/or minced fresh herbs.

Fried Eggs

Heat skillet with 1 to 2 teaspoons butter over medium heat. Break in eggs and cook covered or uncovered (if uncovered, flip over if desired) until done to taste.

Top with seasonings, minced fresh herbs or grated cheese. The secret to frying eggs is not to cook them too rapidly over high heat, as they will toughen. If serving with bacon, cook eggs in bacon drippings, basting them with the drippings as they cook.

BAKED EGGS

Fill each of 2 lightly buttered custard cups with:

2 tablespoons half-and-half or chicken stock

Place cups under broiler just to heat liquid and break into each cup:

1 egg

Season with:

salt and white pepper

Top each egg with:

1 tablespoon coarsely grated Gruyère or Emmenthaler cheese

Bake in 350° oven 6 to 8 minutes or until eggs are set to taste. Garnish with:

minced fresh parsley or chives

Eggs

STEAMED EGGS

Beat until frothy:
3 eggs
Gradually beat in:
2/3 cup hot (not boiling) water
Stir in:
1 cup bean sprouts, crisped in cold
    cold water and well drained
3/4 cup fresh peas
1/2 teaspoon corn oil
4 drops Oriental sesame oil
Pour mixture into shallow
ceramic serving dish and steam
as directed on page 175, 20 minutes, being careful not to let
steaming water boil hard.

SCRAMBLED EGGS

Beat together:
3 to 4 eggs
2 tablespoons milk or water
Herb Salt and pepper to taste
Heat in skillet:
1 tablespoon butter
Pour in eggs, let set slightly
and stir and cook until done to
taste.

Variations:
Let butter brown in skillet before
adding eggs.
To beaten eggs add one of the
following:
• 1 tablespoon wheat germ
• 2 to 3 tablespoons ricotta or
cottage cheese and 1 to 2 tablespoons minced fresh parsley
(reduce milk to 1 tablespoon)
• 1/4 cup grated mild cheese
• 1/4 cup julienne-cut or minced
ham or torn prosciutto
• 1/4 cup sliced fresh mushrooms
• 1 ounce cream cheese (2 tablespoons), cut in small bits
Add one of the following while
cooking:
• 2 tablespoons chopped walnuts
• 1 tomato, diced
• 2 to 3 teaspoons toasted
sesame seeds
• 2 to 3 tablespoons minced
mixed fresh herbs

GREEN SCRAMBLED EGGS
(For Luncheon or Light Supper)

Cook until crisp:
1 to 2 tablespoons minced slab
    bacon
Remove bacon with slotted
spoon and set aside. Sauté in
drippings:
1 tablespoon each minced green
    onion, green pepper and celery
Return bacon to pan. Beat
together:
3 to 4 eggs
1-1/2 tablespoons each milk and
    ricotta or cottage cheese
Herb Salt and pepper to taste
minced fresh herbs of choice
Pour egg mixture over sautéed
vegetables and bacon in pan.
Cook as directed for scrambled
eggs. Garnish with:
tomato slices or wedges

Note: Bacon may be omitted.
Sauté vegetables in 2 teaspoons
butter.

OMELETS

For 2 persons allow:

4 eggs

3 tablespoons water, milk or cream

salt, pepper and minced fresh herbs to taste

Prepare filling (see following suggestions) before beating eggs. Beat eggs with wire whisk in small deep bowl, then beat in water, milk or cream and seasonings. Or beat egg yolks separately with liquid and seasonings, and just before cooking fold in egg whites, beaten stiff but not dry.

Evenly grease a heavy 8- to 9-inch skillet or omelet pan with 2 to 3 teaspoons peanut or corn oil, or half butter and half oil. When a drop of water just sizzles on the skillet, it is hot enough. Pour in egg mixture and after 1 minute lower heat. Cook 7 to 10 minutes, tipping pan in a circular motion occasionally to distribute the liquid egg and loosening edges of omelet along pan with a knife. Approximately 3 minutes before omelet is done, gently score across center. Place filling on one half and fold other half over. Transfer to heated platter and divide into 2 portions. The bottom of the omelet should be crisp and golden, the inside moist, but not runny. For a fluffier, lighter omelet, cook at very low heat 7 to 10 minutes without tipping, spread with filling and bake in 350° oven 5 to 10 minutes. Fold just before serving, or serve open-face.

FILLING SUGGESTIONS FOR PLAIN OMELETS

For plain cheese omelet, allow 1/4 cup grated cheese. For vegetable omelets, allow up to 3/4 cup vegetables, plus optional 2 to 3 tablespoons grated cheese.

- Herb: 1/4 cup mixed minced fresh herbs such as parsley, chives, tarragon, chervil, oregano, basil, thyme.
- Cheese: 1/4 cup grated Parmesan, cheddar, Comté, Gruyère, Monterey Jack; or 2 tablespoons crumbled Roquefort or Gorgonzola. Combine cheese with 2 to 3 tablespoons croutons (optional).
- Minced ham and chopped spinach, heated.
- Hot cooked pasta cut in bits and mixed with grated cheese.
- Hot crisply cooked vegetables such as peas, asparagus.
- Sliced fresh tomatoes with grated cheese.
- Minced cooked ham, small-curd cottage cheese and grated Parmesan.
- Sautéed minced onion, garlic and green pepper, with or without grated cheese.
- Sautéed sliced fresh mushrooms and minced celery, green onions and grated mild cheddar cheese.

SWEET OMELETS

To 4 eggs add 3 tablespoons liquid (water, milk or cream), dash of salt, 1 to 2 teaspoons honey and 1/4 to 1/2 teaspoon ground cinnamon. Vary with grated fresh vanilla bean, allspice, ginger, fresh lemon or orange juice instead of some of the liquid, freshly grated lemon or orange peel, crushed cardamom, coriander, aniseeds, freshly grated nutmeg. Fill with up to 3/4 cup cut-up fresh fruit or whole berries.

Eggs

BASIC METHOD FOR FRITTATAS

This Italian version of an open-faced omelet consists of well-beaten eggs that are combined with a variety of tasty fillings before cooking. For 2, allow 3 or 4 eggs and 1 cup filling. This is a good way to utilize any leftover egg yolks or whites, cooked vegetables, legumes, grains, meats, pasta and/or seafood. The basic method is to beat the eggs, blend in the filling and cook uncovered in heavy 8- or 9-inch skillet until eggs begin to set, about 7 minutes. Broil 1 to 2 minutes until eggs are completely set and top is slightly browned, or slip onto a plate, turn over into skillet and brown other side. Frittatas may be served with a salad and French bread for a filling meal. To serve, cut frittatas into quarters.

PASTA OR BROWN RICE FRITTATA

Heat in heavy skillet:
1 tablespoon olive oil
Pour in mixture of:
3 to 4 eggs, beaten
2 tablespoons minced fresh
   Italian parsley
1 small garlic clove, minced
salt and pepper to taste
2 to 3 tablespoons grated Parmesan cheese
1 cup cooked pasta, cut into bite-size bits, or
1 cup cooked brown rice
Cook as directed in preceding basic method.

SPINACH FRITTATA

Wash and place in saucepan:
1/2 to 1 pound fresh spinach
Cover pan and steam spinach in water that clings to leaves until just wilted. Drain, squeeze out all moisture and chop finely to make 3/4 cup. Set aside. Over low heat sauté 3 minutes in:
1 tablespoon butter or olive oil
1/4 cup chopped green onions
   and some tops
1 small garlic clove, minced
   (optional)
Combine:
reserved spinach
3 to 4 eggs, beaten
1/4 cup chopped Italian parsley
salt and pepper to taste
Pour mixture over onions and cook as directed in preceding basic method.
Serve with:
grated Parmesan cheese, or
mixture of 1/3 cup sour cream
   and 1 small garlic clove,
   minced

RICOTTA FRITTATA

Heat in heavy skillet:
1 to 1-1/2 tablespoons olive oil
Pour in mixture of:
3 to 4 eggs, beaten
1 cup ricotta cheese
2 to 3 tablespoons each grated
    Parmesan or Romano cheese
    and minced Italian parsley
1 small garlic clove, minced
salt and pepper to taste
pinch of freshly grated nutmeg
Cook as directed in preceding
basic method.

GREEN BEAN FRITTATA
WITH MUSTARD SAUCE

In heavy skillet sauté until
tender in:
1 tablespoon olive oil
2 green onions, sliced
1 small garlic clove, minced
    (optional)

Add and stir 1/2 minute:
1/4 cup chopped or torn cooked
    ham
Add:
1 cup cooked halved or julienne-
    cut green beans
1/2 teaspoon Herb Salt
1/4 teaspoon pepper
Pour over ham and beans mixture
of:
3 to 4 eggs, well beaten
1/4 teaspoon salt
1/8 teaspoon each pepper and
    sweet Hungarian paprika
1 tablespoon chopped fresh
    chives (optional)
Stir to evenly distribute beans
and ham. Cook as directed in preceding basic method and transfer
to heated serving platter. Just
before serving drizzle decorative-
ly on top:
Mustard Sauce (following)

Note: Ham may be omitted.
Increase the amount of green
beans to 1-1/4 cups.

MUSTARD SAUCE

Combine, mixing thoroughly:
1 tablespoon homemade or
    Dijon-style mustard
1 tablespoon white vinegar or
    fresh lemon juice
1 teaspoon olive oil
1/2 teaspoon honey or raw
    natural sugar

OTHER FRITTATA
SUGGESTIONS
• Zucchini slices sautéed with
onions.
• Swiss chard as substitute for
spinach.
• Mixture of spinach and sorrel.
• Minced green onions and
grated Parmesan or Romano
cheese mixed in with beaten
eggs.

Eggs

CHEESE SOUFFLÉ

Over low heat stir together in saucepan until foamy:
1 tablespoon each melted butter and unbleached white flour or sifted soy flour
Gradually add, blending well:
2/3 cup milk
3/4 cup grated mild cheese such as Gouda, Edam, cheddar, Gruyère or Emmenthaler
2 tablespoons minced green bell pepper and/or celery
1 tablespoon minced fresh parsley
1/2 teaspoon salt
1/8 teaspoon ground coriander
dash of pepper
Cook and stir until thickened and gradually beat in:
3 egg yolks, beaten
Cook and stir without boiling until smooth and creamy. Cool to room temperature.*
Fold in:
3 egg whites, beaten stiff but not dry
Lightly butter inside surface of 1- to 1-1/2-quart soufflé dish and sprinkle evenly with:
2 tablespoons whole-grain cracker or bread crumbs (optional)

Spoon soufflé mixture gently into dish, place in pan of hot water and bake in 350° oven 50 to 60 minutes until firm and gently browned, or until toothpick inserted in center comes out clean.

Variations: Omit green pepper and coriander and add to sauce mixture 2 cups sliced fresh mushrooms and 1 small garlic clove, minced (optional) sautéed in 1 tablespoon butter, 1/4 teaspoon caraway seeds and 1-1/2 teaspoons minced fresh marjoram.

*At this point mixture may be refrigerated. Before folding in egg whites, bring back to room temperature.

GORGONZOLA SOUFFLÉ

Over low heat stir together in saucepan until foamy:
1 tablespoon each melted butter and unbleached white flour
Gradually stir in:
1/4 cup plus 2 tablespoons (3 fluid ounces) half-and-half or milk

Cook and stir until thick and creamy. Remove from heat and gradually stir in:
3 egg yolks, beaten
Return to heat and add:
2/3 cup crumbled Gorgonzola or Stilton cheese
salt, white pepper and freshly grated nutmeg to taste
Cook and stir without boiling until smooth and creamy. Cool to room temperature.*
Fold in:
2 teaspoons minced fresh chives
3 egg whites, beaten stiff but not dry
Spoon into 2 4-inch individual soufflé dishes, place in pan of hot water and bake in preheated 400° oven 25 to 30 minutes until tops puff up and are evenly browned and toothpick inserted in center comes out clean.

*At this point mixture may be refrigerated. Before folding in egg whites, bring back to room temperature.

GINGER SQUASH SOUFFLÉ

Combine:

1-1/2 cups mashed cooked acorn
   or butternut squash
1-1/2 to 2 tablespoons mild
   honey or molasses
1/4 teaspoon each ground ginger,
   freshly grated nutmeg, salt and
   freshly grated lemon peel
1/8 teaspoon pepper
3 egg yolks, beaten
Fold in:
3 tablespoons ground filberts, or
2 tablespoons sesame seeds
3 egg whites, beaten stiff but
   not dry
Spoon into 1-1/2- to 2-quart
buttered soufflé dish and place
in pan of hot water. Bake in 375°
oven for 35 to 40 minutes or
until toothpick inserted in center
comes out clean and surface is
evenly browned. Garnish with:
1 tablespoon ground filberts, or
minced fresh parsley
Serve with tomato salad or sliced
tomatoes.

MUSHROOM EGG CASSEROLE
(For Brunch or Supper)

Sauté until tender in:
1 tablespoon butter
1-1/2 cups sliced fresh mushrooms
2 tablespoons minced onion, or
1 green onion and some tops,
   sliced
1 small garlic clove, minced
2 teaspoons minced fresh
   marjoram
1/8 teaspoon caraway seeds
   (optional)
Remove from heat and set aside.
Beat together with wire whisk:
4 eggs
3 tablespoons milk
1/2 teaspoon salt
1/8 teaspoon Herb Salt
dash of sweet Hungarian paprika
1 tablespoon chopped fresh
   parsley
2 teaspoons melted and cooled
   butter
In skillet melt:
2 teaspoons butter
When hot add and stir only once
or twice until eggs are just beginning to set:

egg mixture
reserved sautéed mushroom
   mixture
Spoon into a buttered soufflé
form which has been sprinkled
with:
2 to 3 tablespoons whole-grain
   cracker crumbs
Top with:
2 tablespoons whole-grain
   cracker or bread crumbs
2 teaspoons butter, cut in bits
Bake in 350° oven 20 minutes or
until top is golden.
Serve for brunch with whole-
grain breads and crackers,
assorted cheeses and sliced fresh
tomatoes.

Variations:
• Add when sautéing mushrooms
1/4 cup each chopped celery and
finely slivered or shredded
cooked ham.
• Substitute for all or part of
the sautéed mushrooms crisply
cooked fresh peas or green beans.

Eggs

CRÊPES

With wire whisk beat well:
1 egg, beaten
2/3 cup milk
1/2 cup sifted unbleached white
  flour
1/4 teaspoon salt
Transfer to pitcher, cover and refrigerate at least 2 hours or up to 3 days. Heat a 6-inch crêpe pan or heavy skillet and butter lightly. When butter bubbles, lower heat slightly and pour in, stirring batter each time, about 2-1/2 tablespoons batter. Quickly tip pan from side to side to coat bottom of pan. Cook until just golden, turn (using fingers to help) and cook other side 1 minute or until lightly golden. Place on rack and repeat with remaining batter, adding butter to the pan as needed and stacking crêpes as they are cooked. If batter thickens, add milk to make original consistency.
Makes 8 to 10 6-inch crêpes

To fill and bake crêpes: Moisten crêpe filling with a small portion of the sauce. Place 2 to 3 tablespoons of filling on edge of crêpe. Fold over once, fold in sides and roll jelly roll fashion. Cover bottom of small casserole or 2 ramekins with 1/4 of sauce and put filled crêpes seam side down on top of sauce. Cover with remaining sauce and bake in 375° oven 10 minutes or until bubbly. May be made ahead, refrigerated and baked just before serving. Bring to room temperature before baking.
Fillings: Any cooked leftover ham, chicken, turkey, seafood, beef, veal, vegetables, etc. may be used as crêpe filling. Season filling and sauce with grated onion, sherry, chives, parsley, lemon juice, grated cheese, etc. to taste. Use sauce to complement filling, such as Tomato Sauce with seafood or Béchamel Sauce with chicken.

Note: Crêpes may be frozen. Wrap well and defrost in refrigerator. Filled crêpes may also be frozen without additional sauce.

SWEETBREAD FILLING FOR CRÊPES

Combine, adjust seasonings to taste and set aside:
1/2 cup firmly packed, finely
  diced, cooked sweetbreads
  (page 126)
2 ounces mozzarella cheese, cut
  into tiny bits (about 1/4 cup)
1/4 cup ricotta cheese
1/2 teaspoon finely minced fresh
  thyme or lemon thyme
1/4 teaspoon salt
1/8 teaspoon white pepper
dash of cayenne pepper
To make sauce, combine:
1-1/2 cups Béchamel Sauce made
  with half-and-half and liquid
  from cooking sweetbreads
1/2 cup chopped ripe, peeled and
  seeded tomato
salt and white pepper to taste
Fill and bake crêpes as directed.
Garnish each filled crêpe with:
tiny slice of lemon
tiny parsley sprig

CRAB-MUSHROOM FILLING FOR CRÊPES

Sauté 3 to 4 minutes in:
1-1/2 tablespoons butter
1 cup slivered fresh mushrooms
3 tablespoons minced green
    onion and some tops
Sprinkle with:
fresh lemon juice, salt, white
    pepper and cayenne pepper
    to taste
Combine mushroom mixture
with:
1/3 cup grated Gruyère cheese
2 tablespoons minced fresh
    parsley
1-1/2 to 2 teaspoons dry sherry
1/2 to 2/3 cup flaked crab meat,
    marinated 10 minutes in
1-1/2 teaspoons fresh lemon juice
Adjust seasonings and sherry to
taste. Fill crêpes and place in
casserole as directed, using:
1-1/4 to 1-1/2 cups Béchamel
    Sauce made with chicken or
    veal stock or Fish Court
    Bouillon
Sprinkle before baking with:
3 to 4 tablespoons grated
    Gruyère cheese

Bake as directed. Remove from
oven and tuck between and
around crêpes:
avocado slices rubbed with
    fresh lemon juice
Return to oven for 2 to 3 minutes to just heat avocado.

Note: This dish is very rich. If 8
to 10 crêpes are too much, freeze
3 or 4. Wrap tightly before freezing and use within 2 weeks. Make
fresh Béchamel for sauce topping, heat as directed and serve
with poached eggs.

RICOTTA FILLING FOR CRÊPES

Combine:
1 cup ricotta cheese
1 egg, beaten
1/2 to 1 teaspoon minced garlic
1/2 cup minced Italian parsley
freshly grated nutmeg, salt and
    white pepper to taste
Fill and bake crêpes as directed,
using:
1-1/2 cups Tomato Sauce

SPINACH FILLING FOR CRÊPES

Prepare:
1/2 recipe Creamed Spinach
Cool and add:
1 egg, beaten
1/4 cup ricotta cheese
1/2 cup coarsely grated Monterey
    Jack cheese
fresh lemon juice, salt and white
    pepper to taste
Fill and bake crêpes as directed
(filling should not need to be
moistened), using:
1 cup Béchamel Sauce
Sprinkle before baking with:
grated Parmesan cheese

Eggs

QUICHES
(General Directions)

Prepare:
1 unbaked 7-1/2-inch Whole-
    Wheat Pastry shell (page 175)
Arrange on bottom of shell:
1/3 cup firmly packed coarsely
    grated Gruyère cheese
approximately 1-1/2 cups filling
    (suggestions follow)
Pour over filling beaten mixture
of:
2 eggs
2/3 cup half-and-half
1/4 teaspoon salt
1/8 teaspoon white pepper
herbs and/or spices to taste
Top with:
1/3 cup firmly packed coarsely
    grated Gruyère or mozzarella
    cheese or finely grated Par-
    mesan cheese
Bake in 375° oven (if using Pyrex
pie plate, 350°) 35 to 40 minutes
until crust and filling are brown
and toothpick inserted in center
of filling comes out clean.
Garnish with:
chopped fresh herbs of choice
Serve with a salad for a lunch or
light supper.

MUSHROOM FILLING

Turning often, sauté 3 to 4
minutes in:
1 to 2 tablespoons butter
2 cups sliced fresh mushrooms
    (approximately 1/2 pound)
1/4 cup minced green onion and
    some tops
1 small garlic clove, minced
Sprinkle with:
1/4 teaspoon each Herb Salt and
    dried marjoram
Cool and place on cheese layer.
Add to egg mixture:
1/8 teaspoon freshly grated
    nutmeg
2 tablespoons minced fresh
    parsley

GREEN TOMATO FILLING

Arrange on cheese layer:
1 pound green tomatoes, sliced
    (2 3-inch in diameter)
1/4 cup minced onion
1 garlic clove, minced
Sprinkle with:
2 tablespoons each coarsely
    grated cheddar cheese and
    minced fresh parsley
To egg mixture add:
1 teaspoon unbleached white flour
1/4 teaspoon each sweet Hun-
    garian paprika and dried
    oregano

CRAB FILLING

Sauté until soft in:
1 tablespoon butter
1/4 cup minced white of green
    onion
2 tablespoons minced celery
1 garlic clove, finely minced
Combine with:
1-1/4 cups flaked crab meat
    (approximately 6 ounces)
1 tablespoon minced fresh
    parsley
Arrange crab mixture on layer
of cheese. Add to egg mixture:
1/4 teaspoon sweet Hungarian
    paprika
1/8 teaspoon freshly grated
    nutmeg

SHRIMP FILLING

While preparing crust, marinate
in:
1 tablespoon fresh lemon juice
6 ounces cooked shrimp
Drain and pat dry with paper
toweling. Arrange shrimp on
cheese layer. To egg mixture add:
1/8 teaspoon freshly grated
    nutmeg

SPINACH FILLING

Sauté until soft in:
1 tablespoon butter
2 tablespoons minced white of
    green onion
1 small garlic clove, finely
    minced
Combine with:
1 cup well drained, firmly packed
    finely chopped cooked spinach
    (approximately 1 pound)
Arrange spinach mixture on layer
of cheese. Add to egg mixture:
1/8 teaspoon freshly grated
    nutmeg
Before baking, sprinkle top layer
of cheese lightly with:
sweet Hungarian paprika

Variation: Reduce spinach to
3/4 cup and add 1/4 to 1/2 cup
drained minced clams, shrimp or
crab meat, or crisp bacon bits.

ZUCCHINI FILLING

Sprinkle lightly with salt on both
sides and drain in colander for
1 hour to draw out water:
7 ounces zucchini, sliced

Mix together and set aside:
1/4 cup grated Parmesan cheese
1/2 teaspoon Herb Salt
1/4 teaspoon sweet Hungarian
    paprika
1/8 teaspoon each freshly grated
    nutmeg and cayenne pepper
Pat zucchini slices dry and
arrange on cheese layer. Then
arrange on top:
1/4 cup finely minced onion
1 small garlic clove, minced
1 ripe tomato, sliced
Parmesan cheese mixture
Add to egg mixture:
1 teaspoon unbleached white
    flour

PISSALADIÈRE
(Onion and Tomato Tart)

Prepare:
1 unbaked 7-1/2-inch Whole-
    Wheat Pastry shell (page 175)
Sauté until soft in:
1 tablespoon butter
1 cup minced onion
Remove onion from skillet with
slotted spatula and set aside. In
same skillet sauté in:
1 to 2 teaspoons olive oil, or as
    needed
1 small garlic clove, minced

Add and cook over medium heat,
stirring until thickened:
1 pound ripe tomatoes, peeled,
    seeded and chopped
1/2 teaspoon minced fresh
    rosemary leaves
1/4 teaspoon salt
1/8 teaspoon pepper
Adjust seasonings and cool.
Layer in pie shell:
2 tablespoons each grated Par-
    mesan and coarsely grated
    Gruyère cheese
reserved onions
tomato sauce
1/4 cup coarsely grated mozza-
    rella cheese, or
2 ounces mozzarella cheese,
    thinly sliced
Drain, reserving oil, rinse and pat
dry with paper toweling:
1 2-ounce can anchovy fillets
Arrange fillets in spoke pattern
over cheese. In spaces in between
anchovies arrange:
10 to 15 pitted black olives,
    halved
Brush olive halves with anchovy
oil and bake in 350° oven 35 to
40 minutes until crust is golden
and filling is set.

Eggs

EIERPFANNKUCHEN

Beat together with wire whisk:
2 egg yolks, beaten
1 cup milk
1/8 teaspoon salt
1 tablespoon honey
1/8 to 1/4 teaspoon ground
    cinnamon
Stirring gently with wooden
spoon, sift in gradually:
1 cup sifted unbleached white
    flour
Fold in:
2 egg whites, beaten stiff but
    not dry
Transfer batter to a pitcher,
cover and refrigerate 15 minutes
to 2 hours. Heat in a heavy 8- to
9-inch skillet:
1 tablespoon butter
Stirring batter gently, pour in
1/4 of the batter, spreading it out
evenly in skillet, and cook 2 to 3
minutes until underside is golden
and surface has set. Turn and
cook other side 1 minute until
just golden. Slide onto heated
serving plate and keep warm.
Repeat with remaining batter,
adding butter sparingly to skillet
if necessary and making 4 pancakes in all. Serve topped with
hot applesauce or hot Fruit
Compote.

Variations:
• Fresh Fruit: Substitute light
red or rosé wine for the milk in
the batter (optional). Immediately after pouring batter into
skillet, arrange on top sliced
fresh fruit such as plums,
peaches, bananas, apples, pears,
and/or whole berries. Sprinkle
lightly with ground cinnamon.
Just before serving, drizzle
cooked pancakes with honey.
• Sweet Lemon: Drizzle each
cooked pancake evenly with 2 to
3 teaspoons each fresh lemon
juice and honey. Roll up like a
jelly roll and serve immediately
with hot tea.
• Ricotta: Combine 1 cup
ricotta or small-curd cottage
cheese, 1/2 teaspoon ground
cinnamon, 2 tablespoons honey
and 1 teaspoon freshly grated
lemon peel. Spread evenly on
cooked pancakes and roll like
a jelly roll. Place in lightly
buttered shallow baking dish
and broil 3 to 5 minutes until
filling is warmed and edges of
pancakes turn crispy. At table
drizzle honey over each pancake.
• Ham: Top each cooked pancake with a slice of cooked ham.
Roll up like a jelly roll and place
seam side down in lightly buttered shallow baking dish. Pour
over pancakes a mixture of 1/3
cup heavy cream, whipped, 1/3
cup grated Gruyère cheese, and
salt, white pepper and cayenne
pepper to taste. Broil until sauce
is golden and bubbly.

OLD-FASHIONED BAKED APPLE SUPPER

An excellent way to utilize dried bread and leftover bread crusts.

Moisten until soft in:
1 cup milk
3 to 4 slices stale bread
Drain, pressing out any excess milk, and break up bread slightly. Set aside.
Beat together with wire whisk:
3 egg yolks
3 tablespoons softened butter
3 tablespoons honey or raw natural sugar
dash of salt
1/8 teaspoon grated fresh vanilla bean
1 teaspoon freshly grated lemon peel
Fold in:
moistened bread
2 Golden Delicious apples, thinly sliced
3 egg whites, beaten stiff but not dry
Spoon into a buttered casserole, place in pan of hot water and bake in 350° oven 30 minutes. Serve hot as a light supper.

EGG FOO YUNG

Beat together:
4 eggs, beaten
3 tablespoons water
1-1/2 teaspoons Tamari soy sauce
1 tablespoon cornstarch
1/4 teaspoon Oriental sesame oil
Mix in:
2/3 cup crisped and well-drained bean sprouts
1/2 cup ground fresh fish, sliced fresh mushrooms, or minced cooked ham, chicken, shrimp, crab
2 tablespoons each minced green onion, water chestnuts and bamboo shoots
In heavy skillet heat:
2 teaspoons peanut oil, or as needed
Stir egg mixture well to distribute ingredients and ladle about 1/4 cup of mixture into skillet to make a 3- to 4-inch pancake. When egg has started to set, push runny edges up and around each cake to make it uniform. Brown one side, turn and brown other side, turning only once. Repeat with remaining egg mixture, making 8 to 10 pancakes in all.
For gravy, combine:
1/2 cup chicken stock
1-1/2 teaspoons cornstarch
Cook and stir until thickened and pour over egg foo yung.

RED PEPPER RICE TOPPED WITH EGGS

This simple dish is very flexible. Herbs and vegetables can be varied. A good way to use leftover rice.

Sauté in:
1 tablespoon olive oil
1/2 cup chopped onion
3 small garlic cloves, minced
1 red bell pepper, coarsely chopped
Add and combine well:
1/2 to 3/4 cup cooked brown rice
1 small ripe tomato, peeled and chopped
Season while cooking with:
1/2 teaspoon each crumbled dried oregano and basil
salt and pepper to taste
Break onto surface to poach:
3 to 4 eggs
Sprinkle with:
salt, pepper and sweet Hungarian paprika
2 to 3 tablespoons grated Parmesan cheese
Cover and cook over low heat 7 to 10 minutes until eggs have set. Serve for lunch or as a light supper with Simple Tomato Salad.

51

Eggs

COTTAGE CHEESE PANCAKES

Combine:
2 eggs, beaten
2/3 cup small-curd cottage cheese
2 tablespoons unbleached white
    flour, sifted with
1 tablespoon soy flour
1-1/2 teaspoons melted butter
1/4 teaspoon salt
Spooning several tablespoons at
a time onto hot griddle, brown on
both sides, turning only once, in:
1-1/2 teaspoons each butter and
    corn oil, or as needed
Serve with honey and fresh fruit
or applesauce.
Makes 10 3-1/2-inch pancakes

MARSEILLE EGGS

A quick, tasty supper that can be
prepared in advance.

Combine in saucepan over low
heat and simmer 15 to 20 minutes or until thickened:
2 cups Tomato Sauce*
1/3 cup grated mozzarella,
    Gruyère or other light cheese
1/4 cup red wine
1/2 teaspoon each crumbled
    dried oregano and basil
1 bay leaf
Gently mix tomato mixture with:
4 hard-cooked eggs, quartered
Spoon over:
toasted English muffins

*The tomato sauce must be
homemade.

EASY BAKED EGG CASSEROLE

Combine and pour into a buttered casserole:
4 eggs, beaten
3 tablespoons sour cream
salt, pepper and Herb Salt to
    taste
1 cup cooked pasta, diced ham,
    chopped onions, sliced fresh
    mushrooms in any combination
Top with:
1/4 cup grated mild cheese
Bake in 375° oven 35 to 45 minutes or until golden and toothpick inserted in center comes
out clean.

Noodles/Cereals/Legumes

Noodles/Cereals/Legumes

HOMEMADE NOODLES

Beat together:

2 eggs

1 teaspoon corn oil

Sift onto board:

**1-3/4 cups unbleached white
   flour**

1/4 teaspoon salt

Make hollow in center of flour and pour in egg mixture. With fingers and spatula, gradually mix egg and flour until blended. Knead gently until dough is smooth and no longer sticky. Add more flour only if needed. Form into ball and cover with lightly dampened tea towel. Let rest 20 minutes. Divide into 4 equal portions and roll each portion out as thinly as possible on lightly floured board, adding flour as needed. Keep remaining dough covered. Place sheet of dough aside on floured surface and roll out remaining dough. Starting with first sheet, roll half nearest you away from you like a jelly roll, only to midpoint of

sheet. Then roll half farthest from you toward you like a jelly roll to meet other roll in center. With very sharp knife cut into desired widths. With blunt edge of knife, lift at center fold and shake strips free. Place flat on lightly floured waxed paper and proceed with rest of sheets. If strips stick, loosen and sprinkle with flour or cornstarch. Cover with waxed paper and lightly dampened tea towel if not cooking within 10 minutes. Noodles will stay fresh several hours. Or wrap in waxed paper and refrigerate up to 2 days, or freeze. Makes approximately 9 ounces, 4 cups cooked. Enough for main pasta dish for 2. This recipe doubles well.

Green Noodles: Increase flour by 2 to 3 tablespoons and when flour is almost blended into egg mixture, add 3 tablespoons finely minced cooked spinach, squeezed dry.

Cannelloni Variation: Roll dough thinly and cut into 10 4-inch squares. Cook squares a few at a time until al dente in boiling salted water and 1/2 teaspoon olive oil. As they are cooked, remove to oiled cookie sheet and spread out evenly. Turn to coat other side with a little oil and keep covered with tea towel. Fill with any crêpe filling and treat as you would crêpes (page 46), but do not fold in ends. Purchased wonton skins may be substituted for cannelloni skins.

Note: There are several moderately priced pasta machines on the market. If you intend to make much pasta, they are well worth the investment. Use this dough recipe and follow the directions provided by the manufacturer.

GENERAL DIRECTIONS FOR COOKING PASTA

Bring 1-1/2 to 2 quarts water to boil with 1/2 teaspoon salt and 1 tablespoon olive oil. Add, stirring to prevent sticking, 6 to 8 ounces spaghetti or noodles. Continue boiling, stirring occasionally, 10 to 20 minutes for spaghetti or dried noodles, 3 to 4 minutes for homemade or purchased fresh noodles. Pasta should be cooked al dente, just tender. Add 1 cup cold water to prevent further cooking and drain well. Toss with 2 to 3 tablespoons olive oil or as specified in recipe.

SPAETZLE

Into a measuring cup break:
1 egg
Add to measure 1/2 cup:
milk or water
Transfer to large bowl and beat until well blended. Gradually add and stir with wooden spoon until bubbly and elastic:
1 cup unbleached white flour
1/4 teaspoon salt
1/8 teaspoon freshly grated nutmeg
Have ready a large pot of boiling salted water, a bowl of cold water and a buttered baking dish. Place a large fine-mesh strainer in the boiling water. Wet a small cutting board (special boards are available with a handle and tapering end) and place about 1/4 cup of batter on board. With a table knife, spread a portion of batter to end of board, making a thin coating. Dip knife in cold water, and dipping frequently, shred batter directly into the boiling water, making small strands. Use all batter on board and let this portion boil 1 minute or until spaetzle rise to top. Lift strainer to drain and place spaetzle in baking dish. Repeat with rest of batter, keeping cooked spaetzle warm as you work. When all of batter is cooked, stir in:
1 to 2 tablespoons softened butter

Variation: This recipe may be doubled, in which case use water instead of milk. Serve half with first meal. To remaining spaetzle add 1 egg, beaten, 1 teaspoon each chopped fresh parsley and chives, 1/4 teaspoon salt and 1/8 teaspoon pepper. Place in buttered casserole, dot with butter, sprinkle with grated Parmesan cheese and bake in 350° oven 20 minutes.

Noodles/Cereals/Legumes

KIDNAPPER'S CASSEROLE

A stick-to-your-ribs casserole. The hearty flavor varies with the type of cheese used.

Sauté 3 to 5 minutes in:
2 teaspoons corn oil
1/2 cup sliced onion
Combine in bowl with:
2 to 2-1/2 cups cooked flat noodles
1 cup sliced fresh mushrooms
1/2 cup shredded prosciutto or cooked ham (optional)
2/3 cup cubed cheese (Emmenthaler, Gruyère, Edam, Gouda or Colby)
1/2 teaspoon each salt, dried marjoram and dried thyme
1/4 teaspoon pepper
Spoon into buttered 1-1/2-quart casserole which has been sprinkled with:
2 tablespoons whole-grain cracker crumbs
Top with beaten mixture of:
1 egg
2 tablespoons milk

Bake in 400° oven 20 minutes and sprinkle with:
2 to 3 tablespoons grated cheese (as above)
Bake 10 more minutes and garnish with:
1 tablespoon chopped fresh parsley
Serve with colorful tossed salad.

SOUR CREAM PARMESAN NOODLES

This recipe reheats well, so it is worth making a large amount. Serve as a main meal and reheat remainder to serve as an accompaniment to meat or poultry dishes later in the week. The flavor improves with refrigeration and reheating.

Melt together:
2 tablespoons each butter and olive oil

Add and let stand 5 minutes to steep:
2 garlic cloves, minced
In buttered shallow baking dish place:
6 to 8 ounces flat green noodles, cooked al dente
Pour butter-oil mixture over. Combine and mix well with noodles:
1 cup sour cream
1/2 cup grated Parmesan cheese
1/2 teaspoon salt
1/4 teaspoon pepper
Place in 350° oven 15 minutes or until heated through. Just before serving sprinkle with:
1 to 2 tablespoons chopped fresh parsley
Serve as entrée with green beans and Simple Tomato Salad.

Variation: Cut recipe in half and combine noodle mixture with sautéed mixture of 1 tablespoon butter or as needed, 1/2 pound lean ground beef, 1 onion, minced, salt and pepper to taste. Bake in 350° oven 20 minutes.

VANILLA NOODLE CASSEROLE

Beat with wire whisk:
2 egg yolks
Add, stirring with wooden spoon:
**1/2 cup ricotta cheese or small-
curd cottage cheese**
1/2 cup raisins, plumped
3 to 4 tablespoons mild honey
**1 teaspoon freshly grated lemon
peel**
2 teaspoons fresh lemon juice
**1/8 teaspoon grated fresh vanilla
bean**
2 tablespoons softened butter
Fold in:
**3 cups cooked 3/8-inch wide flat
noodles**
**2 egg whites, beaten stiff but
not dry**
Butter a 1-1/2- to 2-quart casserole and sprinkle with:
**2 tablespoons whole-grain cracker
or bread crumbs**
Spoon noodle mixture into casserole and dot top with:
1 tablespoon butter, cut into bits
Bake in 350° oven 30 minutes or
until surface begins to brown.
Serve with fresh fruit salad.

PESTO

In mortar and pestle make
a paste of:
1 to 2 teaspoons minced garlic
**3/4 cup firmly packed, chopped
fresh basil**
**1-1/2 tablespoons minced fresh
Italian parsley**
1/4 teaspoon sea salt
2 teaspoons pine nuts (optional)
Gradually add:
**2 to 3 tablespoons grated Par-
mesan cheese**
Blend mixture thoroughly into:
**3 tablespoons each softened
butter and olive oil**
Toss into freshly cooked noodles
or spaghetti.

Note: If fresh basil is in abundance, double or triple recipe
and freeze up to 2 months.

ORZO (PUNTINE) WITH BROWNED BUTTER

A spaghetti product put out
under several names, orzo is a
small rice-shaped pasta available
in 1-pound packages at Italian
markets.

Bring to boil:
1 quart water
1 teaspoon corn oil
1/2 teaspoon salt
Gradually add:
2/3 to 1 cup orzo
Bring back to boil. Stir and cook
at gentle boil 10 minutes or until
pasta is cooked al dente. Just
before pasta is cooked, melt:
3 tablespoons butter
Cook over medium-high heat
until butter is well browned.
Stir in:
1 teaspoon fresh lemon juice
Drain pasta, return to saucepan
and immediately stir in:
browned butter
Adjust seasonings with:
salt and pepper
Serve as accompaniment to meat
or fowl.

Noodles/Cereals/Legumes

SPAGHETTI WITH ZUCCHINI

Sauté a few slices at a time until golden on both sides in:
2 tablespoons olive oil
1 firm 6- to 7-ounce zucchini, sliced
Remove with slotted spatula and set aside. In same skillet, sauté 2 minutes:
2 garlic cloves, minced
Add and stir well to blend flavors:
1 tablespoon minced fresh basil
1/2 teaspoon Herb Salt
1/4 teaspoon pepper
Return zucchini to skillet and keep warm. In warmed serving bowl combine to coat spaghetti evenly:
6 to 8 ounces spaghetti, cooked al dente
1 tablespoon each grated Parmesan cheese and butter or olive oil
Quickly stir in:
1 egg, beaten
Immediately toss in:
reserved zucchini mixture
Sprinkle generously with:
grated Parmesan cheese
Serve with a tossed salad.

SPAGHETTI WITH BEEF/ MUSHROOM SAUCE

This recipe doubles well and the flavor improves with reheating.

Sauté until onion is transparent in:
2 to 3 tablespoons olive oil
1 medium-size onion, minced
2 garlic cloves, minced
2 cups sliced fresh mushrooms
Add and cook, stirring until browned:
1/4 pound lean ground beef
Stir in:
1-1/2 cups Tomato Sauce
1/4 cup finely chopped green pepper
Cover and simmer 30 minutes to 1 hour, until thickened, adding if desired:
1/2 cup red wine
Adjust seasonings with salt and pepper and serve over:
8 ounces spaghetti, cooked al dente
Serve with a generous amount of Parmesan cheese and a green salad.

MINT SPAGHETTI

Sauté 3 to 5 minutes in:
1/4 cup olive oil
1 cup sliced fresh mushrooms
1 garlic clove, minced
Lower heat and blend in:
1/4 cup minced fresh mint
1/2 cup fresh orange juice
10 to 15 pitted black olives, quartered
5 anchovy fillets, drained and chopped, or
1 to 1-1/2 teaspoons anchovy paste
Heat but do not boil. Pour sauce over:
6 to 8 ounces spaghetti, cooked al dente and tossed with
1 tablespoon softened butter
Sprinkle generously with:
grated Parmesan or Romano cheese
Serve with green salad.

Note: Flavor can be varied by adding capers and minced fresh basil to taste. Use the remaining anchovies for salads, pizza, in stuffed eggs, on crackers, or in gravies or tomato sauces.

ARTICHOKE SPAGHETTI

In heavy skillet or saucepan heat:
**2 tablespoons each olive oil
and butter**
Add, stirring 2 to 3 minutes until
foamy and golden:
**1 teaspoon unbleached white
flour**
Stir in:
**3/4 cup chicken or vegetable
stock**
2 garlic cloves, minced
1 tablespoon fresh lemon juice
**1/4 cup minced fresh Italian
parsley**
salt and pepper to taste
Cook and stir over moderate heat
5 minutes. Add:
**8 cooked artichoke hearts or
bottoms, halved if large**
**2 tablespoons grated Parmesan
cheese**
Lower heat, cover and cook,
basting artichokes several times,
for 5 to 7 minutes. Adjust
seasonings.*
Toss sauce with:
**8 ounces spaghetti, cooked
al dente**
**1/4 pound shredded cooked ham
or prosciutto**

Transfer to heated platter or
bowl and garnish with:
minced fresh parsley
Serve with plenty of grated Parmesan cheese and tossed salad
with Italian Salad Dressing.

*Sauce may be cooled and refrig-
erated at this point.
Reheat gently.

Vegetarian Entrée: Omit ham and
serve with extra Parmesan cheese.

SARDINIAN SPAGHETTI
WITH ANCHOVIES

Heat in skillet:
1/3 to 1/2 cup olive oil
Add, pressing with fork to make
paste-like consistency:
2 to 3 garlic cloves, finely minced
**1 2-ounce can anchovy fillets,
drained**
2 tablespoons chopped fresh basil
Toss with:
**6 to 8 ounces spaghetti, cooked
al dente**
Transfer to heated platter or
bowl and sprinkle with:
**2 tablespoons chopped fresh
Italian parsley**
1/3 cup grated Parmesan cheese
Serve with extra grated Parmesan
cheese and tossed salad with
black olives.

VEGETABLE SPAGHETTI

Sauté until onion is transparent
in:
1 to 2 tablespoons olive oil
1 small onion, chopped
2 to 3 garlic cloves, minced
Lower heat and blend in:
1/4 cup Tomato Paste
**1 cup water, vegetable or beef
stock or red wine**
1 large carrot, thinly sliced
**1/4 to 1/3 cup grated cheddar,
Monterey Jack or mozzarella
cheese**
**1 to 2 teaspoons mixed minced
fresh basil, oregano, thyme
and parsley**
1/2 teaspoon Herb Salt
1/4 teaspoon pepper
Cover and simmer, stirring occasionally, 15 minutes. Sauce
should be thick. Serve over:
**6 to 8 ounces spaghetti, cooked
al dente**
For vegetarian lunch serve
with milk.

Variations: Add chopped celery,
green pepper, mushrooms or
combination when adding carrots.

Noodles/Cereals/Legumes

MACARONI WITH EGGPLANT SAUCE

Combine and place in buttered shallow casserole:
1-1/2 cups cooked elbow
    macaroni, mixed with
3/4 cup Tomato Sauce
salt and pepper to taste
Steam until soft:
1-1/2 cups diced pulp from
    eggplant
Mash and set aside, reserving steaming liquid. Sauté until onion is soft in:
2 teaspoons butter
3 tablespoons very finely minced
    onion
1/4 teaspoon finely minced garlic
    (optional)
Stir in:
mashed eggplant
1 tablespoon each dry white
    wine and reserved cooking
    liquid
crumbled dried oregano or basil
    to taste
salt and pepper to taste
Spread eggplant mixture evenly on macaroni and top with:
1/2 cup grated mozzarella cheese
Bake in 350° oven 15 minutes until macaroni is heated through and cheese is melted.

ORIENTAL NOODLE DISHES

Popular throughout the Orient, main noodle dishes are easy, quick and infinitely varied. They can be served in broth with bits of leftovers or with fresh foods. They can be pan-fried and served with stir-fry meats and/or vegetables. Allow 1/2 pound fresh noodles (homemade or purchased in Oriental and some supermarkets).

NOODLES WITH BROTH

Bring to boil and simmer
10 minutes:
3 cups chicken, pork or beef
    stock
3 to 4 dried forest mushrooms,
    soaked to soften, drained and
    sliced (add soaking water to
    broth)
1/4 pound chicken gizzards,
    thinly sliced
1/2 cup julienne-cut carrots
Add and bring to boil 1-1/2 cups of any combination of the following:
shredded spinach, bok choy,
    Swiss chard, lettuce or Napa
    cabbage leaves, fresh peas,
    sliced water chestnuts, sliced
    bamboo shoots

Simmer 1 to 2 minutes until vegetables are just tender. Cook noodles al dente, drain and place in 2 serving bowls. Pour hot soup over noodles.

Variations:
• Add and simmer in broth a few minutes until cooked quartered chicken livers, shrimp, abalone slices, fish fillet cubes, crab or lobster meat.
• Add and heat through leftover poultry or meat, firm fresh bean curd, cut in squares, quartered hard-cooked eggs.

PAN-FRIED NOODLE DISHES

Cook 1/2 pound fresh noodles in boiling water 2 to 3 minutes, drain immediately and toss with 1 tablespoon peanut or corn oil to prevent sticking. In heavy skillet, heat:
2 tablespoons peanut or corn oil
1/2 teaspoon Oriental sesame oil
Place noodles in hot oil and fry until crispy, turning once and adding more oil if needed. Noodles should be crusty on the outside, soft on the inside. Remove from skillet and keep warm. Prepare any stir-fry recipe and toss with noodles. Serve immediately.

Noodles/Cereals/Legumes

BROWN RICE

Cooking more rice than is needed for a particular recipe saves time and energy. Cooked rice can be used in casseroles, rice puddings, yeast breads, hot cereals, rice patties, salads and soups. It can also be reheated with butter.

Bring to boil:
1-1/4 cups water or stock
1 tablespoon butter (optional)
1/4 to 1/2 teaspoon salt
Add:
1/2 cup brown rice, rinsed in cold water and drained
Bring back just to boil, cover, lower heat and cook 45 minutes until water is absorbed. Do not lift lid and do not stir while rice is cooking. If steaming stops and crackling sounds can be heard after 35 to 40 minutes, the water is absorbed. Remove rice from heat and let stand covered for remainder of cooking time. Makes 2 cups cooked rice

Serving Suggestions:

• Buttered rice: Toss rice with 1 to 2 tablespoons softened butter. Garnish with minced fresh herbs of choice.
• Sesame rice: Add to buttered rice Sesame Butter, Sesame Salt or toasted sesame seeds.
• Savory rice: Before serving, combine rice with 1/3 cup each minced onion and celery that has been sautéed in 2 tablespoons butter.

WHITE RICE

Following preceding instructions for cooking brown rice, using 1/2 cup white rice for each cup of water. Reduce steaming time to 20 minutes. One-half cup raw rice makes 1 cup.

APRICOT RICE

Bring to boil:
1-1/4 cups water
1/2 teaspoon salt
Add:
1/2 cup brown rice
1/4 teaspoon ground cinnamon
1/8 teaspoon freshly grated nutmeg
Cover and cook over low heat 40 minutes. Without stirring, add and replace lid:
1/2 cup fresh green peas
Cook 5 minutes until peas are tender and water has evaporated. Gently stir in:
3 to 5 apricots, quartered
2 to 3 tablespoons grated fresh or unsweetened coconut
2 tablespoons chopped fresh parsley
10 to 15 raw cashews or blanched almonds
Cover and let stand 2 to 3 minutes. Serve as main dish or as an accompaniment.

CHEESE RICE

Combine and heat:
1-1/2 to 2 cups cooked brown rice
1/4 cup vegetable or beef stock
Add:
3/4 cup grated mozzarella cheese
1/4 cup each finely minced celery
    and red or green bell pepper
1/2 cup thinly sliced fresh mush-
    rooms (optional)
1/2 teaspoon salt
1/2 to 1 teaspoon minced fresh
    thyme, or
1/4 to 1/2 teaspoon minced
    fresh savory
Stir with wooden spoon over low
heat until cheese has melted, or
bake in buttered casserole in 350°
oven 20 minutes. Serve with
green salad or cooked vegetable,
or as an accompaniment to
beef patties or broiled fish.

BROWN RICE WITH
NUTS AND FRUIT

Sauté 2 to 3 minutes in:
1 tablespoon peanut oil or butter
1/4 cup chopped fresh
    mushrooms
Combine mushroom mixture
with:
2 cups hot cooked brown rice
1/4 cup slivered almonds or
    cashews in any combination
1/4 cup chopped dried apricots,
    plumped
1/2 apple, finely diced
2 tablespoons chopped fresh
    herbs such as parsley, chives
    and/or thyme
1 tablespoon fresh lemon juice
1 teaspoon freshly grated lemon
    peel
salt to taste
Cover and let stand over low heat
3 to 4 minutes until heated
through. Serve as entrée with
green vegetable.

GREEN RICE

Toss into:
1-1/2 to 2 cups cooked white or
    brown rice
1/3 cup cooked and drained
    chopped spinach
1/4 cup chopped fresh parsley
3 tablespoons grated Parmesan
    cheese
1 teaspoon Tamari soy sauce
1 teaspoon grated onion
1 egg, beaten
salt and pepper to taste
Place in buttered casserole and
bake in 350° oven 15 to 20 minutes until heated through and
egg is set. Garnish with:
chopped hard-cooked egg, or
extra grated Parmesan cheese

Noodles/Cereals/Legumes

RAISIN RICE WITH PEAS

Sauté 5 minutes until kernels
begin to turn white in:
1 tablespoon butter
1/2 cup brown rice
Add without stirring and bring
to boil:
1-1/4 to 1-1/2 cups salted boiling
    water
Lower heat and add:
1/2 cup raisins
Cover and cook over low heat
40 minutes. Without stirring, add
and replace lid:
1/2 cup fresh green peas
Cook 5 minutes or until peas are
tender and water has evaporated.
While rice is cooking, sauté until
onion is transparent in:
1 tablespoon butter
1 onion, thinly sliced
Toss 2/3 of the onions into
cooked rice and peas with:
2 to 3 tablespoons grated fresh or
    unsweetened coconut
Replace lid and let stand 2 to 3
minutes. Garnish with:
remaining sautéed onions
Serve with Carrot Coconut Relish
and Cardamom Peas.

RISOTTO

Heat and keep hot:
1-1/2 to 1-3/4 cups chicken,
    beef, lamb or veal stock
Sauté until rice is golden
brown in:
1-1/2 tablespoons butter and/or
    olive oil
1/2 cup Italian rice
2 teaspoons minced onion
1/2 teaspoon minced garlic
1 tablespoon minced fresh
    Italian parsley
Add and bring to boil until wine
is almost absorbed:
3 tablespoons dry white wine
Stirring and cooking gently until
rice is tender, add 1/4 cup at
a time:
heated stock
With last addition add to stock
to dissolve:
1/8 teaspoon saffron threads
With fork, toss in:
1 tablespoon softened butter
2 tablespoons grated Parmesan
    cheese

CARROT RICE WITH HAM

Bring to boil:
1-1/4 cups water
1/2 teaspoon salt
Add:
1/2 cup brown rice
2 medium-size carrots, thinly
    sliced or coarsely grated
1 medium-size onion, chopped
1 teaspoon minced fresh basil
Cover, lower heat and cook 45
minutes or until rice is cooked.
Toss in:
1 cup diced or shredded
    cooked ham
2 tablespoons chopped
    fresh parsley
1 tablespoon fresh lemon juice
Replace cover and let stand 3 to
5 minutes to heat through.
Adjust seasonings with:
salt and pepper
Garnish with:
red onion rings, or
tomato slices and chopped
    green onions

Vegetarian Entrée: Substitute
1 cup cooked green split peas for
the ham.

LEMON RICE

Beat together and set aside:
2 eggs, beaten
1/4 to 1/2 cup grated Parmesan
  cheese
1-1/2 tablespoons fresh lemon
  juice
1 teaspoon chopped fresh thyme
  or lemon thyme
Toss into:
2 cups hot cooked brown rice
1 tablespoon softened butter
Gently stir in:
egg mixture
Cover and let stand over low heat
3 to 4 minutes until heated
through. Toss in:
2 tablespoons toasted sesame
  seeds, or
1/4 cup chopped or slivered
  almonds, raw cashews or pine
  nuts
Serve with salad.

VEGETABLE SPANISH RICE

In skillet or saucepan with tight-
fitting lid, sauté until kernels
turn white in:
1 tablespoon olive oil
1/2 cup brown rice
Stir in:
1 small onion, chopped, or
3 tablespoons chopped green
  onion
1/2 green pepper, seeded and
  finely chopped
1/4 cup finely chopped celery
2 garlic cloves, minced
1 dried red chili pepper, seeded
  and crushed
1 to 2 ripe tomatoes, peeled and
  diced
Pour over vegetables:
1-1/4 cups boiling water
Cover and steam at low heat 40
to 45 minutes or until moisture
has evaporated and rice is tender.
Serve with Gruyère Salad.

RICE PILAF

Sauté until golden in:
1 tablespoon each butter and
  garlic olive oil
1/2 cup long-grain rice
2 tablespoons finely minced
  onion
2 teaspoons finely minced celery
1 teaspoon finely minced green
  bell pepper (optional)
1/2 teaspoon finely minced garlic
  (optional)
Stir in:
1 cup any rich stock
Cover tightly and simmer over
low heat 20 to 30 minutes until
liquid is absorbed and rice is
tender. Adjust seasonings with
salt and pepper and with fork
stir in:
2 tablespoons minced fresh
  parsley

Noodles/Cereals/Legumes

SAFFRON RICE PILAF

Dissolve in and keep hot:
**1 cup heated beef, chicken or
lamb stock**
1/8 teaspoon saffron threads
Sauté until rice is golden brown
in:
**1-1/2 tablespoons butter and/or
olive oil**
1/2 cup long-grain white rice
2 teaspoons minced onion
1/2 teaspoon minced garlic
Add and stir briefly:
heated stock and saffron
Bring to gentle boil, lower heat to
low, cover tightly and cook 20
minutes or until rice is tender and
liquid is absorbed. Adjust seasonings with salt and pepper and
toss in:
**2 tablespoons minced fresh
parsley, or**
2 teaspoons minced fresh chives

BROWN RICE PILAF
WITH LENTILS

Pour boiling water over and let
stand 1 hour:
3 tablespoons brown lentils
Drain and set aside. In heavy
saucepan with tight-fitting lid,
sauté until kernels turn white in:
**1 tablespoon each olive oil and
butter**
1/2 cup brown rice
**3 tablespoons each minced onion
and celery with some tender
leaves**
**1 tablespoon minced green
pepper**
Stir in:
reserved lentils
**1-1/4 cups chicken or vegetable
stock**
Bring to boil, lower heat to
simmer, cover and cook 45 minutes or until rice is tender and
liquid is absorbed. Remove cover,
adjust seasonings with salt and
pepper and fluff with fork. Serve
as accompaniment to fowl or
meat course.
This recipe doubles well and
can be a vegetarian main meal.
Serve with Simple Tomato Salad
and wedges of feta cheese and
black olives.

HULLED BARLEY PILAF

Pour boiling water to cover over:
**2 tablespoons green or yellow
split peas**
Let stand 30 minutes, drain and
set aside. Sauté until barley is
browned in:
**1-1/2 teaspoons each olive oil and
butter**
1/4 cup hulled barley
**1 tablespoon each finely minced
carrot, onion and celery**
**1/2 teaspoon minced garlic
(optional)**
Add, stir well and bring to boil:
reserved split peas
1 cup any rich stock
Lower heat to simmer, cover and
cook 1 to 1-1/4 hours or until
barley is tender and moisture is
absorbed. Adjust seasonings, toss
with fork to fluff and serve as
accompaniment to meat or fowl.
This recipe doubles well and may
be served as a vegetarian entrée
with fruit salad and ricotta cheese.

BULGHUR PILAF

Sauté until golden in:
2 tablespoons butter
1 cup bulghur
3 tablespoons minced onion
Blend in:
2 cups any rich stock
1/4 teaspoon each salt and
    dried oregano
1/8 teaspoon pepper
Bring to gentle boil, cover and
cook over medium-low heat 15
to 20 minutes or until bulghur is
fluffy and liquid is absorbed.

MILLET

Bring to boil, cover and lower
heat:
1/4 cup millet
3/4 cup water
1/4 teaspoon salt
Simmer 25 minutes until water
evaporates. Remove from heat
and let stand, covered, 10 minutes. Serve plain with butter or
stir in:
2 tablespoons butter
1/4 cup sautéed minced onion
    and/or celery, green bell pep-
    per and mushrooms (optional)
mixed minced fresh herbs or
    dried crumbled herbs of choice
Makes approximately 1-1/4 cups

CHINESE METHOD OF COOKING RICE

This method works best with at
least 1 cup of rice.

Wash well until water runs clean:
1 cup long-grain white rice
Place in 1-quart saucepan and
cover with water to a depth of
1/2 inch above the rice level. Let
stand at least 30 minutes. Over
medium-high heat bring to boil
and boil until water is absorbed
and small hollows appear in rice.
Cover tightly and steam on lowest
heat 20 minutes. This method
lends itself well to one-dish rice
meals—easy and convenient.

RICE WITH BEEF

Prepare 1 cup rice as above. When
water has been absorbed, combine
following and quickly stir in with
fork:
1/2 pound lean ground beef
1 tablespoon Tamari soy sauce
1/4 cup chopped green onions
    and some tops

Cover tightly and cook over
lowest heat 20 minutes. Strew
over top of rice:
3/4 to 1 cup fresh peas
Cover and continue cooking 5
minutes.

RICE WITH MEAT, SEAFOOD OR POULTRY

Prepare 1 cup rice as above. When
water has been absorbed, place
on top of rice:
2 to 3 dried forest mushrooms,
    soaked to soften and cut
    in julienne
1/4 teaspoon each finely minced
    ginger root and garlic
1/4 cup julienne-cut water chest-
    nuts and/or bamboo shoots
2 lop chiang (Chinese sausages),
    parboiled 5 minutes, or
1/2 pound ham, cut in julienne,
    or
1/2 pound raw beef or lamb,
    thinly sliced, or
1/2 pound boneless raw chicken
    or turkey, cut in julienne, or
1/2 pound halved raw shrimp or
    fish fillet, cut in 1-inch squares
Cover tightly and cook over
lowest heat 20 minutes.

LEGUMES

There are 25 or more varieties of dried beans and peas available. The soaking and cooking times will vary depending upon age, variety, where they were grown and how they were processed. Legumes should be well washed and rinsed and imperfect beans or peas discarded. They should always be cooked slowly as rapid boiling causes the skins to break. Be careful not to overcook; they should be tender but retain their shape when done.

Legumes such as soybeans, garbanzo beans, kidney beans and black beans should be soaked. Cover with 3 to 4 times as much water as beans and refrigerate overnight, or bring to boil, simmer 5 minutes, remove from heat, cover tightly and let stand 2 hours. Cooking time for these will vary from 1 to 3 hours. Lentils and split peas, if old, require 1 hour soaking time and about 1 hour cooking time. If the lentils and split peas are new, they need not be soaked and will cook in about 30 to 45 minutes.

For extra flavor, add oil, lemon or lime juice, vegetables such as onion, green pepper, carrot or celery, or garlic, bay leaf, parsley, chili pepper, cumin, salt pork or diced slab bacon to the pot while cooking. Legumes may also be cooked in their soaking water, especially in the case of soybeans, or in stock.

Most legumes will expand 1-1/2 to 3 times their original measurement when cooked.

SPROUTING GRAINS, LEGUMES AND SEEDS

Many grains, legumes and seeds can be sprouted by the following method for mung beans. Sprouting time will vary; check health or natural food stores for information on sprouting times, for uses and for nutritional information.

MUNG BEAN SPROUTS

Soak beans in water to cover overnight. Then pour off water and rinse very thoroughly. Place in shallow pan or in a quart jar placed on its side. Place pan or jar in dark spot or cover with towel. For easier rinsing, fasten cheesecloth or fine mesh screen to opening of jar with rubber band. Rinse with fresh water 2 to 3 times daily. Sprouts are ready to eat in 4 or 5 days. They will turn green if they are given a few hours of sunlight before use. The hulls will usually separate from the sprouted bean and may be eaten with the sprouts. Three tablespoons mung beans, approximately 1-1/2 ounces, will make approximately 2 cups sprouts. Transfer to clean jar immediately, cover and refrigerate up to 2 or 3 days.

SOYBEANS

In saucepan, soak 1 hour at room temperature:
1/4 pound dried soybeans (approximately 2/3 cup)
2 cups water
Cover and refrigerate 12 hours or overnight.
Blend into soybeans and soaking water:
1 tablespoon corn oil
1 teaspoon salt
Add to beans a bouquet garni of:
2 parsley sprigs
1 thyme sprig
1 garlic clove, bruised
1 small onion, cut in large chunks
1 bay leaf
Cover with tilted lid, bring to gentle boil, lower heat and simmer 2 to 3 hours, adding more water as needed, or until tender. Discard bouquet garni. Drain, reserving cooking water, cool and refrigerate.
Makes 2-1/2 cups cooked soybeans

SOYBEAN-MILLET CASSEROLE

Sauté until onion is transparent in:
2 tablespoons butter
1/2 cup minced onion
1/4 cup each minced celery and sliced fresh mushrooms
1 small garlic clove, minced
Combine with:
3/4 cup cooked soybeans
1/2 cup cooked millet
1/2 cup peeled and chopped ripe tomato
2 to 3 tablespoons grated cheddar cheese
1/2 teaspoon Herb Salt
minced fresh or crumbled dried oregano to taste
1 egg, beaten
Spoon mixture into 2 buttered 4-inch soufflé dishes.
Top each with:
1 tablespoon grated cheddar cheese
2 teaspoons bread crumbs
1/2 teaspoon butter, cut into bits
Bake in 350° oven 25 to 35 minutes or until top is golden.
Serve with tossed salad.

Variation: Add to soybean mixture 1/2 cup shrimp meat, marinated in 2 to 3 teaspoons fresh lemon juice.

CRUNCHY SOYBEAN NOODLE CASSEROLE

Sauté in:
1 tablespoon butter
1/2 cup minced onion
Add and stir until browned:
1/2 cup slivered blanched almonds, raw cashews, pine nuts and/or peanuts
2 tablespoons sesame seeds
Add to heat through:
1 cup cooked soybeans
1-1/2 cups cooked flat noodles
Toss in heated serving bowl with:
1/2 cup plain yoghurt
2 tablespoons freshly grated Parmesan cheese
1-1/2 teaspoons Sesame Salt
1/4 teaspoon freshly grated nutmeg
Serve as vegetarian entrée with colorful tossed salad.

Noodles/Cereals/Legumes

LENTILS
COOKED IN RED WINE

Soak, if necessary, at least
1 hour in:
water to cover
1/2 cup brown lentils
Drain and combine with:
1 cup Chianti or other red wine
1/2 cup water
1 1-inch cube slab bacon
1 carrot, sliced
1/2 white part of leek, chopped
1 garlic clove, minced
1 bay leaf
1/2 teaspoon minced fresh thyme
1/4 teaspoon salt
1/8 teaspoon pepper
Bring to boil, lower heat to medium, cover and cook, adding
water or wine if needed, 30 to
45 minutes or until lentils are
tender but still firm. Adjust
seasonings and serve with fresh
vegetable tray, including tomato
wedges, and broiled meat such
as lamb chops.

GARBANZO BEANS

Soak by either method:
1/2 cup garbanzo beans
Bring to gentle boil:
soaked garbanzo beans and soak-
ing water
1/2 teaspoon peanut or soy oil
salt to taste
bouquet garni of:
1 small onion, cut up
2 parsley sprigs
1 oregano sprig
1/4 cup coarsely chopped
celery leaves
Cover with tilted lid and cook
1-1/2 to 2 hours, or until tender,
adding more water if needed.
Drain and cool.

Serving Suggestions:
• Marinate cooled beans in vinegar, olive oil, minced onion, garlic
and fresh parsley, and cumin,
chili powder, salt and pepper to
taste. Serve as accompaniment
or small salad.
• Mash beans and add well-
seasoned chicken, beef or lamb
stock to make thin purée. Heat,
adjust seasoning and sprinkle
with minced parsley. Serve as
soup course.

LENTILS WITH PINEAPPLE

Soak, if necessary, at least
1 hour in:
water to cover
1/2 cup brown lentils
Drain and combine with:
2 tablespoons each finely minced
onion and chopped parsley
1/2 teaspoon minced garlic
1 cup rich beef, chicken or
lamb stock
Bring to boil, lower heat, cover
with tilted lid and simmer 30 to
45 minutes until lentils are just
tender, adding more stock if
needed. Lentils should retain
their shape.
Stir in:
1/2 cup cubed fresh pineapple
Adjust seasoning with:
salt and pepper
Serve as accompaniment to
meat or poultry entrée.

KIDNEY BEAN CASSEROLE

Bring to gentle boil:
1/2 cup kidney beans, soaked by
 either method, with soaking
 water
1/2 teaspoon salt
Cover with tilted lid and simmer
20 minutes. Add bouquet garni of:
1 garlic clove, bruised
2 slices onion
1 small bay leaf
2 parsley sprigs
1 thyme sprig
Continue cooking 20 minutes,
adding water as needed, or until
beans are tender but still retain
their shape. While beans are cooking, sauté until onion is transparent in:
2 tablespoons butter
1/3 cup each chopped onion
 and green bell pepper
1/2 small apple, chopped
1/2 to 3/4 teaspoon Aromatic
 Curry Mixture
Combine with:
1-1/2 cups peeled and diced
 ripe tomatoes
2 tablespoons raw natural sugar
2 teaspoons cider vinegar

Add beans and adjust seasonings
with salt, pepper, sugar and
vinegar. Transfer to casserole and
bake, stirring occasionally, in
350° oven 30 to 40 minutes.
Just before serving sprinkle with:
grated Parmesan cheese

SPLIT PEAS AND NOODLES

Bring to boil:
1/2 cup yellow or green split peas
2 tablespoons each minced onion
 and celery with tender leaves
1/4 teaspoon minced garlic
1/4 teaspoon salt
1/8 teaspoon pepper
1 cup water
Lower heat, cover with tilted lid
and cook slowly 30 minutes, adding more water if needed, until
peas are just tender. Stir in with
fork:
1 cup cooked fine noodles
2 teaspoons minced fresh parsley
2 tablespoons sour cream
1/2 cup peeled and chopped
 ripe tomato
Reheat and adjust seasonings.
If too thick, add and reheat:
chicken or beef stock

FEIJOADA

Bring to gentle boil:
1/2 pound (approximately 1 cup)
 black beans, soaked by either
 method, with soaking water
3/4 teaspoon salt
1/4 pound salt pork, diced
Cover with tilted lid and simmer
1 hour. Add:
1 pound pork shoulder, cut
 into pieces
Continue cooking, adding more
water if needed, until beans
begin to soften. Brown to soften
onion in:
2 teaspoons rendered pork fat
1/2 cup minced onion
1 garlic clove, minced
1/4 to 1/2 dried red chili pepper,
 seeded and crushed
Add to beans and continue cooking until beans are tender.
Blend in:
2 tablespoons tomato paste
Bring back to boil and add:
1/2 pound linguica sausage, par-
 boiled 5 minutes and sliced
Cook 10 minutes more and serve
with:
steamed white rice

Noodles/Cereals/Legumes

COOKED CEREALS

Cooked cereals provide a nutritious breakfast, high in protein. Cereals may be cooked in milk, water or a combination of these, but because of the nutritional value of milk, we recommend it as the cooking liquid. Whole milk scorches easily, so you may prefer using low-fat or reconstituted nonfat dry milk, or placing an asbestos pad between saucepan and burner.

The flavor and texture of cereals can be varied with the addition of fresh or dried fruits, spices, seeds or nuts. Firm fruits, such as apples and some pears, as well as dried fruits may be cooked with the cereal. Softer fruits such as bananas, peaches or berries can be added to cooked cereal. Add spices such as cinnamon, nutmeg, ginger, allspice or grated fresh vanilla bean to the cereal while it is cooking or at the table. Sweeten cooked cereal with natural sweeteners such as raw unfiltered honey, date sugar, real maple syrup or unsulphured molasses; or flavor an unsweetened cereal with 1 tablespoon of peanut butter, 1 teaspoon Tamari soy sauce, 1 teaspoon Sesame Salt or a pat of butter. Top cooked cereal with unsweetened fruit juice or milk and wheat germ, nuts or seeds for flavor, texture and nutrition.

Basic Method
for Cooking Cereals

Bring liquid to a boil. Add 1/4 teaspoon salt and, keeping liquid at a boil, very slowly add cereal, stirring so that each grain is surrounded by the hot liquid. Lower heat, cover and simmer cereal for recommended time. Remove from heat. If very thick cereal is desired, let stand covered for 3 to 5 minutes before serving.

The following cereal and liquid amounts and cooking times are recommended for 2 average servings. Because the processing of grains and therefore the cooking time and amount of cereal and liquid needed vary according to brand, the following information provides only general guidelines and the package directions, if available, should be used. Whole grains generally take 45 minutes to 60 minutes, cracked grains 20 to 30 minutes and flakes and creams, which are quick-cooking, about 5 minutes.

1 cup barley, rye or wheat flakes, 2 cups liquid, 5 minutes.
1/2 cup farina, 2 cups liquid, 3 to 5 minutes.
6 tablespoons rice, cream of, 1-1/2 cups liquid, 5 minutes.
2/3 cup oats, rolled, 1-1/2 cups liquid, 5 minutes.
1/2 cup cornmeal (white or yellow), 2 cups liquid, 15 to 20 minutes.
2/3 cup bulghur, 1-1/3 cups liquid, 15 to 20 minutes.
1 cup buckwheat groats, 2 cups liquid, 20 minutes.
2/3 cup oats, steel cut, 1-1/2 cups liquid, 30 to 45 minutes.
1/2 cup polenta, 2 cups liquid, 50 to 60 minutes.

Note: Cereals such as cornmeal and polenta lump easily. Another method is to mix these with the cold water first and then bring the water to a boil, stirring constantly. Cook, covered, stirring occasionally, for the specified time.

BASIC FAMILIA CEREAL

Combine in a large bowl:
1-1/2 cups rolled oats
1/2 cup rye, wheat or barley
  flakes
1/2 cup each wheat germ and
  raisins
1/2 cup ground or slivered
  almonds and/or hazelnuts
1/2 cup chopped pitted dried
  dates, prunes, apricots and/or
  figs
1/4 cup each sesame seeds, sunflower seeds, grated unsweetened coconut and finely
  chopped dried apples
1/2 cup nonfat dry milk
Serve for breakfast plain or with
fresh fruit and milk, yoghurt or
favorite unsweetened fruit juice;
sweeten with honey or date
sugar, if desired. Store covered
in refrigerator. If dried fruit
hardens, pour over milk or
other liquid and let stand 3 to
5 minutes before eating.
Makes approximately 6 cups

BASIC TOASTED GRANOLA

In large bowl combine 2 cups any
combination of the following:
rolled oats, wheat flakes, rye
  flakes, barley flakes
Add:
1 cup each toasted wheat germ
  and raisins
3/4 cup slivered blanched
  almonds or other nuts
1/4 to 1/2 cup each sesame seeds,
  sunflower seeds and unsweetened grated coconut
1 semisweet apple, coarsely
  grated
1 teaspoon ground cinnamon
1/2 teaspoon salt
1/4 teaspoon freshly grated
  nutmeg (optional)
Blend in to evenly moisten:
1/4 cup safflower, coconut or
  soy oil
1/2 cup mild honey
Spread mixture on lightly oiled
shallow baking pan or cookie
sheet and bake in 300° oven 20
to 25 minutes, stirring often,
until golden. Cool to room temperature, stirring occasionally.
Cover and refrigerate until ready
to use. Serve with fresh fruit and
milk, yoghurt or unsweetened
fruit juice.
Makes approximately 6 cups

Note: Granola can be used in
fruit salads, in fresh fruit omelets,
mixed with applesauce, tossed
into a rice pudding or as a topping
for ice cream.

Variations:
• Add chopped dried fruits such
as apricots, prunes or dates.
• Vary the spices with ginger,
anise, coriander, cardamom and/
or grated fresh vanilla bean.

BASIC FRESH MUESLI

Combine thoroughly:
1 apple, grated
2 to 3 tablespoons raisins
2 tablespoons grated fresh or
  unsweetened coconut
2 to 3 tablespoons toasted wheat
  germ
1/4 cup wheat, oat or barley
  flakes
5 to 6 tablespoons plain yoghurt,
  milk or unsweetened fruit juice
2 teaspoons each fresh lemon
  juice and honey
ground cinnamon to taste
  (optional)
fresh fruits such as peaches,
  bananas, grapes (optional)

Noodles/Cereals/Legumes

PIZZA
(Two Meals from One Recipe)

For the dough, combine and heat to lukewarm:
1/4 cup milk
1 teaspoon mild honey
Stir in and let stand 15 minutes until bubbly:
1 tablespoon active dry yeast, or
1 cake yeast, crumbled
Sift together in bowl:
2-3/4 cups unbleached white flour
1/2 teaspoon salt
Make hollow in center and pour in:
yeast mixture
1/2 cup water, at room temperature
1/4 cup milk, at room temperature
2 tablespoons olive oil or melted and cooled butter
Knead with hands, turn out onto lightly floured board and knead 10 minutes or until smooth and elastic, using additional flour only to prevent sticking. Place in oiled bowl, turn to coat top with oil, cover with tea towel and let rise in warm place 1 hour or until double in bulk. Turn out onto floured board, knead briefly, divide dough in half and roll into 2 rounds. Brush 2 6- to 7-inch pizza pans lightly with olive oil and pat dough into them to fit evenly, making a rim slightly thicker than bottom dough. Coat top of dough lightly with olive oil and bake in 425° oven 10 minutes. Dough will puff slightly; prick gently with tines of fork to release steam. Sprinkle pizzas with:
3/4 cup grated mozzarella cheese
Spread evenly over cheese:
Quick Tomato Sauce (following)
At this point, freeze one of the pizzas for another meal. Defrost and treat as first pizza.
In order given, top remaining pizza with:
1 cup sliced fresh mushrooms
1/4 green bell pepper, chopped or cut in julienne
1 or 2 Turkish or Italian pickled peperoncinis, minced or cut in julienne (optional)
1/2 cup julienne-cut salami or cooked ham
8 to 10 pitted black olives, halved
1 teaspoon finely minced fresh oregano
1-1/2 tablespoons toasted wheat germ
1 cup grated mozzarella cheese
Bake in 425° oven 20 to 30 minutes until golden and cheese is melted.

Note: Substitute 3/4 cup whole-wheat flour for 3/4 cup of the unbleached flour. Topping may be varied according to taste and ingredients on hand. Pizza dough may also be rolled into rounds and placed on a cookie sheet. Form rim while on cookie sheet.

QUICK TOMATO SAUCE

Sauté until onion is soft in:
2 to 3 tablespoons olive oil
1 onion, minced
2 to 4 garlic cloves, minced
Stir in:
3 tablespoons tomato paste
1/2 cup water
2 to 3 ripe tomatoes, peeled and quartered (1-1/4 pounds)
1/2 teaspoon each salt and sweet Hungarian paprika
1/4 to 1/2 dried red chili pepper, seeded and crushed
3/4 teaspoon minced fresh oregano
1/2 teaspoon minced fresh thyme
1-1/2 teaspoons minced fresh basil
1 to 2 bay leaves
Cover and cook over low heat, stirring occasionally, 30 minutes. Add last 5 minutes of cooking time:
1/2 teaspoon anchovy paste (optional)

Vegetables

Vegetables

The method of cooking fresh vegetables depends upon the vegetable and your preference. Except for firm vegetables such as beets and potatoes, we recommend vegetables be cooked only until just tender. This conserves vitamins and minerals and adds texture to the meal. Included with the following method instructions are lists of some of the vegetables that best lend themselves to that particular method. However, there are no hard or fast rules.

Allow approximately 2 cups sliced, chopped, shredded or grated vegetables for 2 persons as an accompaniment to an entrée, allowing for the fact that some vegetables cook down more than others.

STEAMING

Steaming over boiling water is one of the best ways to insure crisp cooking and minimum vitamin and mineral loss. If you don't have one of the collapsible perforated steaming racks that expands to fit any size saucepan, substitute a colander, strainer or perforated tray. Place rack in a saucepan filled with 1 inch of water, place vegetables on rack, cover saucepan tightly and bring water to rapid boil. Lower heat, and keeping water at gentle boil, cook until vegetables are just tender. Save steaming water for stocks and sauces. When steaming vegetables, plan on cooking extra to be used for soups, vinaigrette salads and casseroles. Further steaming instructions are given with individual vegetable recipes.

Recommended for Steaming:
artichokes, asparagus, beans, broccoli, cauliflower, carrots, kohlrabi, bok choy, Brussels sprouts, cabbage, corn on the cob, celery, peas, sunchokes, summer squash

BUTTER STEAMING

Melt 2 tablespoons butter in saucepan. Add vegetables and seasonings of choice. Cover and steam over medium heat until vegetables are just tender.

Recommended for Butter Steaming:
Brussels sprouts, shredded cabbage, carrots, celery, cucumbers, small whole onions, peas and snow peas, summer squash, sunchokes, spinach, celeriac, tiny new potatoes, whole or sliced

STIR-FRYING

For 2 persons, allow 1-1/2 to 2 cups prepared vegetables. Heat wok or heavy skillet and add 1 tablespoon peanut oil, 1 slice ginger root, 1 small garlic clove, bruised, and 1/4 teaspoon crumbled dried red chili pepper. When oil sizzles, lower heat slightly and add vegetables, stirring constantly with chopsticks or fork to coat vegetables with oil. If cooking more than one vegetable, add first those that require the longest cooking time. Cook and stir 1 to 5 minutes and add, depending upon vegetable, 2 to 3 tablespoons water or stock. Leafy vegetables will need little or no water. Cover and steam until just tender. Add, stirring gently, 1/2 tablespoon Tamari soy sauce, a dash of raw natural sugar (optional), a dash of Oriental sesame oil and salt to taste.

For vegetarian stir-fry, allow 3 cups prepared vegetables; sauté with ginger and garlic 1 tablespoon whole or slivered almonds. Just before serving toss in 1/4 to 1/2 teaspoon Oriental sesame oil and 2 firm fresh bean-curd cakes or 2 to 3 freshly scrambled eggs. Top with toasted sesame seeds or chopped roasted peanuts.

Recommended for Stir-Frying: asparagus, cut on diagonal; carrots, turnips, celeriac, cut in julienne; green or red bell pepper, kohlrabi, cut in small chunks or in julienne; celery, green or wax beans, cut on diagonal; whole snow peas or small young whole green beans; shelled peas; crisped and drained bean sprouts; coarsely cut lettuce, cabbage, Napa cabbage, bok choy, Swiss chard, spinach, beet greens, mustard greens; eggplant cut in chunks or strips; cauliflower or broccoli flowerets; sliced zucchini, bamboo shoots, water chestnuts

BOILING

Boiling is the least recommended method because nutrients are lost in the cooking water. Very firm vegetables, however, require this method. When possible, the cooking water should be reserved for stocks or other use. Potato water, for example, is excellent for baking breads. If boiling tender vegetables such as home-frozen beans, cook rapidly in covered saucepan until barely crisp.

Recommended for Boiling: beets, potatoes, rutabagas, turnips, parsnips

TOPPINGS FOR VEGETABLES

• Add to butter-steamed vegetables 2 tablespoons toasted sesame seeds, toasted pine nuts (good with carrots) or sunflower seeds, toasted grated fresh unsweetened coconut, toasted blanched almonds or toasted chopped cashews.
• Sesame Salt
• Garlic Butter
• Lemon or Orange Sauce: Toss into hot steamed vegetables such as carrots, peas and broccoli, 1 tablespoon butter and mixture of 1 tablespoon fresh lemon or orange juice, 1-1/2 teaspoons mild honey, 1/4 teaspoon freshly grated lemon or orange peel and salt to taste.

Vegetables

ARTICHOKES

To trim large artichokes, cut tough stem evenly off bottom, cut 1 inch of leaves off top, and with scissors snip off 1/2 inch of remaining leaf tips. To trim small artichokes cut off all tough leaves; leave whole or halve and remove choke if developed. When cut, artichokes discolor, so as you work place them immediately in cold water to which lemon juice or vinegar has been added. This will help crisp mature artichokes and rid those fresh from the garden of insects. Place in the refrigerator and let soak 30 minutes to 1 hour.

If steaming large artichokes, add lemon juice and chopped onion to steaming water and sprinkle a little lemon juice and olive oil over tops.

ARTICHOKES COOKED IN STOCK

Select a saucepan with a tight-fitting lid. It should be large enough to hold 2 artichokes, close together, standing upright. In the saucepan sauté 5 minutes in:
1 tablespoon olive oil
2 tablespoons chopped onion
1 garlic clove, minced
1 teaspoon minced fresh oregano
Add:
2/3 cup any stock*
1 teaspoon fresh lemon juice
Place artichokes in saucepan and spoon juices over. Add to bring depth of liquid to 2 inches:
additional stock
Cover, bring to boil, lower heat and cook at gentle boil 30 to 45 minutes, adding additional stock if needed. Cooking time will depend upon size and age of artichokes; when leaves pull off easily, they are cooked. Remove from pan and turn upside down for 3 minutes. Stand upright on serving plates and serve with small bowls of one of the following: melted or browned butter, melted butter combined with cooking stock and/or lemon juice, Hollandaise sauce, mayonnaise.

*Use a stock which will complement your entrée. (Lamb stock is especially good for cooking artichokes.) Reserve stock for poaching eggs, for soups, gravies, etc. Artichokes can also be cooked along with stew meat.

FRIED ARTICHOKES

Trim, soak and pat dry:
12 to 14 small artichokes,
   approximately 1 ounce each
Cut in half from top to bottom and dip in:
1 egg, beaten with
1 teaspoon fresh lemon juice
Coat with:
1/3 cup Seasoned Bread Crumbs,
   or as needed
In heavy skillet, heat:
1 tablespoon each garlic olive
   oil and butter
Over medium heat and adding oil and/or butter as needed, brown artichoke halves on both sides, turning once. Cook until tender, approximately 10 to 15 minutes.

ASPARAGUS

For 2 persons, allow 3/4 to 1 pound asparagus, depending upon age and variety. Snap ends off where they break easily and scrub stalks well with vegetable brush, being careful not to snap off tips.

STEAMED ASPARAGUS

If you do not have a steamer, stand asparagus upright in a coffee pot so that tips cook evenly. Steam until just tender crisp. Sprinkle with salt and pepper.

Dress with:
- Melted butter; top with buttered seasoned bread crumbs and chopped hard-cooked eggs. Sprinkle with paprika.
- Browned Butter
- Melted butter and lemon juice
- Melted butter; top with buttered bread crumbs and grated cheese and broil to melt cheese.

Or top with:
- Sliced almonds browned in butter; add lemon or lime juice to taste.
- Hollandaise or Aioli Sauce

BEANS, GREEN OR WAX

For 2 persons, allow 1/2 pound beans. Trim ends. If very small and tender, leave whole. For more mature beans, cut lengthwise, or snap or cut into pieces, or cut thinly on diagonal. Cooking time depends upon variety and age. Beans may be stir-fried, butter steamed, or steamed, or boiled if home frozen. Never salt beans until after they have been cooked. If boiling, add a sprig of summer savory to rapidly boiling water with the beans. Cook quickly, drain, reserve water for stocks and toss with:
- Butter, salt and pepper
- Butter, salt, pepper and sautéed mushrooms; fresh dill
- Butter, salt, pepper and freshly grated nutmeg to taste
- Sliced almonds browned in butter
- Butter and 2 to 3 tablespoons sunflower seeds

GREEN BEANS IN TANGY SAUCE

Sprinkle freshly cooked beans with:
salt or Herb Salt
Beat until creamy:
1 egg yolk
2 teaspoons fresh lemon juice
1/2 teaspoon raw natural sugar
1/4 teaspoon mustard seed, or
1/8 teaspoon dry mustard
Pour over beans and serve immediately.

BEETS

Wash well and boil until tender in salted water to cover. Peel, slice and use in salad recipes. To serve hot, toss with butter, salt and pepper, or with Tangy Sauce seasoned to taste with grated fresh horseradish. Beet greens may be prepared like spinach. Beet cooking water may be served as a cold vegetable drink.

Vegetables

BROCCOLI

One head of broccoli is too much for 2 persons, but the unused portion keeps well if refrigerated in a plastic bag. Cut off and discard tough ends of stalks and lightly peel off any tough skin. To assure even cooking, slit thick stalks from bottom up to top; or break into flowerets and cut up stems into strips or slices. Dress steamed broccoli or toss flowerets and stems with:

• Melted or Browned Butter
• Melted butter with lemon juice
• Lemon or Orange Sauce
• Lemon-Garlic Butter Sauce
Top broccoli with:
• Seasoned bread crumbs, chopped hard-cooked eggs and bits of butter. Sprinkle with paprika.
• Hollandaise or Mornay Sauce
• Mayonnaise seasoned to taste with curry powder.

BAKED BROCCOLI EGG SUPPER

Steam 5 to 7 minutes:
2-1/2 cups coarsely chopped broccoli
Place in buttered casserole and sprinkle with:
salt and pepper
Set aside. Sauté until onion is transparent in:
1 tablespoon butter
1/4 cup chopped onion
Add and cook, stirring, 2 minutes until golden:
1 tablespoon unbleached white flour
Remove from heat and gradually stir in:
1 cup milk
Return to heat and cook, stirring, until sauce thickens. Add and heat to melt:
1/2 cup grated mild cheddar cheese
1/4 teaspoon salt
1/8 teaspoon each white pepper and freshly grated nutmeg
Pour sauce over broccoli. Make 2 to 4 hollows in mixture with back of spoon. Break into hollows:
2 to 4 eggs
Top with:
3 tablespoons grated mild cheddar cheese
Bake in 375° oven 15 minutes or until eggs are set.
Garnish with:
chopped fresh parsley
Serve with Simple Tomato Salad and buttered whole-grain toast.

Variations:
• Omit salt and add 1/4 cup shredded cooked ham or prosciutto with broccoli.
• Omit cheese topping and sprinkle with 3 tablespoons seasoned bread crumbs. Dot with butter.
• Sauté 1/2 cup sliced fresh mushrooms with the onion.

CAULIFLOWER

Trim leaves from small cauliflower and break into flowerets.
Or, if leaving whole, cut out
core.* Steam flowerets or whole
cauliflower just until tender, or
boil whole cauliflower in salted
water with 1 tablespoon lemon
juice and 1 teaspoon unbleached
white flour. Serve topped with:
• Mornay Sauce
• Hollandaise Sauce
• Browned Butter
• Melted butter and crumbled
Gorgonzola cheese
• Melted butter and sesame seeds
• Seasoned buttered bread crumbs
and chopped hard-cooked eggs

*Core may be cut into julienne
and eaten raw or prepared in the
same way as celeriac, sunchokes
or water chestnuts.

HUNGARIAN CAULIFLOWER IN SOUR CREAM SAUCE

Steam 7 to 10 minutes until
just undercooked:
2-1/2 cups cauliflowerets
Remove cauliflower and set
aside. Reserve steaming water.
Sauté 3 minutes in:
1 tablespoon butter
1/4 cup chopped onion
Remove from heat and stir in:
1-1/2 teaspoons sweet Hungarian
    paprika
Quickly add to prevent paprika
from turning bitter:
2 tablespoons cauliflower
    steaming liquid
Stir in and heat:
1 ripe tomato, peeled and
    chopped
1/2 red or green bell pepper,
    finely chopped
1/2 teaspoon Herb Salt
Blend in slowly binder of:
2 tablespoons cauliflower
    steaming liquid
3 tablespoons sour cream
1/2 tablespoon unbleached
    white flour or sifted soy flour
Add:
reserved cauliflowerets

Cover and cook 5 minutes until
sauce has thickened and cauliflower is just done. Do not boil.
Top with:
2 fried eggs
Serve with rye bread and butter
and tomato wedges.

BRUSSELS SPROUTS

Allow approximately 3/4
pound Brussels sprouts for 2
persons. Trim sprouts and make
slashes in bottom. Sauté in butter
and season with salt and pepper;
butter steam with salt and
pepper; or steam and serve
dressed with butter and a sprinkling of Sesame Salt.

Vegetables

CABBAGE

For 2 persons, cut 1 small cabbage into 2 to 4 wedges, or shred cabbage to make 3 cups.

• Cut cabbage into wedges and steam or boil until just tender. Dress with melted butter and salt and pepper.

• Butter steam shredded cabbage. Season with salt and pepper and sprinkle with caraway seeds.

• Butter steam shredded cabbage with fresh peas and sliced water chestnuts.

CABBAGE ROLLS WITH VEGETABLE FILLING

Blanch 2 to 3 minutes just to wilt and set aside:

4 large or 6 medium-size white, Napa or savoy cabbage leaves

Combine for filling:

1/2 cup each chopped fresh mushrooms and cooked brown rice or millet

1/3 cup finely minced carrot

1/4 cup finely chopped onion

1 small ripe tomato, peeled and diced

2 tablespoons each chopped bell pepper and celery or celeriac

2 garlic cloves, minced

1/2 teaspoon Herb Salt

1 teaspoon chopped fresh thyme or basil

1/8 teaspoon each pepper and finely minced fresh rosemary

1 egg, beaten

1 tablespoon wheat germ (optional)

Place a portion of filling on core end of cabbage leaf, roll once, fold in sides and roll like a jelly roll. Repeat with remaining leaves. Set aside. In a saucepan, combine and heat:

1 cup Tomato Sauce

1/4 cup dry white wine

1/4 to 1/2 dried red chili pepper, seeded and crushed

Place rolls seam side down in sauce and spoon sauce over tops of rolls. Bring to gentle boil, lower heat, cover and simmer gently 30 minutes. Serve with sour cream, chopped fresh parsley, brown rice or millet and milk.

Note: If using small center leaves of cabbage, layer blanched leaves and filling in casserole to a depth of about 2 inches. Pour sauce over and bake in 350° oven 30 minutes.

Use rest of cabbage in Fruit Coleslaw, or as a steamed vegetable accompaniment. Rolls may be prepared ahead and cooked just before dinner.

CARROTS

Scrape lightly and cut off tip and stem end. Grate, slice or cut in julienne to make approximately 2 cups.

• Butter steam and toss with 2 to 3 tablespoons milk or half-and-half, Herb Salt and white pepper to taste; garnish with chopped fresh chives.

• Steam and toss with butter and toasted pine nuts, minced fresh dill and parsley and/or lemon juice.

• Butter steam with 2 teaspoons mild honey. Season with Herb Salt and white pepper to taste.

• Steam and dress with Sesame Butter.

• Butter steam and sprinkle with Sesame Salt.

• Steam and toss with Lemon or Orange Sauce; garnish with fresh dill.

CELERIAC (CELERY ROOT)

A root vegetable available almost year round. Varying in size, the small ones are more tender and can be used raw in salads or as an appetizer. Peel skin with sharp knife, cutting out any imperfections. Cut as desired and if not using immediately, sprinkle with fresh lemon juice to prevent discoloration.

BREADED CELERIAC

Peel and trim:
2 1/2-inch thick round slices celeriac, approximately 4 inches in diameter
Bring celeriac slices to boil with:
2 tablespoons fresh lemon juice
1/2 teaspoon salt
boiling water just to cover
Cover saucepan, lower heat and steam 7 to 10 minutes or until just tender. Drain, cool and sprinkle each side of celeriac slices with:
salt
Dip slices in:
1 egg, beaten
Sandwich each slice between:
2 large thin slices mild cheddar, Gouda, Edam or Gruyère cheese

Dip again in egg and coat with:
1/2 cup toasted wheat germ, Seasoned Sesame Coating or Seasoned Bread Crumbs
If time permits, chill at least 1 hour to help keep coating intact when browning. (May also be made several hours ahead, covered and refrigerated.) Sauté approximately 10 minutes until both sides are golden brown in:
1 tablespoon corn or peanut oil, or as needed

CORN ON THE COB

Purchase unhusked corn, checking size and color of kernels. When preparing corn, cook extra for use in other dishes such as soups, stuffed vegetables or meatloaf. Cut kernels from cob and store refrigerated up to 3 days or freeze.
• Soak unhusked corn in water 1 hour. Broil over charcoal, turning often, 30 to 40 minutes until corn is tender and husks are almost charred.
• Steam husked corn standing upright, stem end down, until tender, about 7 to 10 minutes. Serve with butter, salt and pepper.

EGGPLANT

There are 2 types of eggplant available—the large oval-shaped ones and the small slender Oriental variety called aubergines. One large eggplant is too much for 2 persons. To store eggplant, cover cut end with plastic wrap and refrigerate up to 2 days.

BAKED EGGPLANT

Slice 4 slices 1/4 inch thick from:
1 oval eggplant, peeled if desired
Sprinkle both sides of slices with salt and let stand on paper toweling 30 minutes. Pat dry.
Dip into mixture of:
3 to 4 tablespoons mayonnaise
1 teaspoon very finely minced onion
Coat with mixture of:
3 to 4 tablespoons Seasoned Bread Crumbs
1 tablespoon grated Parmesan cheese
Place on cookie sheet and bake in 350° oven 15 minutes or until eggplant is tender and coating is browned.

Vegetables

EGGPLANT MUSHROOM RATATOUILLE

In heavy saucepan, sauté until onion is transparent in:
2 tablespoons olive oil, or as needed
1 onion, chopped
2 garlic cloves, minced
1-1/2 cups diced unpeeled eggplant
Blend in and mix well:
2 cups Tomato Sauce
Then add:
1/2 green bell pepper, sliced
1 ripe tomato, peeled and diced
1 cup sliced fresh mushrooms
1/4 to 1/2 dried red chili pepper, seeded and crushed
1/2 teaspoon Herb Salt
1/4 teaspoon pepper
2 bay leaves
1 teaspoon each minced fresh oregano and basil
1/2 teaspoon minced fresh thyme
Cover and simmer gently 15 minutes. Discard bay leaves and serve with brown rice.

Variation: Substitute zucchini for half or all of mushrooms.

EGGPLANT CURRY

Brush lightly with:
olive oil
4 to 6 slices unpeeled eggplant
Sprinkle lightly with:
salt and turmeric
Broil eggplant slices on both sides to just soften. Set aside.
In a skillet, sauté until onion is transparent in:
1-1/2 tablespoons butter
1 onion, sliced
1 garlic clove, minced
Sprinkle with:
1 tablespoon Aromatic Curry Mixture
1/4 to 1/2 dried red chili pepper, seeded and crushed
Stir 2 minutes over low heat and blend in:
1 cup coconut milk
Bring to gentle boil, lower heat and cook and stir until thickened. Return eggplant to skillet and add:
1 tablespoon white vinegar or fresh lemon juice
Simmer slowly until sauce is very thick, being careful not to overcook eggplant. Serve with millet and bean sprout or bean curd salad or fresh fruit.

EGGPLANT PARMESAN

Halve and remove pulp, leaving a 1/4-inch thick shell from:
1 1-pound eggplant
Steam shells approximately 7 minutes or until slightly softened.
Sprinkle inside of shells with:
Herb Salt
grated Parmesan cheese
Dice pulp to make 1-1/2 cups* and combine with:
1/4 cup chopped fresh mushrooms or cooked ham
1/2 cup grated Parmesan cheese
1/3 cup Tomato Sauce
1/2 teaspoon Herb Salt
1/2 to 1 teaspoon chopped fresh oregano
Mound mixture into reserved shells and place in shallow baking pan filled with 1/2 inch water.
Bake in 350° oven 30 minutes or until eggplant mixture is tender. Serve with tomato salad and brown rice.

*Unused pulp can be used for Macaroni with Eggplant Sauce or in Eggplant Mushroom Ratatouille.

Vegetables

FENNEL

Fennel, also called sweet anise, has a distinct licorice flavor and is available in the market in the early winter months. The bulb, stalks and feathers can all be eaten.

FENNEL WITH MIXED VEGETABLES

The flavor of the fennel combined with the other vegetables makes this dish a nice complement to many meals. It is good with Russian Herring Fillets in Custard, rice and a green salad.

Sauté 2 to 3 minutes in:
1 tablespoon each corn oil and butter
1 small carrot, sliced
3/4 cup each sliced fresh mushrooms and cauliflowerets
1/4 cup sliced fennel bulb
Sprinkle with:
1/2 teaspoon salt
Add and steam 10 minutes:
1/2 cup water
Bind with:
1/4 cup milk, half-and-half or dry white wine
1 tablespoon cornstarch
Adjust seasonings with salt and pepper and blend in:
1 to 2 teaspoons butter

KOHLRABI

Select small, young kohlrabi. With a sharp knife, peel tough skin, being careful not to cut too deeply. Four to 6 small kohlrabi will make approximately 2 cups diced. Cooking time varies with size and age. Home-grown kohlrabi, when very young, is excellent raw.

KOHLRABI IN DELICATE SOUR CREAM SAUCE

Sprinkle lightly with:
salt
unbleached white flour
2 cups 1/2-inch dice kohlrabi
Sauté diced kohlrabi until golden in:
1 to 2 tablespoons butter or corn oil
Sprinkle evenly with:
1 teaspoon unbleached white flour
1/8 teaspoon ground cinnamon
dash of white pepper
Cover with:
1/2 cup sour cream
Top with:
1 ripe tomato, peeled and diced
Cover saucepan and cook gently over low heat 15 minutes. Remove from heat and let stand, covered, 10 minutes.
Top with:
generous amount of chopped fresh parsley
Serve with a light meat such as broiled ground beef patty.

MUSHROOMS

Select firm mushrooms of uniform size. If the cut end of the stem is still white, the mushrooms are at their freshest. Store refrigerated in plastic bag up to 2 days. Do not wash until ready to use and then only wipe gently with dampened paper toweling; do not peel. Use the entire mushroom, including the flavorful stem, unless otherwise specified. If only the caps are needed, reserve stems for soup stocks, sauces, sautés, etc. One half pound equals approximately 2 cups sliced.

• Sauté in butter with minced garlic; sprinkle while cooking with marjoram or oregano. Season with salt and pepper to taste.

• Sauté as above, sprinkle with a little unbleached white flour and cook and stir gently 3 minutes. Stir in milk or half-and-half and cook and stir until thickened.

• Add torn prosciutto to sautéed mushrooms.

• Add caraway seeds to taste to sautéed mushrooms.

MUSHROOMS IN BUTTERMILK SAUCE

Melt until bubbly:
2 tablespoons butter
Sprinkle with:
2 tablespoons unbleached white flour
1 teaspoon finely minced onion
Cook and stir 3 minutes. Gradually add:
1-2/3 cups buttermilk
1/8 teaspoon each dry mustard, salt, freshly grated nutmeg and white pepper
Cook and stir until thickened. Add:
3 cups sliced fresh mushrooms
Cover and cook over medium heat 7 to 10 minutes or until mushrooms are tender. Add:
1/2 cup minced fresh parsley
If sauce is too thick, thin with a little more buttermilk. Adjust seasonings and serve as an accompaniment or as supper or luncheon dish on toasted whole-grain bread.

ONIONS, SMALL

Select small white onions of uniform size, allowing 8 to 10 for 2 persons. To peel, blanch 2 minutes, drain and slip skins off. Thinly slice stem end off and score stem end lightly. Cooking time will depend upon size.

• Butter steam until tender. Add dry sherry and half-and-half to taste.

• Butter steam with stock or dry red wine; let liquid cook away to glaze, shaking pan often.

• Butter steam with fresh minced sage.

• Steam and combine with Cream Sauce or Béchamel Sauce.

FRESH PEAS

Depending upon maturity of peas, allow 1 to 1-1/2 pounds unshelled peas for 2 persons, approximately 1-1/2 cups shelled.

• Steam and serve with Lemon or Orange Sauce; garnish with fresh mint.

• Butter steam with minced fresh parsley or chervil.

• Butter steam with shredded lettuce.

Vegetables

CARDAMOM PEAS

Bring to boil:
1/4 cup water
Add, cover and boil 2 to 3 minutes until just tender crisp:
1-1/2 cups fresh peas
Drain off all but 1 tablespoon of the cooking water, reserving remainder for stock. Quickly toss peas with:
1/2 teaspoon salt
1/4 teaspoon each pepper and crumbled dried marjoram
1/8 to 1/4 teaspoon freshly ground cardamom
Adjust seasonings and stir in:
1 tablespoon chopped fresh parsley
Garnish with:
fresh chives cut in 1-inch lengths

PEA PODS (SNOW PEAS)

Snow peas, also called pea pods, can be stir-fried or butter steamed. Trim ends and string, if necessary. Allow 1/2 pound for 2 persons.

POTATOES

New white and red potatoes should never be peeled, for the skin is flavorful and nutritious. Simply scrub gently and cut out any imperfections. Russet, Idaho or other baking potatoes should be scrubbed well before baking and the skin also eaten.

SCALLOPED POTATOES WITH BASIL

Slice thinly:
3/4 to 1 pound potatoes
Making 2 layers, layer in shallow well-buttered baking dish:
potato slices
3 to 4 tablespoons grated onion
sprinkling of salt, pepper and unbleached white flour
bits of butter
Pour in:
1/4 cup each milk and any rich stock
Tuck in and around potatoes:
4 to 5 fresh basil leaves, coarsely chopped
Bake in 325° oven 45 minutes to 1 hour, adding milk and/or stock if needed, until potatoes are just tender.

IRISH BAKED POTATOES WITH CABBAGE

Steam until tender:
2 cups shredded white cabbage
Mash together with:
2 6-ounce potatoes, boiled and peeled
2 tablespoons butter
1 tablespoon plain yoghurt or sour cream
Add:
1/4 cup minced onions, sautéed until transparent in
1 to 2 teaspoons butter
Spoon into buttered casserole.
Top with:
1/4 cup grated cheddar cheese
Bake in 350° oven 35 minutes, or until cheese is melted and surface is evenly browned.

STEAMED POTATOES AND BEANS

In heavy saucepan with tight-fitting lid heat:
2/3 cup any rich stock
Arrange in saucepan:
2 to 3 medium-size white or red potatoes, thinly sliced
1 cup diagonally cut fresh green beans
2 summer savory sprigs
Cover, bring to gentle boil and simmer 10 minutes or until potatoes and beans are just tender. Discard savory and season with:
salt and pepper to taste
If stock has not cooked away, remove lid and let most of juices boil off. Sprinkle with:
minced fresh parsley

SOUFFLÉ-BAKED POTATOES

Bake in 375° oven 45 minutes to 1 hour:
2 6-ounce baking potatoes
Make a slash lengthwise on top of potato skin and scoop out potato pulp, keeping skins intact. Mash pulp together with:
1/3 cup sour cream
1 tablespoon softened butter
Herb Salt and white pepper to taste
Return mixture to skins and sprinkle each with:
1 tablespoon grated mild cheese
Bake in 375° oven until top is browned and potato is heated through.

Variations:
Add to potato mixture one of the following:
• 2 slices bacon, fried crisp and crumbled
• 2 to 3 tablespoons finely minced celery
• 1/4 cup minced fresh mushrooms
• 1/4 cup sautéed chopped onions
• 1/4 cup mixed leftover vegetables or meats

POTATO PANCAKES

Combine:
1 egg, beaten
1 cup grated raw potatoes (about 6 ounces)
1/2 teaspoon salt
1/2 tablespoon fine bread crumbs
dash of baking powder and pepper
Heat in heavy skillet until bubbly:
1 teaspoon each butter and corn oil
Stirring well, spoon half of potato mixture into hot butter and oil, making 3 4-1/2-inch pancakes. Brown, turn to brown other side, adding butter or oil as needed, and repeat with rest of potato mixture. Serve with applesauce.

Variation: Add to potato mixture 1 tablespoon finely minced ham or grated carrot.

Vegetables

SCOTCH POTATO PATTIES

Boil and peel:
1 pound potatoes
Force through ricer to make 2 cups and in large bowl combine with:
1 egg yolk
1 hard-cooked egg, finely chopped
2 teaspoons softened butter
1/2 teaspoon each Herb Salt and dry mustard
1/4 teaspoon white pepper
Form into 9 or 10 patties 2 inches in diameter and 1/2 inch thick. Coat evenly on both sides with mixture of:
1/4 to 1/3 cup bread crumbs
1 tablespoon toasted wheat germ
1/4 teaspoon Herb Salt
Refrigerate for at least 1 hour. Brown on both sides in:
corn or peanut oil, as needed
Serve hot as accompaniment to meat or vegetable entrée, or with thick gravies. Patties will keep up to 1 week if tightly wrapped and refrigerated. To reheat, broil 3 minutes per side, or spread with a little softened butter and heat in 350° oven.

CHEESE-BAKED POTATOES

Scrub well and cut in half lengthwise:
5 to 6 small potatoes (approximately 1 pound)
Arrange potato halves in buttered casserole or ovenproof skillet.
Combine:
1 cup milk
1 garlic clove, minced
1/2 dried red chili pepper, seeded and crushed
1/2 teaspoon Herb Salt
1/4 teaspoon sweet Hungarian paprika
1/8 teaspoon pepper
1/2 teaspoon caraway seeds
Pour milk mixture over potatoes and top with:
1/3 cup grated Gouda or cheddar cheese
Bake in a 350° oven about 40 minutes. Sprinkle with:
1/3 cup additional grated Gouda or cheddar cheese
Continue baking another 20 minutes. Serve hot from casserole or skillet with a tossed salad.

Note: This recipe can easily be enlarged for a party. Use 1 cup milk and 2/3 cup grated cheese for each pound of potatoes.

SPINACH

Allow 2 bunches of spinach, approximately 1-1/2 to 2 pounds, for 2 persons. The amount depends upon the size of leaves and stems. Discard tough stems and break up large leaves. Nutmeg, lemon juice and peel, mushrooms and sesame seeds all complement the flavor of spinach.
• Butter steam 2 tablespoons finely minced onion and 1/2 teaspoon finely minced garlic. Add spinach and butter steam until just wilted and tender. Remove lid and let liquid boil away. Season to taste with salt, pepper, freshly grated nutmeg and fresh lemon juice.
• Bruise 2 to 3 garlic cloves and place on bottom of saucepan. Add spinach, cover and steam in water clinging to leaves until just tender. Sprinkle with fresh lemon juice.

CREAMED SPINACH

Butter steam spinach as above and cool. Chop finely or if smoother consistency is desired, purée in blender. Combine with:
1/2 cup hot Béchamel Sauce
Reheat and adjust seasonings and garnish with:
chopped hard-cooked egg, or hard-cooked egg wedges, and/or croutons
lemon wedges

COCONUT SPINACH

Cook, covered, in water that clings to leaves until spinach is just wilted and tender:
1 to 1-1/2 pounds spinach
Set aside and sauté in:
1 tablespoon butter
1/3 cup minced onion
Stir in:
1/4 cup coconut milk
2 tablespoons crushed blanched almonds, cashews or pine nuts
1/2 teaspoon salt
1/4 teaspoon seeded and crushed dried red chili pepper
reserved spinach
Reheat and serve in heated bowl.

SUMMER SQUASH

Purchase summer squash that are firm and have good, even color. Wash and trim ends but do not peel. Varieties include zucchini, scallop (also called pattypan or summer squash) and yellow (also called crookneck or straight-neck). Allow 6 to 10 ounces for 2 persons, depending on cooking method and variety.

SAUTÉED YELLOW SQUASH

Sauté, covered, 3 minutes in:
2 tablespoons butter
1/2 medium-size sweet red onion, thinly sliced
1/2 garlic clove, minced
Add and continue cooking, covered, until just tender:
8 to 10 ounces yellow squash, sliced
Season to taste with:
salt and pepper
Remove lid and let most of moisture boil away. Sprinkle generously with:
minced fresh parsley, dill or chervil

YELLOW SQUASH WITH MUSHROOMS

Sauté until mushrooms are golden in:
1 tablespoon butter
3/4 cup sliced fresh mushrooms
1/4 cup sliced onion
Combine with:
1-1/2 cups steamed sliced yellow squash
Season with:
Herb Salt and white pepper to taste
Garnish with:
chopped fresh parsley

BROILED ZUCCHINI HALVES

Cut in half lengthwise and blanch 3 minutes:
2 3-ounce zucchini
Place in shallow buttered baking dish and spread cut side with:
softened butter
Sprinkle with:
Seasoned Bread Crumbs and/or grated Parmesan cheese
paprika
Broil under medium heat until zucchini are tender and topping is crispy.

Vegetables

ZUCCHINI PANCAKES

Grate to make 3 cups:
9 to 10 ounces zucchini
If very fresh, drain in colander
30 minutes.
Combine gently with:
2 eggs, beaten
3 tablespoons toasted wheat germ
2 teaspoons unbleached white
    flour or sifted soy flour
1 tablespoon chopped fresh
    parsley
2 tablespoons grated Parmesan
    or Edam cheese
1/2 teaspoon Herb Salt
1/4 teaspoon pepper
Heat in a skillet:
1 tablespoon corn or peanut oil,
    or as needed
Spoon zucchini mixture into hot
oil, forming pancakes about 4
inches in diameter. Brown on
first side 3 to 4 minutes. Turn
and brown second side. If turned
too soon, pancakes will fall apart.
Serve with lettuce and tomato
salad or tomato and onion salad
and whole-grain bread or crackers.

SAUTÉED ZUCCHINI SLICES

Cut into 1/4-inch slices:
1 8- to 10-ounce zucchini
Sprinkle with:
Herb Salt and pepper
Sauté to brown on both sides in:
2 tablespoons butter and/or
    garlic olive oil, or as needed

Variation: Before browning, dip
in beaten egg and coat with
Seasoned Bread Crumbs mixed
with grated Parmesan cheese.

ZUCCHINI CASSEROLE

Wash, trim and cut into slices:
10 ounces zucchini
Cook 10 minutes until soft in:
1 cup chicken stock
Drain, reserving broth, and mash
zucchini. Cool zucchini and combine with:
1/4 cup whole-grain bread or
    cracker crumbs
Gently stir in:
1 egg, lightly beaten
2 tablespoons melted and cooled
    butter
1/2 teaspoon salt
1/4 teaspoon pepper
2 tablespoons grated onion
3/4 cup chopped cooked ham, or
1 cup sliced fresh mushrooms

Transfer mixture to lightly buttered soufflé dish or casserole,
or 2 small deep-dish casseroles.
Top with:
3 tablespoons whole-grain
    bread or cracker crumbs
2 teaspoons melted butter
Bake in 375° oven 45 minutes or
until mixture is slightly puffed
and crumbs are browned. If
using individual dishes, reduce
cooking time to 30 minutes.
While zucchini is cooking, heat:
reserved broth
chicken stock to make 2 cups
1 small carrot, very finely grated
1/2 teaspoon Herb Salt
1/8 teaspoon pepper
1 to 2 tablespoons minced fresh
    parsley
Serve the broth as an appetizer
while waiting for the casserole.
Serve casserole with a green
salad and buttered toast rubbed
with garlic or sprinkled with
Herb Salt.

SAUTÉED GRATED ZUCCHINI

Sauté until just tender in:
2 to 3 tablespoons butter
3 cups very coarsely grated
    zucchini (approximately 9
    ounces)
1/2 teaspoon salt
1/4 teaspoon pepper

BAKED SHREDDED ZUCCHINI

Combine:
2 cups coarsely grated zucchini
    (approximately 6 ounces)
1/4 cup grated Parmesan cheese
1 egg, beaten
1/2 teaspoon salt
1/4 teaspoon pepper
Transfer to buttered baking dish
and bake in 350° oven 20 minutes.

WINTER SQUASH

Acorn, banana, Hubbard,
spaghetti and butternut are just
some of the many winter squash
available almost all year round.
They store well and the larger
varieties are sometimes sold by
the piece. Allow 2/3 to 1 pound
for 2 persons. Halve whole squash
and remove seeds and fibers
before baking. If steaming, peel
and dice. Complementary seasonings include nutmeg, ginger,
cinnamon and allspice.

BAKED ACORN SQUASH

Cut in half lengthwise:
1 acorn squash
Remove seeds and fibers from
cavity and place skin side down
in shallow baking dish filled
with:
1/2 inch water
Place in cavity of each half:
2 tablespoons dry sherry
1 tablespoon butter
1 teaspoon honey or raw natural
    sugar
sprinkling of freshly grated
    nutmeg
Bake in 350° oven 45 minutes
to 1 hour until soft.

PUMPKIN PURÉE

Place in buttered pan skin side
up:
1-1/2 to 2 pounds pumpkin, cut
    in pieces
Bake in 325° oven 1 hour and 15
minutes, or until tender. Remove
pulp and put through sieve, food
mill or blender.
Makes approximately 1 cup purée

Vegetables

SUNCHOKES (JERUSALEM ARTICHOKES)

Sunchokes are a root vegetable available in supermarkets and easily grown in the home garden. Scrub well, trim, but do not peel. Cook by any method or eat raw.

- Combine raw minced sunchokes with meatloaf or stuffings.
- Add raw minced or julienne-cut sunchokes to freshly cooked beans, peas or spinach to add texture.
- Boil until soft, rub off skins and mash with butter, salt and pepper; serve plain or in combination with mashed, butter-steamed carrots.
- Thinly slice sunchokes to make 1-1/2 cups and combine with 2 tablespoons softened butter, 1 teaspoon fresh lemon juice and 1/4 teaspoon white pepper. Cover and bake in 350° oven 15 minutes or until just tender, stirring several times.
- Cut in 1-inch slices and bake in roasting pan with lamb or other roast.

- Butter steam and dress with Sesame Salt and Tamari soy sauce.
- Butter steam and sprinkle with minced fresh parsley and rosemary.

SWISS CHARD

Swiss chard may be treated in the same way as spinach. Because it does not cook down as much, less will be needed. Do not discard stems unless they appear very tough. Cut stems on diagonal and cook for a few minutes before adding leaves, cut up if very large.

SWEET POTATOES AND YAMS

For 2 persons, allow 2 6- to 7-ounce sweet potatoes or yams. Scrub and bake in 350° oven 50 minutes until soft. Serve with butter, salt and pepper.

YAMS IN ORANGE CASES

Bake in 350° oven 50 minutes or until soft:
2 yams
While yams are baking, cut a 1-inch slice off top of:
2 oranges, approximately 3 inches in diameter
With serrated knife, cut out pulp, leaving a shell 1/2 inch thick. Save juices and orange sections. Turn orange shells upside down and set aside.
When yams are baked, remove pulp from skins and mash with:
3 tablespoons softened butter
Season to taste with:
salt and pepper
mild honey
fresh orange juice
freshly grated lemon peel
Spoon into reserved orange shells and dot with:
bits of butter
Bake in 350° oven 15 minutes or until heated through.
Serve with reserved orange sections.

TOMATOES

Ripe, full-flavored tomatoes are seasonal. When there is an abundance, take advantage of the many ways they can be utilized. Tomatoes can be canned, but if freezer space allows, the easiest way to preserve them is to simply bag, seal and freeze. When canned tomatoes are needed in recipes, or when sauce recipes call for ripe tomatoes, remove from freezer, place in one layer, and defrost just until skins peel off easily. Chop and use immediately so juices don't drain off.

BROILED TOMATO HALVES

Halve tomatoes crosswise, place on baking sheet, spread with mayonnaise and top with buttered seasoned bread crumbs mixed with minced fresh basil or mint. Dot with a little butter and sprinkle with paprika. Broil under medium heat until tomatoes are softened and tops browned.

BAKED TOMATOES

Slice tops off:
2 large ripe tomatoes
Scoop out pulp and seeds, leaving a shell at least 1/2 inch thick. Turn upside down to drain. Reserve pulp for soup or sauce. Sprinkle shells with salt and pepper.
Fill with one of the following:
• Creamed Spinach mixed with grated Parmesan cheese to taste
• Corn from cooked corn on the cob, mixed with finely minced red or green bell peppers, onion and fresh parsley
• Sautéed mushrooms
• Cooked grains moistened with a little stock
Top with:
• Buttered seasoned bread crumbs
Place in shallow baking dish and bake in 350° oven 15 minutes or until filling is heated and tomato shell is just tender. Sprinkle with:
minced fresh parsley

FRIED TOMATOES

Slice red or green tomatoes 1/2 inch thick, dip in egg beaten with a little fresh lemon juice or dry sherry or sake, then in seasoned bread crumbs mixed with grated Parmesan cheese. Brown slowly on both sides in butter and/or garlic olive oil.

STEAMED BEAN CURD

Place in shallow ceramic serving dish:
3 firm fresh bean curd cakes, cut in 1-inch squares
2 green onions, chopped
1 small garlic clove, finely minced
1 slice ginger root, finely minced
1/2 dried red chili pepper, seeded and crushed
1/2 cup minced bamboo shoots
1/4 cup minced water chestnuts
3 to 4 dried forest mushrooms, soaked to soften and minced
Drizzle over all a mixture of:
2 teaspoons Tamari soy sauce
1/2 teaspoon Oriental sesame oil
Steam as directed on page 175 for 10 minutes.
Serve with steamed white rice and salad with Miso Dressing.

Vegetables

SAUTÉED VEGETABLES WITH EGGS

Sauté until onion is transparent in:
1 tablespoon olive oil
1/2 cup chopped onion
1 small garlic clove, minced
Add and cook, stirring, 1 to 2 minutes:
1/2 cup each coarsely chopped green bell pepper, peeled ripe tomato and fresh mushrooms
Break onto surface of vegetables:
2 to 4 eggs
Sprinkle to taste with:
salt, pepper and sweet Hungarian paprika
minced fresh or crumbled dried oregano
Cook, uncovered, over low heat until eggs have set.
Serve for supper with hash browns.

Note: Vegetables may be varied according to what is on hand.

STUFFED BELL PEPPERS

Cut tops from:
2 to 3 large green or red bell peppers
Seed peppers and blanch 2 minutes; set aside. Mince the tops and set aside.
Sauté until onion is transparent in:
1 tablespoon peanut or corn oil
1/3 cup chopped onion
3/4 cup chopped fresh mushrooms
Combine mushroom mixture with:
1 cup cooked brown rice or bulghur
1/2 semi-tart apple, grated
1 egg, beaten
reserved minced green or red pepper tops
1/4 teaspoon salt
1/8 teaspoon pepper
Fill peppers with rice mixture and set aside. In a saucepan of a size to hold upright peppers close together, bring to a gentle boil:
1 to 1-1/2 cups Tomato Sauce
1/2 teaspoon minced fresh thyme
1 bay leaf
salt and pepper to taste
Place filled peppers in sauce, cover, lower heat and cook 15 to 20 minutes. Garnish with:
1 tablespoon chopped fresh parsley

ALMOND PATTIES

Combine:
1/2 cup slivered, blanched almonds
2 tablespoons each toasted wheat germ and sesame seeds
1 tablespoon minced celery or green onion
1 egg yolk, lightly beaten
6 tablespoons ricotta cheese
1/4 to 1/2 teaspoon Herb Salt
dash of freshly grated nutmeg or Aromatic Curry Mixture
minced fresh or crumbled dried herbs to taste
Form into 4 1/2-inch thick patties. Gently roll in:
1 to 2 tablespoons toasted wheat germ
Cover and refrigerate at least 1 hour, overnight or all day.
Over low heat, brown patties on both sides in:
1 tablespoon peanut or safflower oil, or as needed
Serve with a green salad and Saffron Rice Pilaf.

Fish and Seafood

Fish and Seafood

Fresh seafood should be eaten within 24 hours of purchase. If desired, marinate fish in fresh lemon juice for 10 to 15 minutes before cooking to bring out the flavor. If fresh fish is not available, this marinating will help to improve the flavor and texture of frozen fish. When the fish loses its translucency and flakes easily with a fork, it is done. Watch carefully so that it does not overcook and toughen. Fish steaks may be substituted for the fillets in the recipes that follow.

EASY FISH FILLETS

Wash and pat dry:
2 5- to 6-ounce firm white fish fillets
Sprinkle with:
1 tablespoon fresh lemon or lime juice
Let stand 10 minutes and season lightly on both sides with:
Herb Salt
pepper
Sauté approximately 6 to 7 minutes per side in:
1 tablespoon olive oil
After turning, while second side is cooking, top fillets with:
2 tablespoons chopped green onions and some tops
1 or 2 ripe tomato slices
2 tablespoons chopped green bell pepper
1/2 to 1 tablespoon chopped fresh basil
When fish is cooked, sprinkle with:
minced fresh parsley

STEAMED FISH

Place in shallow ceramic serving dish:
1 10- to 12-ounce firm white fish fillet or steak
Sprinkle lightly with:
salt and pepper
Drizzle over fish:
1-1/2 teaspoons each Tamari soy sauce and corn oil
1 teaspoon sake or dry sherry
Top with:
1 tablespoon finely chopped green onions
1 thin slice ginger root, finely minced
1 small garlic clove, finely minced
Steam as directed on page 175, 10 to 15 minutes depending upon thickness of fillet or steak.

CHEESE-BAKED FISH FILLETS

Pat dry and place in shallow buttered baking dish:

2 5- to 6-ounce firm white fish fillets

Combine and pour over fillets:

3/4 cup sour cream
1/3 cup grated Parmesan, Gruyère or Emmenthaler cheese
2 teaspoons fresh lemon juice
1 small onion, finely minced or grated
1/4 teaspoon Herb Salt
1/2 small dried red chili pepper, seeded and crushed (optional)

Sprinkle with:

sweet Hungarian paprika

Bake in 350° oven 15 to 20 minutes or until fish flakes easily when tested with a fork. Do not overcook. Garnish with:

chopped fresh parsley

TARRAGON BAKED FISH FILLETS

Pat dry and place in shallow buttered baking dish on layer of:

1 small onion, sliced
2 5- to 6-ounce firm white fish fillets

Sprinkle each fillet with:

salt, Herb Salt and pepper
1-1/2 teaspoons minced fresh tarragon

Pour over fillets:

2 tablespoons fresh lemon juice

Garnish each fillet with:

2 lemon slices
1 fresh basil leaf or 1 bay leaf

Dot each fillet with:

1 teaspoon butter

Bake in 350° oven 15 to 20 minutes or until fish flakes easily with fork. Do not overcook. Serve with sautéed fresh mushrooms, escarole salad and buttered toast sprinkled with Herb Salt.

CORNMEAL FISH FILLETS

Wash and pat dry:

2 5- to 6-ounce firm white fish fillets

Marinate 10 minutes in:

1 tablespoon fresh lemon or lime juice

Coat fillets with mixture of:

1/4 cup yellow cornmeal
2 tablespoons grated Parmesan cheese
1/4 to 1/2 teaspoon fennel seeds, crushed

Sauté gently to brown both sides, approximately 12 minutes in all in:

1 tablespoon each garlic olive oil and butter

Transfer to heated platter and garnish with:

lemon slices
minced fresh parsley

Fish and Seafood

HUNGARIAN FISHPAPRIKAS

Slice into 1-1/4-inch strips:
1 8-ounce firm white fish fillet
Sprinkle generously with:
fresh lemon juice
sweet Hungarian paprika
Set fillets aside.
Sauté, covered, 5 minutes in:
1 tablespoon butter
2 cups chopped white cabbage
Add and steam 15 minutes:
2 to 3 tablespoons water
1/4 teaspoon Herb Salt or salt
**1/8 teaspoon freshly grated
  nutmeg**
In separate pan, sauté until
onions are transparent in:
1 tablespoon butter
3/4 to 1 cup chopped onion
2 garlic cloves, minced
Remove from heat and quickly
stir in so paprika does not turn
bitter:
**1 tablespoon sweet Hun-
  garian paprika**
1-1/2 to 2 tablespoons water

Blend onion mixture into
cabbage and add:
**1 small red bell pepper, cut in
  julienne**
**1/4 teaspoon seeded and crushed
  dried red chili pepper**
**1 cup peeled and diced ripe
  tomatoes**
Cook, covered, 15 minutes.
Gently add:
reserved fish slices
Cover and cook over low heat
10 minutes or until fish is tender
and flakes easily. Remove fish
and keep warm.
Bind sauce with mixture of:
1/3 cup sour cream
2 tablespoons white vinegar
1 tablespoon soy flour, sifted
Transfer sauce to heated platter
and place fish on top.
Garnish with:
**chopped fresh parsley
  and dill**

Note: The Hungarians use pike
for this recipe. The herbs may
also be added to sauce a few
minutes before serving to
infuse their flavor.

BREADED FISH FILLETS

Wash and pat dry:
**2 5- to 6-ounce firm white fish
  fillets**
Marinate 10 minutes in:
**1 tablespoon fresh lemon or
  lime juice**
Coat each fillet with mixture of:
2/3 cup fine bread crumbs
**1/2 teaspoon each salt and sweet
  Hungarian paprika**
1/4 teaspoon pepper
Sauté gently to brown both sides,
approximately 12 minutes in all
in:
**1 tablespoon each garlic olive oil
  and butter**
By the time the fillets are
browned they should be tender
and flake easily. Do not overcook. Sauté any extra bread
crumb coating along with the
fillets, remove fillets to heated
platter and add to crumbs:
1 tablespoon melted butter
Sprinkle buttered crumbs over
fillets and garnish with:
lemon wedges
parsley sprigs

FISH FILLETS STEAMED IN MILK AND DILL

Sauté to just soften in:
1 tablespoon butter
2 young leeks, white and some green, sliced
Place half the leeks in bottom of lightly oiled saucepan and set remainder aside. Rinse and pat dry:
2 5- to 6-ounce firm white fish fillets
Coat evenly with mixture of:
1/4 cup toasted wheat germ
1 tablespoon soy flour, sifted
1/2 teaspoon salt
1/4 teaspoon white pepper
Sauté 3 minutes per side in:
1 tablespoon each corn or peanut oil and butter, or as needed
Place fillets on bed of leeks in saucepan and sprinkle with:
reserved leeks
salt and pepper
Combine and pour over fillets:
any unused breading mixture
3/4 cup milk
2 tablespoons chopped fresh dill
Cover and let steam at low heat 10 minutes. Adjust seasonings and transfer to heated platter. Garnish with:
butter curls
lemon wedges
dill sprigs
Serve with cooked spinach and new potatoes.

FISH FILLETS IN LEMON-PARSLEY SAUCE

Rinse and pat dry:
2 5- to 6-ounce firm white fish fillets
Sprinkle both sides evenly with:
salt
Dip in:
1 egg white, lightly beaten with fork
Roll in mixture of:
1/3 cup toasted wheat germ
1/2 teaspoon Herb Salt
1/4 teaspoon white pepper
Sauté 5 to 7 minutes per side in:
1 tablespoon each olive oil and butter
While fillets are cooking, prepare sauce. Melt until bubbly:
1 tablespoon butter
Stir in and cook and stir 3 minutes:
1 tablespoon unbleached white flour
Blend in:
1/2 cup milk or half-and-half
2 tablespoons fresh lemon juice
1/4 teaspoon salt
Cook and stir until thickened and beat in:
1 egg yolk
Cook and stir without boiling until sauce is quite thick.
Stir in:
3 tablespoons minced fresh parsley
Transfer fish fillets to heated platter and pour sauce over. Serve with new potatoes and lettuce salad with sliced fresh mushrooms and/or slivered almonds.

Variation: Add 1/4 cup slivered almonds to the sauce.

Fish and Seafood

YUCATAN RED SNAPPER FILLETS

Pat dry and place in shallow buttered baking dish:
2 5- to 6-ounce red snapper fillets
Sauté until soft in:
1 tablespoon garlic olive oil
1/4 cup chopped onion
Add and cook, stirring, 3 minutes:
1/4 cup sliced pimiento-stuffed olives
1/4 cup chopped red or green bell pepper
1/2 to 1 teaspoon ground or crushed coriander seed
1/2 dried red chili pepper, seeded and crushed
Stir in:
3 tablespoons each fresh lemon and orange juice
1/4 teaspoon salt
1/8 teaspoon pepper
Pour mixture over fillets, and bake, uncovered, in 375° oven 15 to 20 minutes or until fish flakes easily. Do not overcook. Transfer fillets to heated platter and pour juices over them. Garnish with:
minced fresh parsley or coriander
chopped hard-cooked egg
shredded iceberg lettuce
Serve with steamed white rice.

POACHED SALMON IN SORREL SAUCE

Sprinkle generously with:
fresh lemon juice
2 6- to 7-ounce salmon steaks
Let stand 10 minutes. Place on greased rack in shallow saucepan filled with:
Fish Court Bouillon to cover
Cover, bring to gentle boil and cook 6 to 8 minutes or until salmon flakes easily. Cooking time will depend upon thickness of salmon steaks. Remove and keep warm.
In skillet or saucepan, melt until bubbly:
1 tablespoon butter
Add and cook until sorrel turns dark:
1 cup firmly packed chopped sorrel
Sprinkle with:
1 tablespoon unbleached white flour
Cook and stir 3 minutes and gradually add:
1/2 cup each reserved court bouillon and half-and-half
Cook and stir until thickened. Adjust seasonings with:
salt, white pepper and fresh lemon juice
Pour sorrel sauce over salmon steaks.

SARDINIAN SAGE FISH

Wash and pat dry:
1 10-ounce fresh tuna or other firm white fish fillet
Cut into pieces about 2 inches by 2 inches.
Coat pieces with:
unbleached white flour or rice flour
Brown lightly 3 to 4 minutes in:
1 tablespoon olive oil
Add:
1/2 cup chopped onion
1 garlic clove, minced
Continue cooking until fish is almost tender. Combine, add to pan and heat:
1/2 to 3/4 cup Tomato Sauce
2 to 2-1/2 tablespoons white vinegar
Sprinkle with:
1/2 to 1 teaspoon finely minced fresh sage
1/2 teaspoon finely minced fresh basil or oregano
1/8 teaspoon freshly grated nutmeg
salt to taste
Add if needed to make sauce consistency:
1 tablespoon olive oil
Transfer to heated platter. Serve with rice and shredded escarole salad with olives.

SMOKED FISH RICOTTA SOUFFLÉ

With wire whisk beat until creamy:
2 egg yolks
1 tablespoon each milk and softened or melted and cooled butter
Add, stirring with wooden spoon:
3 tablespoons farina
1 cup ricotta cheese
3 tablespoons grated Edam cheese
2 tablespoons minced fresh Italian parsley
1 tablespoon minced celery (optional)
1/2 teaspoon salt
1/4 teaspoon baking powder
1/8 teaspoon sweet Hungarian paprika
Fold in:
1 cup flaked smoked fish such as halibut or mullet (approximately 8 ounces with skin and bones)
2 egg whites, beaten stiff but not dry
Spoon into lightly buttered soufflé or casserole dish and bake in 400° oven 30 to 35 minutes until surface is evenly browned and toothpick inserted in center comes out clean.

FRESH TUNA ORIENTAL

Cut into strips approximately 2 inches long and 1/2 inch wide:
6 ounces fresh tuna fish or other firm white fish fillets
Sprinkle pieces with:
salt
Tamari soy sauce
In wok or skillet, gently stir-fry fish 2 to 3 minutes in:
1 tablespoon peanut oil
Remove fish and juices to plate and set aside. Add to pan and stir-fry 2 minutes in:
1 tablespoon peanut oil
1/4 cup slivered blanched almonds
1 slice ginger root
1/4 teaspoon ground cardamom
Add and stir-fry 2 minutes:
1/4 cup chopped white part of leek
2 to 3 dried forest mushrooms, soaked to soften and sliced
1/3 cup sliced bamboo shoots
1 tablespoon julienne-cut green bell pepper
Add and bring to steam:
3 to 4 tablespoons sake, dry white wine or dry sherry
1 to 2 tablespoons Tamari soy sauce

Steam 1 to 2 minutes and gently stir in:
reserved fish and juices
Reheat and bind with:
2 tablespoons water
1 teaspoon cornstarch
Add and just heat through:
1/4 to 1/3 cup cut-up fresh pineapple

TARRAGON TUNA PATTIES

With fork mash:
1 7-ounce can water or oil pack tuna fish or salmon, drained
Blend in:
1/4 cup minced onion
1/2 teaspoon Herb Salt
1/4 teaspoon pepper
2 tablespoons chopped fresh celery stalk and leaves, or
1/2 teaspoon dried celery leaves
1/2 to 1 teaspoon chopped fresh tarragon
1 egg, beaten
1 tablespoon toasted wheat germ
Form mixture into 4 patties and brown, turning once, approximately 4 minutes per side in:
1 to 2 tablespoons garlic olive oil
Serve on:
lettuce leaves
Garnish with:
lemon wedges

Fish and Seafood

RUSSIAN HERRING FILLETS IN CUSTARD

A simple but excellent dish and a delight to guests. If increasing portions, allow 1 fillet per person. One sauce recipe is enough for up to 4 fillets.

Lightly sprinkle with:
Herb Salt, pepper and unbleached white flour
2 6-ounce fresh herring fillets
Brown quickly on both sides in:
1 to 2 tablespoons corn oil
Arrange on top:
1 small onion, very thinly sliced into rings
Pour over fillets mixture of:
3/4 cup sour cream
1 egg, beaten
2 tablespoons chopped fresh chives
Cover and cook over low heat 10 minutes without stirring. Sauce will set to custard consistency.
Note: If herring is unavailable, substitute red snapper.

SCALLOP COQUILLE

Wash and halve or quarter if large:
1/2 pound scallops
Pat dry and marinate 10 minutes in:
2 teaspoons fresh lemon juice
Place scallops and juice in saucepan with:
1/4 cup minced green onion and some tops
1/3 cup dry vermouth
1/4 teaspoon minced fresh thyme
1/8 teaspoon each salt and white pepper
Bring to boil, cover, lower heat and simmer, shaking pan often, 2 minutes or until just tender. Do not overcook. With tongs, remove scallops to 2 ramekin dishes. Bring juices to boil and reduce by half. In separate saucepan, melt until bubbly:
2 tablespoons butter
Blend in and cook and stir 3 minutes:
2 teaspoons unbleached white flour
Stirring constantly, gradually add:
2/3 cup half-and-half
reduced scallop cooking liquid
Cook and stir over medium-low heat until thickened. Pour over scallops. Sprinkle over each ramekin:
1-1/2 tablespoons seasoned fine bread crumbs
Bake in 350° oven 10 minutes or until bubbly and heated through. Garnish with:
minced fresh parsley or watercress sprigs

PRAWNS IN GORGONZOLA

Shell, devein and butterfly:
8 to 10 large prawns (approximately 8 to 10 ounces)
Sauté prawns quickly until they turn white in:
2 tablespoons butter
1 garlic clove, finely minced
Do not overcook.
Add and stir until creamy:
1-1/2 tablespoons fresh lemon juice
1/4 cup crumbled Gorgonzola cheese
Garnish with:
minced fresh parsley
Serve immediately with hot buttered rice and a green salad.

Poultry

Poultry

CHICKEN

Chickens vary in size. Allow approximately 3/4 pound per person. When cooked, the light meat should be white and tender; the juices of the dark meat should run clear when the meat is pierced with a fork.

MARINATING CHICKEN

Marinating chicken before preparing will insure seasoned flavor throughout. The marinating process, when using salt water or wine marinade, will also serve to tenderize the meat. The salt water marinade is especially good for frozen chickens, since some of the flavor is lost in freezing and the marinade soaking serves to "plump" the chicken back to the texture of a fresh bird.

Marinating can be done at room temperature up to 1 hour. For longer periods, cover and refrigerate up to 12 hours until needed. Use ceramic or glass containers.

SALT WATER MARINADE

For a 2-1/2- to 3-pound fryer, cut into serving pieces and place in large bowl with a mixture of 1 to 1-1/2 tablespoons salt and 2 to 3 cups ice water to cover. Let stand at least 1 hour. Drain and let dry 15 minutes or pat dry with paper toweling. For half a cut-up chicken, halve the salt water mixture. For a whole roasting fryer, double the salt water mixture.

LEMON MARINADE

Pour over half a cut-up fryer 2 tablespoons lemon juice. Let stand 30 minutes to 1 hour.

LEMON-GARLIC MARINADE

Sprinkle each piece of half a fryer on both sides with salt and pepper. Place pieces in a bowl and pour over them 2 tablespoons fresh lemon juice. Tuck between chicken pieces 2 small garlic cloves, minced, and optional crushed bay leaves. Cover and refrigerate 2 to 3 hours. Remove chicken, drain and pat dry.

WINE MARINADE

In a large bowl, marinate in white or rosé wine, or dry sherry to cover, half a fryer, cut in serving pieces. Cover and let stand in cool place or refrigerator 2 to 3 hours or overnight. Bruised whole garlic cloves, bay leaves and/or lightly crushed peppercorns may be added for variation. Good for turkey and also red meats. For meats, substitute red wine or burgundy for white or rosé wine or dry sherry.

EASY METHODS OF COOKING CHICKEN

- Butter steam with addition of 1/4 cup chicken stock.
- Brush with melted butter and dry sherry and sprinkle with minced fresh tarragon or oregano. Bake in a 350° oven 35 to 40 minutes.
- Brush with Tamari soy sauce and honey and sprinkle lightly with five-spice powder. Bake in a 350° oven 35 to 40 minutes.

CHICKEN SAUTÉ SEC

Pat dry:
1-1/2 pounds fryer chicken,
    cut up
Brown on all sides in:
2 tablespoons olive oil
Sprinkle with salt and pepper
and remove from skillet. Wipe
out skillet and sauté 2 minutes
in:
2 tablespoons butter
1 small onion, minced
1 garlic clove, minced
Add and sauté 3 minutes:
1 cup sliced fresh mushrooms
Return chicken pieces to skillet
with:
1/2 cup dry white wine
1 or 2 fresh sage leaves
Cook over medium heat,
uncovered, 25 minutes, turning
occasionally, or until chicken is
tender. Juices should almost
cook away; add more wine if
necessary. Remove sage leaves
and adjust seasonings to taste.

GINGER STEAMED CHICKEN

Place in shallow ceramic serving
dish:
1-1/2 pounds fryer chicken, cut
    in serving pieces
Sprinkle with:
1/2 teaspoon salt
3 green onions and tops, cut in
    2-inch lengths
1/4 cup thinly sliced ginger root
1/3 cup dry white wine
Steam as directed on page 175, 45
minutes or until chicken is tender.

CHICKEN IN WINE AND TOMATO SAUCE

Marinate in salt water or wine
marinade:
1-1/2 pounds fryer chicken, cut
    into serving pieces
Drain and pat dry. Turning once,
brown 10 minutes in:
1 tablespoon each butter and
    corn oil
Add:
1/2 cup chopped onion
1 to 2 tablespoons minced celery
1 garlic clove, minced
1 ripe tomato, peeled and diced
1/2 teaspoon each sweet Hun-
    garian paprika and Herb Salt
1/4 teaspoon pepper
Pour over chicken pieces
a mixture of:
1/2 cup Tomato Sauce
1/4 cup Chianti or other red wine
1 tablespoon cider vinegar
Cook, covered, over medium heat
25 to 30 minutes or until chicken
is tender. Stir in:
1/4 cup sour cream
1-1/2 teaspoons each minced
    fresh parsley and chives
Replace cover and let stand 2 to
3 minutes to allow flavors to
blend. Adjust seasonings to
taste. Serve with hot buttered
noodles or Spaetzle, green salad
with vinegar and oil dressing.
Recipe doubles and reheats well.

Poultry

ITALIAN CHICKEN WITH ANCHOVIES AND OLIVES

An exciting dish that can be easily doubled. Serve for guests if doubling, as it does not reheat well.

Marinate in salt water or white wine marinade:

1-1/2 pounds fryer chicken, cut into serving pieces, or
1 large chicken breast, halved
Drain and pat dry. Brown on all sides in:
1 tablespoon each garlic olive oil and butter
Remove from skillet and set aside. Add to skillet and sauté 5 minutes:
1/4 cup chopped onion
1 garlic clove, minced
Blend in and let simmer 1 to 2 minutes:
1/2 to 3/4 cup dry white wine
1-1/2 tablespoons white vinegar
1 teaspoon chopped fresh oregano
2 bay leaves
1/3 cup sliced fresh mushrooms (optional)

Return chicken to skillet, cover and cook over medium heat 30 minutes. Transfer chicken to heated serving platter. Discard bay leaves and to sauce add:
1/2 teaspoon anchovy paste
2 tablespoons halved or quartered pitted black olives
salt and pepper to taste
Let stand 2 to 3 minutes and pour over chicken.

HUNGARIAN CHICKEN IN PAPRIKA GRAVY

Marinate in salt water or rosé wine marinade:
1-1/2 pounds fryer chicken, cut into serving pieces
Pat dry and set aside.
Sauté 5 minutes or until onion is transparent in:
2 tablespoons butter
1 medium-size onion, chopped
Remove from heat and add, stirring constantly:
2 teaspoons sweet Hungarian paprika
Return to heat and immediately add:
2 tablespoons water

Stir until smooth and cook to reduce liquid by half. Place chicken in skillet, skin side down and sprinkle generously with:
salt
Sauté uncovered 5 minutes, turn chicken pieces, lower heat and cook 30 to 40 minutes or until tender, adding after 15 minutes cooking:
1 small red bell pepper, chopped
1 ripe tomato, peeled and chopped
2 tablespoons rosé wine
Remove chicken to heated platter and keep warm. Add to pan juices smooth mixture of:
1/2 cup sour cream
1 tablespoon unbleached white flour
1/4 cup water or rosé wine
1/4 teaspoon salt
Bring to gentle simmer and cook without boiling, stirring constantly, 5 minutes or until sauce is creamy and a rich pink-orange color. Pour sauce over chicken and serve with buttered noddles or Spaetzle and a butter lettuce salad.
This recipe doubles well and is almost better when reheated.

SPICY CHICKEN WITH COCONUT MILK

Marinate in salt water or lemon marinade:
1-1/2 pounds fryer chicken, cut into serving pieces, or
1 large chicken breast, halved
Drain and pat dry. Sprinkle with:
salt and sweet Hungarian paprika
Brown chicken pieces in:
2 tablespoons butter
After 10 to 15 minutes add:
1/2 cup chopped onions
1 garlic clove, minced
1/4 cup grated blanched almonds
1/4 teaspoon seeded and crushed dried red chili pepper
1 bay leaf
1/2 teaspoon salt
1-1/2 to 2 tablespoons fresh lemon juice
2 teaspoons mild honey
Pour over all:
1 cup coconut milk
Sprinkle with:
1/3 cup grated fresh or unsweetened coconut
sweet Hungarian paprika
Cover and cook over medium-low heat 30 minutes or until tender. Serve with Saffron Rice Pilaf and Carrot Coconut Relish.

BALINESE CHICKEN

Delicious and spicy, yet light.

Wash and pat dry:
1-1/2 pounds fryer chicken, cut into serving pieces, or
1 large chicken breast, halved
In wok or heavy skillet brown covered, turning once, over medium-low heat 30 minutes or until tender in:
1 tablespoon rendered chicken fat and/or corn oil
While chicken is cooking, in dry skillet sauté, stirring often, over medium-low heat 10 minutes mixture of:
1/4 cup finely minced onion
1 garlic clove, finely minced
1/2 teaspoon finely minced ginger root
1 tablespoon chopped slivered blanched almonds
1/4 teaspoon seeded and crushed dried red chili pepper
1/4 to 1/2 teaspoon freshly ground coriander
Remove chicken from wok or skillet and deglaze pan with:
1/4 cup dry white wine
Let reduce slightly and add:
1/4 cup chicken stock
2 teaspoons Tamari soy sauce
1/2 to 1 teaspoon mild honey
reserved onion mixture

Cook and stir 3 minutes, return chicken pieces to sauce and reheat. Spoon sauce over, cover and let stand 3 minutes. Serve over brown rice with green salad or vegetable.

CHICKEN TANDOORI

Make 2-inch long and 1/2-inch deep slits in:
1-1/2 pounds fryer chicken, cut in serving pieces
Coat well with:
1 recipe Tandoori Marinade
Cover and refrigerate, turning pieces occasionally, for at least 2 hours or overnight. Place chicken in shallow roasting pan and pour over it marinade remaining in pan and:
2 tablespoons melted butter, cooled
Bake in 400° oven 15 minutes. Reduce heat to 350° and continue baking 25 to 30 minutes until chicken is tender and crisp. Serve with brown rice and tossed salad of butter lettuce, tomato wedges and onion rings.

Poultry

DRIED FRUIT CHICKEN CURRY

Marinate in salt water or lemon marinade:

1-1/2 pounds fryer chicken, cut into serving pieces, or

1 large chicken breast, halved

While chicken is marinating, soften in:

3/4 cup water

1/2 cup dried apples

1/4 cup each dried pitted prunes and raisins

Drain chicken and pat dry. Brown on all sides in:

1 tablespoon each peanut oil and butter

Remove and set aside. In same skillet, adding more oil or butter if needed, sauté 3 to 4 minutes:

1/2 cup finely chopped onion

Blend in and cook 2 minutes:

1/2 teaspoon salt

1 tablespoon Aromatic Curry Mixture

Stir in:

dried fruits and soaking water

1 tablespoon each red wine vinegar and fresh lemon juice

Return to skillet:

reserved chicken

Bring to boil, lower heat, cover and simmer 20 to 30 minutes or until tender, adding if needed:

not more than 1/4 cup water

Serve on heated platter or bed of rice and garnish with:

1/2 cup shelled unsalted raw peanuts

1 banana, sliced and lightly sautéed in butter

Recipe doubles and reheats well.

BREADED FRIED CHICKEN

Marinate in salt water or white wine marinade:

2 chicken legs and thighs, disjointed

Pat dry and coat with:

rice flour

Dip in mixture of:

1 egg, beaten

1 teaspoon fresh lemon juice

Coat with mixture of:

1/2 cup fine bread crumbs

1/2 teaspoon each salt and sweet Hungarian paprika

1/4 teaspoon black pepper

If time permits, refrigerate in single layer for 1 hour so coating will better adhere to chicken while frying. Chicken may also be prepared up to this point in the morning.

In heavy skillet with lid, heat:

2 tablespoons garlic olive oil

1 tablespoon butter

Brown chicken pieces without touching, covered, over medium-low heat 15 minutes. Turn and brown other side 15 minutes, removing lid last 5 minutes. Chicken should be cooked through but still moist and golden brown. Transfer to heated platter and keep warm. Deglaze skillet over high heat with:

1/2 cup chicken stock or dry white wine

Scrape up any bits on bottom of pan, let liquid cook down by half and pour over chicken. Sprinkle with:

minced fresh parsley

Poultry

BARBECUED BROILERS WITH VERMOUTH

Over very low heat, cook
10 minutes:
5 tablespoons butter
1 garlic clove, bruised
Basting frequently with half the
butter, broil 10 minutes per side
over charcoal or under broiler
to brown well:
1 young broiler chicken, halved
Transfer to baking dish, discard
garlic and pour over chicken:
remaining butter
2 tablespoons dry vermouth
Sprinkle with:
salt, pepper and sweet Hun-
garian paprika
2 tablespoons each minced fresh
parsley and green onions
with some tops
Cover with lid or foil and bake in
350° oven 20 minutes, or until
chicken is tender. Remove to
heated platter, pour juices over
and garnish with:
lemon wedges
parsley sprigs
Serve with Rice Pilaf or mashed
or riced potatoes and a green
vegetable or salad.

CHICKEN WITH MUSHROOMS IN WINE SAUCE
(Two Meals from One Recipe)

This French-inspired chicken dish
is excellent reheated.

Sprinkle with:
salt and pepper
1 3-pound fryer chicken, cut into
serving pieces
Marinate, covered, for 2 to 3
hours in:
3/4 cup dry white or light rosé
wine
Remove chicken pieces and pat
dry; reserve wine. Sauté chicken
pieces until golden brown in:
2 tablespoons butter or rendered
chicken fat
Remove chicken from skillet. Add
to skillet and sauté 2 minutes:
1 onion, finely chopped
1 garlic clove, minced
Sprinkle with:
1 teaspoon unbleached white flour
Cook and stir for 2 minutes.
Deglaze pan with:
reserved wine

Return chicken to skillet and
add:
1/2 teaspoon salt
1/8 teaspoon each pepper and
sweet Hungarian paprika
1-1/2 teaspoons chopped fresh
basil
2 bay leaves
3 parsley sprigs
1 small celery stalk, cut in half, or
2 teaspoons dried celery leaves
Cover skillet and let simmer over
medium heat 30 to 35 minutes or
until chicken is tender. Transfer
chicken to heated serving platter
and keep warm. Discard bay
leaves, parsley and celery stalk.
Add to skillet and cook
5 minutes:
2-1/2 to 3 cups sliced fresh
mushrooms (3/4 pound)
Mix together and add to skillet:
1/4 cup half-and-half
1 egg yolk, beaten
2 to 3 tablespoons sauce from
skillet
Cook and stir to thicken sauce.
Adjust seasonings to taste and
pour over chicken.

LEMON ROAST CHICKEN
(Two Meals from One Recipe)

Wash and pat dry inside and out:
1 3-pound fryer chicken
Rub inside and out with:
2 tablespoons softened butter
2 tablespoons fresh lemon juice
Sprinkle inside and out with:
salt and pepper
Place in cavity of chicken:
3 oregano sprigs
4 garlic cloves, bruised
4 slices lemon
Roast in 450° oven, back side up, 10 minutes. Turn over and roast another 10 minutes. Lower heat to 350° and, basting with pan juices, continue roasting 45 minutes or until juices run clear when thighs are pierced with a fork. Transfer to heated platter and pour over chicken:
2 tablespoons fresh lemon juice
Reduce pan juices by half and pour over chicken. Garnish with:
lemon wedges
Serve with parslied new potatoes and a green vegetable.
This chicken reheats well. Debone, place in shallow pan, cover and reheat with pan juices and extra chicken stock.
Or serve cold.

SESAME BAKED CHICKEN
(Two Meals from One Recipe)

Marinate in salt water marinade:
1 3-pound fryer chicken, cut into serving pieces
Pat dry and coat with:
1 cup Seasoned Sesame Coating
Place on lightly greased pan and bake in 350° oven 45 minutes to 1 hour until crispy brown and juices from thighs run clear when pierced with a fork. Baste several times during cooking time with juices that collect on bottom of pan. If chicken is very lean, last 10 minutes of cooking dot with butter to moisten any coating areas that are still dry. Serve with salad and baked winter squash.

Note: This chicken is excellent cold. For picnic fare, accompany with potato salad, fresh tomatoes, spinach salad.

Variation: Dip chicken pieces in mixture of 1/4 cup each melted butter and half-and-half. Coat with 1/2 cup sesame coating and place in buttered baking dish. Pour remaining melted butter and half-and-half over and surround with broccoli flowerets. Cook as directed.

BUTTERMILK CORNMEAL CHICKEN
(Two Meals from One Recipe)

Marinate in salt water marinade:
1 3-pound fryer chicken, cut into serving pieces
Drain, pat dry and dip pieces in:
3/4 to 1 cup buttermilk
Coat on all sides in mixture of:
1/3 cup yellow cornmeal
1/4 cup each soy flour, sifted, grated Parmesan cheese and unbleached white flour
2 teaspoons Herb Salt
1 teaspoon sweet Hungarian paprika
Place chicken in well-buttered or oiled shallow baking pan and bake in 350° oven 45 minutes or until chicken tests done. Baste several times with juices that collect in pan. If chicken is very lean, last 10 minutes of cooking time dot with butter to moisten any breaded areas that are still dry. Serve with baked potatoes and a cooked green vegetable or salad. Serve leftovers cold later in the week.

Note: Refrigerate any unused breading mixture and use on ground beef patties, chops, chicken giblets, liver.

Poultry

CHRISTMAS ROAST CHICKEN

Marinate in salt water marinade:
1 3- to 4-pound fryer chicken
Drain and pat dry. Rub chicken inside and out with:
olive oil
Sprinkle inside and out with:
salt, pepper and sweet Hungarian paprika
Place in cavity:
1 recipe Apple-Raisin Stuffing (following)
Place chicken in oiled or buttered roasting pan and surround with:
1/2 onion, finely chopped
Roast in 450° oven 15 minutes.

While chicken is roasting, parboil in salted water 4 to 5 minutes:
3 carrots, halved lengthwise and then crosswise
4 white onions, approximately 1-1/2 inches in diameter
6 to 8 small potatoes, unpeeled and lightly scrubbed (approximately 1 to 1-1/4 pounds)
Add to roasting pan:
2 cups chicken stock
2 whole garlic cloves, bruised
1 to 2 teaspoons grated fresh lemon peel
Arrange around chicken:
parboiled vegetables
Lower oven heat to 325°, cover and roast 45 minutes. Remove cover and roast chicken 15 minutes longer until chicken is tender and golden. Transfer chicken and vegetables to heated platter and keep warm. Bind pan juices with mixture of:
1/4 cup water
1-1/2 tablespoons cornstarch
When thickened, blend in:
1/3 to 1/2 cup light red wine
Cook and stir 5 minutes and adjust seasonings with salt and pepper. Serve in gravy bowl.

APPLE-RAISIN STUFFING

Combine and mix well with hands:
3 cups grated Golden Delicious or semisweet apples
1/3 cup raisins or sultanas, plumped
1/4 cup minced celery
3 tablespoons grated carrot
2 tablespoons grated almonds
1-1/2 tablespoons each minced onion and fresh Italian parsley
1 tablespoon fresh lemon juice
1/2 teaspoon salt
1/4 teaspoon each ground cinnamon and freshly grated nutmeg
Adjust seasonings and pack into cavity of bird. Sew or skewer shut. Excellent for goose, in which case double or triple recipe as required. Stuffing is also good reheated.

CHICKEN À LA ASTRID
(Two Meals from One Recipe)

Marinate in double recipe lemon-garlic marinade:
1 3-pound fryer chicken, cut into serving pieces
Pat dry and sprinkle each piece on both sides with:
salt and pepper
Place chicken pieces in shallow roasting pan and add:
4 small onions, quartered
2 tablespoons melted butter
Sprinkle evenly with:
sweet Hungarian paprika
Roast in 450° oven 10 minutes.
Combine and heat:
reserved marinade and garlic, mixed with water, chicken stock or dry white wine to measure 3/4 cup
1 cube frozen beef stock concentrate, or
1 to 2 teaspoons Tamari soy sauce
1/2 teaspoon seeded and crushed dried red chili pepper
Lower oven heat to 375° and pour mixture over chicken. Add:
1 green bell pepper, cut into 1-1/2 by 1-inch julienne
1 large or 2 small unpeeled potatoes, cut into eighths or fourths

Continue roasting chicken, basting 3 or 4 times, 40 minutes. Remove chicken to heated platter and add to pan juices:
2 tablespoons quartered green or black olives
1/3 cup dry white wine
binder of:
2 tablespoons water
1 teaspoon cornstarch
Cook and stir over low heat 2 minutes or until thickened. Pour sauce over chicken and serve with brown rice and a green salad. This recipe makes 4 servings, but is excellent reheated. Cool and refrigerate; reheat in juices later in the week.

Variations:
• Omit green pepper and olives; add sliced cooked artichoke hearts to pan juices with wine.
• Add to gravy 2 teaspoons tomato paste.

CHICKEN LIVERS IN WINE

Marinate 1 hour in:
port or Marsala to cover
1/2 pound chicken livers, halved if large
Sauté until onion is transparent in:
3 to 4 tablespoons butter
1/4 cup minced onion or green onion and tops
Pat livers dry and sprinkle very lightly with:
unbleached white flour
Add to onions and sauté 3 minutes or until livers stiffen.
Stir in:
1 tablespoon fresh lemon juice
1/3 cup port or Marsala
1/2 teaspoon minced fresh sage
1/4 teaspoon salt
1/8 teaspoon white pepper
Cook over medium-low heat, stirring occasionally, 6 to 8 minutes. Livers should still be slightly pink in center. Adjust seasonings and serve with rice and a tossed green salad with oil and vinegar dressing.

Variation: Sauté with the livers 1/2 cup sliced fresh mushrooms and/or julienne-cut green bell pepper.

Poultry

CORNISH HENS

Halve and pat dry:
1 large Cornish hen
Marinate 1 hour in mixture of:
**1-1/2 tablespoons Tamari soy
    sauce**
1 tablespoon sake or dry sherry
1 teaspoon mild honey
**1/2 teaspoon finely minced gar-
    lic (optional)**
Broil over hot coals, basting with
marinade and turning several
times, 35 to 40 minutes or until
tender.

DUCKLING WITH OLIVES

Marinate covered and refrigerated in large deep bowl at least
1 hour in:
3 to 4 cups water to cover
**1-1/2 to 2 tablespoons salt, dis-
    solved in water**
**1 whole 4- to 5-pound duckling,
    trimmed of excess fat**
Drain and pat dry. Place duckling
breast side up in deep, lightly
oiled roasting pan and bake in
350° oven 30 minutes, basting
frequently, until browned.
Pierce breasts and thighs to
release fat. Transfer to heated
platter and keep warm while
preparing sauce. Pour off all
except 2 tablespoons of the fat
that has collected in pan. Heat
fat in pan over medium-low heat
and add, stirring until golden
brown:
**1 tablespoon unbleached white
    flour**
Add, stirring until
thickened:
1-1/2 cups chicken stock
1 cup dry white wine
**15 each black and green olives,
    pitted and quartered**
salt and pepper to taste
bouquet garni of:
    1 bay leaf
    3 parsley sprigs
    1 sprig each savory and thyme
Return duckling to sauce, cover
and roast approximately 1 hour
and 20 minutes. Uncover, baste
several times, and cook 10 minutes longer. Discard bouquet garni,
remove duck to serving platter
and adjust sauce seasonings. Garnish carved or whole duckling
with:
parsley sprigs
lemon or orange twists
Serve sauce on side; accompany with shredded escarole salad
or green vegetable and brown rice.

Note: If there are leftovers, this
duckling reheats well, or remove
meat from bones and use diced
meat in soups or for hash and
make stock from the bones.

TURKEY MEATLOAF
SCARBOROUGH FAIR

Combine:
2/3 cup mashed potatoes
1 egg, beaten
Add and blend well:
1 pound raw ground turkey
**1/2 cup peeled and chopped
    ripe tomato**
**2 tablespoons finely minced
    onion**
**1/2 teaspoon freshly grated
    lemon peel**
1 teaspoon salt
1/4 teaspoon pepper
1/4 cup chopped fresh parsley
1/4 teaspoon minced fresh sage
**1/8 teaspoon finely minced fresh
    rosemary**
1/4 teaspoon minced fresh thyme
Form into loaf shape in shallow
baking dish. Bake in 350° oven
50 to 60 minutes. Transfer to
heated platter and keep warm.
Make gravy from drippings if
desired. Serve with small baked
potatoes with butter and/or sour
cream and minced chives and a
green salad.

Note: If turkey mixture seems
too moist, add 2 to 3 tablespoons
bread crumbs.

Meat

Meat

RENA'S POT ROAST
(Two Meals from One Recipe)

Trim excess fat off:
1 3-pound chuck roast
Season with salt and pepper and dust with flour. Brown on all sides in:
2 tablespoons rendered beef fat, or as needed
Remove from skillet and stir in:
1 tablespoon flour
Gradually blend in:
1 cup water
Cook and stir until thickened and then add:
salt and pepper
until gravy is so briny and hot that it is almost inedible; this takes courage, but is the secret of the pot roast.

Place roast in a Dutch oven and over it place:
4 medium potatoes, peeled and quartered
4 to 6 carrots, quartered
2 green bell peppers, seeded and cut in strips
2 to 3 onions, quartered
3 to 4 celery stalks, cut up (optional)
Pour over all:
1 28-ounce can tomatoes with liquid
gravy from skillet
Cover and simmer on top of stove or in 350° oven 2-1/2 to 3 hours. Twenty minutes before serving add:
1/4 cup dry sherry
To serve, remove roast to heated platter and surround with vegetables. Strain cooking juices into another pot and bind with:
3 tablespoons water
2 teaspoons cornstarch
Adjust seasonings with salt and pepper and serve in a bowl with the roast.
The roast is even better reheated. If there is any gravy left over, serve over noodles with a salad for a light supper.

GERMAN-STYLE GOULASH

In stewing pot fry until crisp:
1/4 cup diced slab bacon
Remove with slotted spoon, drain and set aside. In drippings remaining in pot, brown over medium heat, a portion at a time without allowing them to touch:
1 pound beef stew meat, cut into chunks
A brown crust should form on bottom of pot. When all meat is browned return meat to pot and add:
1 cup water
reserved bacon
1 onion, sliced into rings
2 garlic cloves, minced
1/2 teaspoon each Herb Salt and pepper
1 or 2 ripe tomatoes, peeled and cubed
1 tablespoon tomato paste
1/2 teaspoon dried celery leaves
1 bay leaf
1 tablespoon minced green bell pepper
1/8 teaspoon each crumbled dried thyme and rosemary
cayenne pepper to taste

Lower heat, cover and cook approximately 2 hours or until meat is tender, adding more water as needed. Adjust seasonings and serve with mashed potatoes and butter-steamed carrots.

Variation: Last half hour of cooking, add 1/4 to 1/2 cup burgundy, 3/4 cup sliced fresh mushrooms, 1 cup thinly sliced carrots and 3 to 4 small potatoes, sliced. Continue cooking, adding beef stock or more wine if needed. Adjust seasonings and serve as a meal in one dish.

BEEF POT PIE

Prepare:
1 recipe Whole-Wheat Pastry
    (page 175)
Marinate 1 hour in:
1 cup burgundy
1 bay leaf
1 garlic clove, bruised
3/4 pound beef stew meat, cut
    in 3/4-inch cubes

Drain and pat meat dry. Reserve marinade. Shake in paper bag to coat meat well with:
1/4 cup unbleached white flour
1/2 teaspoon salt
1/4 teaspoon pepper
Shake excess flour from meat and brown cubes a few at a time, not touching, in:
1 tablespoon each butter and
    garlic olive oil
With last batch of meat brown:
1/4 cup chopped onion
1 garlic clove, minced
Return browned meat to skillet and deglaze skillet with:
reserved marinade
Lower heat and add:
1/2 cup beef stock
1/2 cup burgundy
1 ripe tomato, peeled and
    chopped
1 teaspoon Tamari soy sauce
1 bay leaf
1 sprig each thyme and parsley
1/2 teaspoon salt
1/4 teaspoon pepper
Cover and cook stirring occasionally at gentle simmer for 1 hour. Add and continue cooking, stirring occasionally and adding wine as needed, until vegetables and beef are tender:

1 cup diagonally cut carrots
1 medium-size onion, cut in
    eighths and separated
2 to 3 dried forest mushrooms,
    soaked to soften and slivered
mushroom soaking water
Gravy should be thick and flavorful. Discard bay leaf and sprigs. Adjust seasonings and transfer to 2 individual 4-inch pot pie dishes. Let cool slightly while rolling out pastry. Roll pastry into 2 5-inch rounds. Place on top of dish and fold edges under. Crimp edges, pushing down gently on rim of dish. Cut a small design in center of pastry with pastry cutter or sharp knife and loosen slightly to allow steam to escape while baking. Bake in 350° oven 25 minutes or until crust is golden.

Meat

FILET MIGNON

Sprinkle with:
2 teaspoons fresh lemon juice
2 filets mignons
Let stand 1 hour and pat dry.
Sauté quickly, depending upon
thickness, in:
1-1/2 teaspoons each butter and
   olive oil
Filets should be browned on the
outside, pink or very pink in
the center, according to taste.
Sprinkle lightly with:
salt
Add to skillet and let cook down
by half:
1 cube frozen beef stock concentrate, thawed
Heat:
1 to 2 tablespoons cognac
Pour over filets and flame, shaking skillet to distribute flaming
cognac. (Have potholder ready
to move skillet from fire if flame
is too high.) Transfer filets to
heated serving plates and pour
juices over. Garnish with:
watercress sprigs
Serve with sautéed mushrooms
and Soufflé-Baked Potatoes.

HERB-SEASONED MEATBALLS IN SOUR CREAM SAUCE

Mix thoroughly and form into
balls 1-1/4 inches in diameter:
1/2 pound lean ground beef
1/3 cup chopped onion
1 garlic clove, minced
1 egg, lightly beaten
3 tablespoons toasted wheat germ
1/2 teaspoon salt
1/4 teaspoon pepper
1-1/2 teaspoons each chopped
   fresh parsley, chives and dill
Without allowing to touch,
brown well on all sides 10 minutes in:
1-1/2 tablespoons each corn oil
   and butter
Pour over mixture of:
3/4 cup sour cream
1 egg yolk, lightly beaten
1 tablespoon fresh lemon juice
1/8 teaspoon freshly grated
   nutmeg
Cover and heat 2 to 3 minutes.
Do not boil. Transfer to heated
serving dish and garnish with:
1 tablespoon chopped fresh
   parsley
Serve with buttered egg noodles
and sliced fresh fruit.

BELL PEPPER AND SWISS CHEESE MEATLOAF

Combine:
1 pound lean ground beef
1 egg, beaten
1/2 cup each minced green bell
   pepper and coarsely grated
   Gruyère or Emmenthaler
   cheese
2 tablespoons bread crumbs or
   toasted wheat germ
1/2 to 1 teaspoon each Herb Salt
   and minced fresh thyme
1/4 teaspoon sweet Hungarian
   paprika
1/8 teaspoon pepper
Form into loaf in shallow baking
dish and bake in 325° oven 1
hour. Make gravy from drippings
if desired.

Variation: Bake meatloaf topped
with 1 cup thick Tomato Sauce.

Note: Refrigerate leftover meatloaf. Reheat or use in sandwiches
or to stuff bell peppers, tomatoes,
zucchini or onions.

ITALIAN BAKED ZUCCHINI WITH BEEF

Cook over low heat 15 minutes:
3/4 cup Tomato Sauce
2 tablespoons minced green
 bell pepper
1/2 teaspoon each minced fresh
 oregano and basil
1/4 teaspoon minced fresh thyme
pinch minced fresh rosemary
1 teaspoon fresh lemon juice
1 whole clove
While sauce is heating, sauté
until transparent in:
1 tablespoon olive oil
1 onion, chopped
Add, stirring until browned:
1/2 pound lean ground beef
salt and pepper to taste
Remove from heat and layer
meat mixture in buttered shallow
baking dish alternately with:
1 6- to 7-ounce zucchini, sliced
 in rounds
1/2 cup sliced fresh mushrooms
seasoned tomato sauce
Top with:
1/4 cup grated mozzarella cheese
1/8 to 1/4 teaspoon freshly
 grated nutmeg
Bake in 375° oven 30 minutes.
Serve with brown rice, buttered
noodles or garlic bread and a
green salad with Italian Dressing.

SHEPHERD'S CASSEROLE

Steam or blanch until tender:
1/2 (small) head savoy or white
 cabbage
Drain and set aside. Cook 15 minutes or until soft:
3 or 4 medium-size potatoes
While potatoes are cooking,
sauté in:
1 tablespoon butter
1/2 cup chopped onions
1/2 pound lean ground beef
1/4 teaspoon salt
1/8 teaspoon pepper
1-1/2 teaspoons minced fresh
 marjoram
Peel potatoes and mash with:
1/3 cup milk
2 teaspoons butter
salt and pepper to taste
Separate cabbage leaves and layer
half of leaves in buttered 1-1/2-
quart baking dish. Top with
onion and beef mixture and
sprinkle lightly with:
salt and pepper
Cover with remaining cabbage
leaves and top with:
mashed potatoes
3 tablespoons grated mild cheese
Bake in 375° oven 15 to 20 minutes until potatoes are golden
and cheese is melted.

ONION MEATLOAF WITH MUSHROOM SAUCE

Sauté until browned in:
2 tablespoons butter
1 cup minced onion
Combine with:
1 pound lean ground beef
1 egg, beaten
1/2 teaspoon Herb Salt
1/8 teaspoon pepper
1/4 cup bread crumbs or toasted
 wheat germ
Form into loaf in shallow baking
dish. Bake in 325° oven 1 hour.
Transfer to heated platter and
keep warm. Deglaze pan juices
with:
1/2 to 3/4 cup dry white or rosé
 wine
Stir in:
1 cup sliced fresh mushrooms,
 sautéed in
1-1/2 tablespoons butter
binder of:
 1 tablespoon water
 1 teaspoon cornstarch
1 teaspoon minced fresh thyme
Simmer until thickened. Combine:
2 tablespoons sauce
2 tablespoons sour cream
Return to rest of sauce and stir
well. Serve meatloaf with sauce
on side.

Meat

HAMBURGERS

Soften in:
1/3 cup milk
**1 to 2 slices whole wheat or
white bread**
Squeeze out milk and combine
with:
**1 to 1-1/3 pounds lean ground
beef or lamb**
1 egg, beaten
**1 tablespoon each catsup, grated
onion and Tamari soy sauce**
1 garlic clove, finely minced
1/4 teaspoon pepper
**1/2 teaspoon finely minced
fresh thyme**
Form into 4 to 6 patties. Wrap
half the patties well and freeze.
Broil remaining patties and serve
with one of the following
toppings.

TOPPINGS FOR
HAMBURGERS,
STEAKS AND CHOPS

• Prepare 1/2 cup Béchamel
Sauce made with beef stock. Just
before serving add to hot sauce 1
to 2 tablespoons crumbled Gorgonzola cheese.

• Mash 1/2 avocado with 1/2
teaspoon each fresh lemon juice
and grated onion. Add 2 tablespoons diced ripe peeled tomato and salt, white pepper and
chili oil to taste.
• Mixture of 1/3 cup sour cream,
1 tablespoon crumbled Gorgonzola cheese, 1 teaspoon each
minced green onion and green
bell pepper.
• Mixture of 1/4 cup sour cream,
2 tablespoons mayonnaise, 2 to
3 pimiento-stuffed or black
olives, minced.
• 1 cup sliced fresh mushrooms,
3 tablespoons chopped green
onion, 1/4 teaspoon minced garlic and 1/2 teaspoon minced
fresh oregano sautéed in 1 to 2
tablespoons butter and seasoned
to taste with salt and white
pepper.
• Mixture of 1/4 cup mayonnaise, dry mustard to taste and
thinly sliced Bermuda onions.

• Mixture of 1/3 cup plain
yoghurt, 2 teaspoons minced
green onion, 1/4 teaspoon finely
minced garlic and minced fresh
mint, salt and white pepper to
taste.
• Hollandaise or Béarnaise Sauce

CHILI CON CARNE

Prepare and cook for 1 hour:
1 recipe Chili Sauce
Then add:
**1/2 pound sautéed lean ground
beef**
**1/2 cup soaked kidney beans
and their soaking water**
Cover and cook over low heat
1 hour or until beans are tender,
adding beef stock, tomato juice
or water if mixture becomes too
thick. The last 10 minutes of
cooking add:
**1/4 cup chopped green bell
pepper (optional)**
Adjust seasonings and serve with
rice and a green salad.

STEAMED STUFFED PEPPER BOATS

Combine and set aside:
1/2 pound lean ground beef
1 green onion and top, minced
1/2 teaspoon minced fresh ginger root
1/4 teaspoon minced garlic
1/2 tablespoon water
1 tablespoon cornstarch
1 teaspoon each Tamari soy sauce and sake or dry sherry
1/4 teaspoon salt
Cut into quarters lengthwise and then in half again crosswise to make boat-shape sections:
1 large green bell pepper
Remove seeds and fill each piece with beef mixture, pressing well to hold. Place in shallow ceramic serving dish and steam as directed on page 175 for 20 minutes. Just before serving sprinkle with:
1/2 teaspoon Oriental sesame oil (optional)

Variation: Substitute ground pork for beef and increase cooking time to 30 minutes.

BAKED OXTAILS

Sprinkle with:
salt, pepper, sweet Hungarian paprika and unbleached white flour
2 pounds oxtails
Brown on all sides, a few at a time so pieces don't touch in:
2 tablespoons garlic olive oil, or as needed
Remove and set aside. Adding more oil if needed, brown:
1/2 carrot, diced
small celery stalk and tender leaves, finely chopped
1/2 onion, chopped
2 tablespoons minced fresh parsley
1-1/2 teaspoons minced fresh oregano or marjoram

Return oxtails to skillet and deglaze pan over high heat with:
1/2 cup red wine or Marsala
Let reduce by half and add:
1 cup beef stock
Cover and cook over medium-low heat, adding more stock and/or wine if needed, 2 hours or until oxtails are tender. Remove oxtails and set aside. Strain juices and thicken with binder of:
2 tablespoons red wine or Marsala
2 teaspoons cornstarch
Adjust seasonings and set aside. Spread oxtails evenly on all sides with:
Dijon-style or champagne mustard
Place on rack in baking pan and sprinkle with:
buttered bread crumbs
Bake in 375° oven 15 minutes or until nicely browned. Reheat sauce and serve with oxtails.

Meat

HASH

Boil until almost tender:
2 to 3 medium-size potatoes
Cool, peel and cut into 1/2-inch dice; set aside. Sauté until onion is transparent in:
1 tablespoon butter
1/4 cup minced onion
1 tablespoon minced celery
2 teaspoons minced green bell pepper (optional)
1/2 teaspoon minced garlic (optional)
Add and stir gently:
reserved potatoes
1-1/2 cups diced leftover cooked meat or poultry
1/4 cup any rich stock
salt and pepper to taste
Cook, adding more stock if needed, until heated through. If desired, continue cooking until bottom is browned. Turn hash over and make two hollows in surface. Break into each hollow:
1 egg
Cover and cook until egg is set. Garnish with:
sprinkling of minced fresh parsley
Serve with Chili Sauce.

CALVES' TONGUE

In saucepan place:
2 calves' tongues, approximately 6 to 7 ounces each, soaked 20 minutes in ice water and drained
1 cup each water and dry white wine, or to cover
1 small onion, chopped
1 small carrot, chopped
1 small celery stalk and leaves, chopped
2 garlic cloves, bruised
4 parsley sprigs
2 oregano sprigs
1 thyme sprig
1 bay leaf
6 peppercorns, lightly crushed
1 teaspoon salt
Bring to boil, cover, lower heat and simmer 1 hour or until tongues are tender. Remove cover and let cool. Then cover and refrigerate overnight. Reheat just until stock is liquid, remove tongues and set aside. Strain cooking liquid and cool and refrigerate. Trim fat and membrane from tongues and slice thinly. Serve as a sandwich meat, or in vinaigrette. Tongue does not keep more than 3 days refrigerated. Freeze up to 2 weeks.

CREAMED CALVES' TONGUE

Prepare, using reserved cooking liquid in place of stock:
1-1/2 cups Béchamel Sauce
Season to taste with:
salt, white pepper and freshly grated nutmeg
Cut tongue into julienne to make 2 cups. Add to sauce and heat. Adjust seasonings and serve with brown rice or other grain and a green vegetable.

Variation: Add to sauce and tongue 1 to 2 hearts of palm, sliced, and heat gently.

CALVES' TONGUE IN TOMATO SAUCE

Bring to gentle boil:
1-1/2 cups Tomato Sauce
2 tablespoons minced fresh Italian parsley
Add and cook until almost tender:
3/4 cup fresh green peas
Stir in and reheat:
2 cups julienne-cut cooked calves' tongue
Just before serving, blend in:
2 to 3 tablespoons red wine vinegar

QUICK-FRY LIVER

Sauté until beginning to soften
in:
2 tablespoons butter
1-1/2 cups sliced onions
Add:
**8 to 10 ounces calves' or baby
    beef liver, sliced into 5/8-inch
    wide strips**
Sauté together over moderately
high heat 3 to 4 minutes or until
liver is browned on all sides.
Serve with Rice Pilaf and a
green salad.

SAUTÉED CALVES'
LIVER AND ONIONS

Combine:
1/4 cup sake or dry sherry
**1 to 2 tablespoons Tamari soy
    sauce**
2 garlic cloves, bruised
2 to 3 thin slices ginger root
Add and turn to coat evenly:
**2 slices calves' or baby beef liver
    (approximately 4 to 5 ounces
    each)**
1 large onion, thinly sliced
Let stand several hours. (If
marinating in the morning,
cover and refrigerate.) Remove

liver slices, pat dry and set aside.
Strain marinade and discard garlic and ginger. Set marinade aside
and sauté onions, covered, over
medium heat until softened and
slightly browned in:
**1 tablespoon each corn oil and
    butter**
Sprinkle liver slices lightly with:
flour
Push onions aside, raise heat
slightly and, adding more oil
and/or butter if needed, sauté
liver until browned on both sides,
turning only once. Liver should
be pink inside; if overcooked it
will toughen and lose flavor.
Raise heat and stir in:
**1 to 2 tablespoons reserved
    marinade**
Serve immediately with:
**sprinkling of minced fresh herbs
    such as parsley, chives, sage,
    marjoram**

BROILED CALVES'
OR BEEF LIVER

Brush lightly with:
melted butter
**2 4- to 5-ounce slices calves' or
    baby beef liver**
Broil 6 inches away from broiler
2 to 3 minutes per side. Serve
with:
Lemon-Garlic Butter Sauce

SAUTÉED LIVER IN
APPLE-SOUR CREAM SAUCE

Stirring constantly, sauté over
high heat 1 minute in:
2 tablespoons butter
2 onions, sliced in rings
1/2 apple, sliced into thin wedges
Lower heat, cover and let steam
3 minutes until apples are
browned and onions transparent.
Remove from pan and set aside.
Stirring constantly, sauté 5 to 7
minutes, adding more butter if
needed:
**1/2 pound baby beef liver, cut in-
    to 5/8-inch wide strips**
Remove from heat and stir in:
reserved onion and apples
**salt and ground cinnamon to
    taste**
3/4 cup sour cream
Reheat 2 to 3 minutes; do not
boil. Just before serving, stir in:
**2 to 3 tablespoons chopped fresh
    parsley**
Serve with buttered rice and
a green salad.

Meat

SWEETBREADS

Soak in ice water to cover several hours or overnight:
1 pound veal sweetbreads
Place in saucepan with:
1 cup dry white wine
2 tablespoons fresh lemon juice
1/2 teaspoon salt
1 small carrot, cut up
1 small celery stalk and leaves, cut up
1 small onion, chopped
3 parsley sprigs
1 thyme sprig
1 small bay leaf, crumbled
8 peppercorns, lightly crushed
water to cover
Bring to boil, cover, lower heat and simmer 10 to 15 minutes depending upon size of sweetbreads. Cool, cover and refrigerate overnight in cooking liquid. Remove skin, fat and membrane and break sweetbreads into 1-1/2-inch pieces. Reheat liquid, strain and reserve.

Suggestions for Using Cooked Sweetbreads:

• Skewer and broil over hot coals, basting with a mixture of melted butter and dry sherry.
• Combine with leftover cooked chicken and ham in a Béchamel Sauce. Adjust seasonings with salt, white pepper, powdered thyme and minced fresh parsley. Serve on toast or as a pot pie.
• Sauté in butter with sliced fresh mushrooms, chopped onion, minced garlic and minced fresh oregano. Serve with salt and white pepper.

BREADED SWEETBREADS

Beat together:
1 egg, beaten
2 teaspoons fresh lemon juice
Select 12 to 14 uniform-size pieces of cooked sweetbreads and dip in:
egg mixture
Coat evenly with:
3/4 cup Seasoned Bread Crumbs
Refrigerate at least 1 hour to keep coating intact while browning. Brown sweetbread pieces, without touching, on all sides in:
2 teaspoons each butter and/or garlic olive oil, or as needed
Transfer to 2 ramekins and set aside.
Adding butter to make about 1 tablespoon, sprinkle skillet with:
1 tablespoon unbleached white flour
Cook and stir 3 minutes and gradually add:
1/2 cup each half-and-half and reserved sweetbread cooking liquid
Cook and stir until thickened; keep hot over very low heat, stirring occasionally. In separate skillet sauté until golden in:
1 tablespoon butter and/or garlic olive oil
2/3 cup sliced fresh mushrooms, sprinkled with
1/2 teaspoon finely minced oregano
1/8 teaspoon white pepper
Season to taste with salt and add to warm sauce. Pour over sweetbreads and bake in 350° oven 10 minutes or until bubbly and heated through. Sprinkle with:
minced fresh parsley or chives

Meat

VEAL STRIPS WITH MUSHROOMS

Cut into small strips:
1/2 pound thinly sliced veal from leg
Dredge lightly with:
unbleached white flour
Brown in:
1 tablespoon each butter and olive oil
meat strips
1 small onion, cut in slivers
Remove meat and onion with slotted spoon and sprinkle into pan:
1-1/2 teaspoons unbleached white flour
Blend in:
1/4 cup dry white wine or chicken or veal stock
Return meat and onions to skillet and add:
1 cup sliced fresh mushrooms
Stir and cook 2 minutes and blend in:
1/3 cup half-and-half
Reheat without boiling and sprinkle with:
minced fresh parsley
Serve with buttered noodles or Spaetzle and artichokes.

Variations:
• Substitute pork from loin or steak for the veal; use pork stock.
• Substitute calves' liver for the veal.
• Omit mushrooms. When adding flour to skillet, add 1 teaspoon curry powder or to taste. Serve with rice and garnish with fresh fruit.

VEAL CHOPS WITH CHEESE TOPPING

Marinate 1/2 hour in:
1 tablespoon fresh lemon juice
2 large or 4 small veal chops
Pat dry and sprinkle lightly with:
salt, white pepper and sweet Hungarian paprika
Brown slowly on both sides in:
2 tablespoons butter, or
1 tablespoon each butter and garlic olive oil
Cover and cook over medium-low heat 20 minutes, adding:
1/4 cup veal or chicken stock or dry white wine
Top each chop with:
slice of Fontina, Jarlsburg or similar cheese
Cover and cook until cheese melts. Transfer to heated serving plates and pour pan juices over. Serve with Orzo in Browned Butter and vegetable or green salad.

VEAL KIDNEY CHOPS

Dust lightly with:
salt and pepper
unbleached white flour
2 large or 4 small veal kidney chops
Brown over medium-low heat on both sides in:
2 tablespoons butter, or as needed
Raise heat and add:
3 tablespoons Madeira
2 tablespoons brandy
Bring to boil, lower heat, cover and cook 15 to 20 minutes until almost tender. Remove chops from pan and add to juices:
1/3 cup half-and-half
1/4 to 1/2 teaspoon Dijon-style mustard
2/3 cup sliced fresh mushrooms, sautéed in
1 tablespoon butter
Return chops, cover and simmer, turning chops several times, 10 minutes. Adjust sauce seasonings and transfer to heated platter. Sprinkle with:
1/4 cup minced fresh parsley

VEAL SCALLOPS WITH LEMON

Marinate 1 hour in:
1 to 2 teaspoons fresh lemon juice
8 to 10 veal scallops (10 to 12 ounces), pounded gently until very thin
Pat dry and dredge lightly with:
unbleached white flour
Sauté quickly to lightly brown on both sides in:
1-1/2 tablespoons butter
Transfer to heated platter and keep warm. Deglaze skillet with:
2 cubes frozen beef stock concentrate, thawed
Reduce by half and add:
1 tablespoon capers
2 to 3 teaspoons fresh lemon juice
1/2 teaspoon freshly grated lemon peel
Return veal to sauce, cover and cook 2 to 4 minutes until just tender. Serve immediately with lemon wedges and steamed asparagus.

VEAL SCALLOPS WITH MUSHROOMS

Sauté until mushrooms are golden in:
1 tablespoon butter
1-1/2 cups sliced fresh mushrooms, sprinkled with minced fresh oregano and white pepper to taste
1/2 teaspoon finely minced garlic
Sprinkle with:
salt to taste
Transfer to heated serving platter and keep warm. In same skillet, adding butter as needed, sauté quickly to brown both sides:
8 to 10 veal scallops (10 to 12 ounces), pounded gently until very thin and lightly dredged with unbleached white flour
Add and bring to boil:
1/4 cup Marsala or Madeira wine
1 cube frozen beef stock concentrate, thawed

Cook 2 to 4 minutes until veal is tender. Place veal on mushrooms and reduce pan juices slightly. Season with:
salt and white pepper to taste
Pour juices over veal and mushrooms and garnish with crab legs heated in a little butter. Sprinkle with:
minced parsley

VEAL SCALLOPS WITH CHEESE AND PROSCIUTTO

Sauté veal scallops as above and remove from juices. Pour half the juices in shallow baking dish. Arrange veal scallops in dish and place on top of each scallop to cover:
1 strip prosciutto or thin slice cooked ham
1 thin slice Gruyère or Emmenthaler cheese
Bake in 400° oven 5 minutes or until cheese is melted. Pour remaining juices over and garnish with avocado rings or slices.

Meat

OSSO BUCO

Have butcher saw into 3-inch crosswise pieces:
2 medium veal shanks (about 1-1/2 pounds each)
Wipe with damp paper toweling and marinate 1 hour in:
2 tablespoons fresh lemon juice
Pat dry and roll in:
unbleached white flour
Without allowing pieces to touch, brown well on all sides in:
2 tablespoons butter, or as needed
Lower heat slightly and pour over:
2/3 cup dry white wine
Cook, turning pieces occasionally, 10 minutes or until wine has almost evaporated. Add:
2 to 3 ripe tomatoes, peeled and cut up
1/4 teaspoon salt
1/8 teaspoon pepper
Cover and cook over low heat, adding veal or beef stock if needed, 1-1/2 hours or until meat is very tender and starts to fall off bones. Cooking time will depend upon quality of the veal. (At this point meat may be cooled and refrigerated to be reheated later.) Transfer meat to heated serving platter and keep warm. Stir into juices in pan, mixture of:
3 tablespoons minced fresh parsley
1 teaspoon fresh lemon juice
1/2 teaspoon freshly grated lemon peel
1 teaspoon anchovy paste
Cook and stir 2 minutes, adjust seasonings and pour over meat. Serve with Risotto and a green salad.

WIENER SCHNITZEL

Trim fat from:
2 veal round steaks, or
2 veal chops, boned
Pound with meat pounder or edge of heavy plate until very thin, being careful not to cut or tear meat.
Beat together:
1 egg, beaten
1 tablespoon water or fresh lemon juice
Dip slices in egg mixture and then in mixture of:
1/2 cup Seasoned Bread Crumbs or toasted wheat germ
1 tablespoon rice flour or sifted soy flour
1/2 teaspoon salt
1/4 teaspoon pepper
2 tablespoons grated Parmesan cheese
If time allows, refrigerate 1 hour to help keep coating intact when cooking.
Sauté slices until lightly browned on both sides, 7 to 10 minutes in all, in:
1 tablespoon corn oil or butter, or as needed
Garnish with:
lemon wedges
Serve with Hot Potato Salad.

Variation: Substitute chicken breasts, pork cutlets or chops or venison steaks, cutlets or chops for the veal.

STEAMED BEAN CURD WITH PORK AND SHRIMP

Place in shallow ceramic serving dish:

2 firm, fresh bean-curd cakes, cut in 1-inch squares

Combine and strew over bean curd:

1/4 pound each ground lean pork and minced raw shrimp

2 tablespoons minced green onion and tops

2 teaspoons cornstarch

1 teaspoon each Tamari soy sauce and sake or dry sherry

3 dried forest mushrooms, soaked to soften and minced

2 tablespoons minced bamboo shoots (optional)

Drizzle over all:

1 teaspoon each peanut oil and Tamari soy sauce

4 to 6 drops Oriental sesame oil (optional)

Steam as directed on page 175 25 minutes.

Serve with steamed white rice and stir-fried vegetable.

STEAMED PORK

Combine:

1/2 pound ground lean pork, or

1/4 pound each ground pork and finely minced ham

2 teaspoons cornstarch

1 teaspoon each Tamari soy sauce and sake or dry sherry

1/4 cup chopped water chestnuts (optional)

1/4 cup finely chopped green onions and tops

1/4 teaspoon salt

Pat mixture firmly into shallow ceramic serving dish, building up sides slightly. Arrange on top:

3 to 4 dried forest mushrooms, softened and sliced

Drizzle with:

1 teaspoon peanut oil

4 to 6 drops Oriental sesame oil (optional)

Steam 30 minutes as directed on page 175.

Serve with steamed white rice and stir-fried vegetables.

Note: The meat mixture may be prepared ahead and refrigerated until ready to steam.

Variation: Substitute for half the pork 1/2 pound minced raw shrimp.

PORK CHOP PILAF

In small Dutch oven or flame-proof casserole with tight-fitting lid, brown on both sides 10 to 15 minutes in:

1 tablespoon butter or rendered pork fat

2 3/4-inch thick pork chops, trimmed of most of fat and sprinkled with salt and pepper

Remove chops and sauté 4 minutes, adding butter as needed:

3/4 cup chopped onion

1/4 cup chopped celery

Add and sauté 5 minutes:

1/2 cup brown rice

Blend in:

1 to 1-1/4 cups chopped un-peeled pears (1 to 2 pears)

2 tablespoons raisins, plumped

1/4 teaspoon freshly ground cardamom

1 cup heated pork or chicken stock

Place pork chops on top of rice mixture. Bring to boil, cover, lower heat and cook 1 hour until rice is tender and moisture is absorbed. Do not stir while rice is cooking. Pilaf may also be baked in 350° oven 1 hour.

Meat

BAKED PORK CHOPS IN MUSHROOM BURGUNDY SAUCE

Sprinkle lightly on both sides with:
salt and pepper
2 6-ounce pork chops, trimmed of most of fat
Sauté until gently browned on both sides in:
1 tablespoon butter or rendered pork fat
Remove chops from skillet and place in shallow buttered baking dish. In same skillet, sauté, stirring, 1 to 2 minutes:
1 onion, minced
1 cup sliced fresh mushrooms
Sprinkle with:
1/4 teaspoon salt
1/8 teaspoon pepper
1 teaspoon unbleached white flour
Blend in and cook and stir until thickened:
3/4 cup burgundy

Add to sauce:
1 bay leaf
1-1/2 teaspoons minced fresh thyme
2 teaspoons minced celery
Pour sauce over chops, cover and bake in 350° oven 1 hour or simmer gently on medium heat 45 minutes or until tender. Remove chops and keep warm. Blend into sauce mixture of:
1 egg yolk, beaten
2 tablespoons sour cream
1/4 cup milk or half-and-half
Cook and stir without boiling until thickened. Adjust seasonings and pour over pork chops. Serve with Potato Pancakes and applesauce.

BAKED PORK SPARERIBS

Rub well with:
2 tablespoons hoisin sauce*
1-1/2 to 2 pounds pork spareribs
Place ribs on rack in baking pan and spread on top mixture of:
1 ripe tomato, peeled and chopped
3 tablespoons grated onion
Let stand 1 to 2 hours. Pour over ribs:
1/4 cup sake or dry sherry
Bake on rack in 325° oven with 1/2 inch of water in bottom of pan 1-1/2 hours until browned and tender, basting occasionally. Serve with baked yams and stir-fry green vegetable.

*Hoisin sauce is available in cans in Oriental markets. It keeps indefinitely if transferred to jar with lid and refrigerated. If not available, substitute mixture of 2 tablespoons Tomato Catsup, 1 teaspoon cider vinegar and 2 drops of mild honey.

CAULIFLOWER, HAM AND CHEESE SKILLET BAKE

Steam 5 to 7 minutes:
2 cups cauliflowerets
Place cauliflowerets in one layer in a skillet coated lightly with:
safflower or corn oil
Sprinkle with:
salt and white pepper
freshly grated nutmeg
1/4 cup grated Gruyère or Emmenthaler cheese
Cover with:
2 ripe tomatoes, thinly sliced
Top with:
2 to 3 slices cooked ham (approximately 3 ounces)
1/4 cup grated Gruyère or Emmenthaler cheese
Sprinkle again with:
salt and white pepper
freshly grated nutmeg
Dot with:
1 tablespoon butter, cut in bits

Cover skillet and cook over low heat 5 minutes. Remove from heat and let stand, covered, 10 minutes. Just before serving sprinkle with:
2 to 3 tablespoons toasted wheat germ
minced fresh parsley

Note: May be baked in a casserole. Bake in 325° oven 10 minutes or until cheese melts and turns golden.

HAM AND POTATO SCALLOP

Sauté until lightly browned in:
1 tablespoon butter
1/4 cup minced onion
1 cup shredded cooked ham
Set aside.

Layer in buttered casserole and sprinkle lightly with:
salt and pepper
3/4 to 1 pound unpeeled red or white potatoes, sliced 1/8 inch thick
1/2 cup sliced fresh mushrooms
Top with:
3/4 cup finely grated Gruyère or Emmenthaler cheese
browned onion and ham mixture
Combine, scald and pour over:
1/2 to 2/3 cup milk or half-and-half
1/4 teaspoon salt
1/8 teaspoon mustard seed or dry mustard
Sprinkle over top:
1/4 teaspoon crumbled dried marjoram
Dot with:
1 tablespoon butter
Bake in 375° oven 30 to 40 minutes or until potatoes are tender.
Sprinkle with:
1 to 2 tablespoons chopped fresh parsley

Meat

FRENCH LAMB RAGOUT
(Two Meals from One Recipe)

Marinate in refrigerator overnight in:
1-1/2 cups red wine
2 pounds lean lamb, cut into
   1-1/2-inch cubes
1 onion, chopped
2 garlic cloves, minced
10 to 12 peppercorns, lightly
   crushed
1 teaspoon salt
1 teaspoon minced fresh thyme
1/8 to 1/4 teaspoon minced fresh
   rosemary
Remove lamb cubes with tongs,
reserving marinade. Pat cubes dry
and brown cubes on all sides,
without allowing pieces to touch,
in:
1 tablespoon each butter and
   corn or peanut oil
1 1-inch cube salt pork
Transfer lamb and salt pork to
a 3- to 4-quart baking dish with
lid. Pour over:
unstrained seasoned marinade

Slice into 2-inch pieces and add
to lamb:
2 carrots
1 parsnip
1 small celery stalk
1 white of leek and some green
Cover dish and cook in a 350°
oven 2-1/2 hours, stirring gently
several times. Last 45 minutes of
cooking add:
2 4-ounce zucchini, sliced
1/4 eggplant, chopped
1/2 cup chopped celeriac
As sauce is thin, transfer ragout
and sauce to deep bowls and
sprinkle with:
chopped fresh parsley
Serve with French bread and
escarole salad.

Note: If thicker sauce is desired,
dust meat with unbleached white
flour before browning.

CURRIED LAMB SPARERIBS

Bake on rack in roasting pan,
turning once, in 400° oven for
40 minutes:
1-1/2 to 2 pounds meaty lamb
   ribs, lightly sprinkled with salt
   and cut into serving pieces
Remove ribs and set aside.
Deglaze baking pan with:
1/2 cup water
Skim off any fat and reserve pan
juices. In large saucepan sauté in:
1-1/2 teaspoons each garlic
   olive oil and butter
1/2 cup chopped onion
Add and cook and stir 2 minutes:
1 tablespoon Aromatic Curry
   Mixture
Blend in mixture of:
reserved pan juices
3/4 cup plain yoghurt
1/2 teaspoon salt
Place ribs in saucepan, turn to
coat with sauce, bring to gentle
boil, lower heat, cover and let
simmer 1 hour or until lamb is
tender, adding more water to
sauce as needed. Serve with
brown rice and Sautéed
Shredded Zucchini.

LAMB AND VEAL MEATBALLS

Combine:
1/2 pound each lean ground
    lamb and veal
1/4 cup each chopped tomato
    and minced cooked Swiss
    chard or spinach
1 teaspoon fresh lemon juice
1 egg, beaten
1 tablespoon each grated onion
    and carrot
1 teaspoon finely minced fresh
    oregano
1-1/2 tablespoons grated Parme-
    san or Romano cheese
1/2 teaspoon minced garlic
2 tablespoons minced fresh parsley
2 tablespoons wheat germ or fine
    bread crumbs
1/2 teaspoon salt
1/4 teaspoon white pepper

Chill and form into 40 meatballs,
about 1 inch in diameter. Sauté
slowly on all sides until browned
and cooked through, adding butter if needed. Remove to plate.

Cool half the meatballs, wrap and
freeze. Make gravy from pan
juices, return rest of meatballs to
gravy and reheat. Adjust seasonings and sprinkle with:
minced fresh parsley

Note: For a main meal soup, defrost meatballs and reheat in
lamb, veal or chicken stock with
leftover pasta, rice or vegetables.
Or reheat in enough stock to
moisten and use as filling for
Arab bread, tortillas or rolls.

Variation: For meatloaf, shape
full recipe into loaf shape and
bake in 350° oven 45 to 50
minutes.

LAMB SHANKS

Dredge with:
unbleached white flour
2 large lamb shanks, cracked
Brown on all sides under broiler
and set aside.
Sauté until onion is transparent
in:
2 to 3 tablespoons butter
1 onion, sliced
1 garlic clove, minced
Blend in and stir 1 to 2 minutes:
**1/2 teaspoon each salt, ground
    cumin and sweet Hungarian
    paprika**
**1/4 teaspoon each raw natural
    sugar and pepper**
1/8 teaspoon cayenne pepper
Stir in:
1 cup red wine
**1 cube frozen lamb stock con-
    centrate**
1 cup tomato purée, or
**1-1/2 cups peeled and chopped
    ripe tomatoes**
1 large sprig oregano
Return lamb shanks to pot, cover,
bring to boil, lower heat and simmer, adding more wine if needed,
1-1/4 hours or until shanks are
very tender. Transfer to heated
serving platter and sprinkle with:
1/3 cup minced fresh parsley

Meat

ROAST LEG OF LAMB

Have butcher cut 2 to 4 1-inch thick steaks from:
1 6- to 7-pound leg of lamb
Freeze steaks for broiling or pan-frying.
Make 6 to 8 shallow slits in surface of roast and insert in each:
a sliver of garlic
Place roast in ceramic or glass pan and sprinkle with:
salt and pepper
ground cumin and chili powder
1/4 cup chopped onion
Pour over:
1/3 cup Marsala
2 tablespoons olive oil
Marinate at room temperature, turning often, 4 hours or longer.

Remove roast to rack in roasting pan. Pour marinade over and roast in 300° oven, basting occasionally, about 1 hour, adding if needed:
Marsala, lamb stock or water
Remove from oven and coat lamb with mixture of:
2 tablespoons each wheat germ and fine bread crumbs
2 tablespoons mixed minced fresh herbs such as parsley, marjoram, oregano and/or thyme
2 tablespoons olive oil, or as needed to make spreading consistency
Return lamb to oven and continue roasting 1/2 hour. Transfer to heated serving platter and let rest 10 minutes before carving. If making gravy, strain liquid.

Note: Use any leftover lamb for lamb curry, to add to barley soup, or reheat in gravy or pan juices.

LAMB MEATLOAF

Combine and chill:
3/4 pound lean ground lamb
1 egg, beaten
2 tablespoons minced onion
1 tablespoon minced green bell pepper
1 teaspoon minced garlic (optional)
1/4 cup corn kernels from cooked corn on the cob (optional)
1/3 cup diced, peeled ripe tomatoes
1 teaspoon minced fresh oregano
3 tablespoons fine bread crumbs or toasted wheat germ
1/2 teaspoon salt
1/4 teaspoon pepper

Combine:
1/4 cup finely diced Monterey Jack cheese
2 tablespoons toasted sesame seeds (optional)
Pat meat mixture into a rectangle. Place cheese and sesame seeds down center and form into meat loaf shape. Place on baking pan and bake in 300° oven 30 minutes. Raise heat to 350° and surround loaf with:
2 5- to 6-ounce thinly sliced unpeeled red potatoes
Spread potatoes with:
softened butter
Sprinkle potatoes with:
salt and pepper
Bake 30 minutes until meat is done and potatoes are crisp. Serve with Baked Shredded Zucchini.

FONDUE BOURGUIGNONNE

This is a meal that can be cooked at the table in a fondue pot or electric skillet. Fondue forks or chopsticks are used to hold the ingredients in the hot liquid until cooked to taste. Allow 3/4 to 1 pound cubed beef or lamb from a tender cut and arrange on platter. Let stand at room temperature 1/2 hour before cooking. Rub fondue pot or skillet with a cut clove of garlic and heat 1 cup peanut oil and 1/4 pound butter, or 1-1/2 to 2 cups chicken, beef or lamb stock to 375°. Place an assortment of dips and condiments in small bowls and serve with French bread and a salad. If using stock as cooking liquid, include vegetables such as snow peas, cauliflowerets, shredded greens.

Dips: Hollandaise or Béarnaise Sauce, Aioli Sauce, Chili Sauce, Herb Butter or Lemon-Garlic Sauce, Tomato Sauce, Browned Butter.

Condiments: Minced parsley, chilies, garlic and onions, mustard, paprika, capers.

VENISON STEAKS AND CAKES

A favorite Midwest meal during hunting season.

Combine:
1/4 cup unbleached white flour
1 teaspoon salt
1/4 teaspoon pepper
1/4 teaspoon powdered sage
Dip into flour mixture to coat evenly:
2 venison tenderloin steaks (4 to 5 ounces each)
Heat in heavy skillet:
2 tablespoons each corn oil and butter
Brown steaks 7 to 10 minutes per side over moderate heat. Serve with hot griddle cakes topped with real maple syrup and applesauce or cranberry sauce.

Meat

STIR-FRY MEALS

The stir-fry method of cooking is ideal for 1 or 2 persons. Quick, easy, light and nutritional, meats and/or vegetables may be prepared for cooking ahead of time and refrigerated until ready to use.

For 2 servings allow:
1/2 pound meat, seafood or fowl
Toss with:
2 teaspoons Tamari soy sauce
2 teaspoons sake or dry sherry
1/8 teaspoon raw natural sugar
   (optional)
1/8 teaspoon salt
Set aside. Prepare:
1-1/2 cups julienne-cut or sliced
   vegetables, torn greens and/or
   bean sprouts in any
   combination
Heat a wok or heavy skillet until very hot. Add:
1 to 2 tablespoons peanut oil

Lower heat slightly and heat until oil sizzles.
Add and stir-fry 1 minute:
2 thin slices ginger root
2 small garlic cloves, bruised
1/4 to 1/2 teaspoon seeded and
   crushed dried red chili pepper
   (optional)
Add meat, seafood or fowl mixture and cook, stirring constantly, until just tender. Remove from wok or skillet with slotted spatula and set aside. Adding more oil if needed, toss in vegetables and cook and stir 1 to 3 minutes (depending upon vegetable) to coat well with oil. Add 2 to 3 tablespoons water (leafy vegetables need only the water clinging to leaves after washing), cover and bring to steam. Cook 2 to 5 minutes or until vegetables are just tender crisp. Return meat, seafood or fowl to skillet and add:
1/4 teaspoon Oriental sesame oil

Reheat quickly. If desired, thicken with binder of:
3 to 4 tablespoons water or
   chicken or other complementary stock
2 teaspoons cornstarch
Serve with steamed white rice.

Variations:
• Before adding meat, sauté 6 to 8 whole blanched almonds with the garlic and ginger until slightly browned.
• Substitute 1/4 cup whole blanched almonds and 3 to 4 dried forest mushrooms, softened and cut in julienne, for meat, seafood or fowl. Increase vegetables to 2-1/2 cups.
• Add with vegetables, sliced water chestnuts and/or bamboo shoots.
• Just before serving, add and stir gently into mixture 1 firm fresh bean-curd cake, cut into cubes.

Meat and Seafood Suggestions:
• skirt or flank steak or lamb from leg, sliced very thinly across grain
• veal, fowl, pork, lamb or ham cut in julienne
• whole shrimp, abalone strips, crab meat, lobster meat
• firm fish fillets, cut into cubes

Vegetable Suggestions: See Stir-Frying method in Vegetable chapter.

STIR-FRY BEEF AND TOMATO

Toss together and set aside:
1/2 pound skirt or flank steak, sliced very thinly on diagonal across grain
2 teaspoons Tamari soy sauce
2 teaspoons sake or dry sherry
1/8 teaspoon raw natural sugar
1/8 teaspoon salt

In heated wok or heavy skillet heat until oil sizzles:
1 tablespoon peanut oil
Add and stir-fry 1 minute:
2 thin slices ginger root
2 small garlic cloves, bruised
1/4 to 1/2 teaspoon seeded and crushed dried red chili pepper
Add and stir-fry 2 to 3 minutes:
reserved flank steak mixture
Remove meat. Adding oil if needed, stir-fry 2 to 3 minutes:
1 small onion, cut in eighths and separated
1/2 green bell pepper or mild green chili pepper, cut in small chunks
Add:
2 ripe tomatoes, cut in eighths
Cover, bring to steam and return meat to wok or skillet.
Stir in:
1/4 teaspoon Oriental sesame oil
Reheat and serve immediately over steamed white rice.

MONGOLIAN BEEF OR OR LAMB

Coat well with mixture of:
2 teaspoons hoisin sauce (page 132)
1/4 teaspoon chili oil
3/4 pound beef or lamb, cut in 1-inch cubes*
Set aside. In heated wok or heavy skillet heat until oil sizzles:
1 tablespoon peanut oil
Add and stir-fry 1 minute:
2 thin slices ginger root
2 small garlic cloves, bruised
Add and stir-fry 1 to 2 minutes:
reserved meat mixture
Add:
1 cup cubed bamboo shoots
Continue stir-frying until meat is well browned and tender. Adjust seasoning with more chili oil and salt. Serve over steamed white rice.

*Use tender cut of meat such as top sirloin or leg of lamb.

Meat

SHISH KEBABS

Shish kebabs are a quick and easy meal. Most types of meat, poultry or seafood can be used with or without vegetables such as mushrooms, water chestnuts, cherry tomatoes, green or red peppers, onions and new potatoes. The fast-cooking meats may be skewered and broiled separately from the vegetables. If combining on the skewer, it will be necessary to parboil potatoes, onion sections and green or red bell pepper sections before skewering. Vegetables such as eggplant or zucchini and mushrooms may also be skewered but do not marinate; brush with a mixture of olive oil, fresh lemon juice and oregano while barbecuing or broiling.

Allow 3/4 to 1 pound meat, poultry or seafood for 2 persons.

Cut into 3/4-inch cubes (leave foods such as shrimp and lamb kidneys whole) and marinate several hours in any of the following marinades. While cooking, baste with marinade, strained if desired.

Lamb: Combine 2 tablespoons each fresh lemon juice and olive oil, 1 garlic clove, finely minced, 2 to 3 tablespoons minced fresh mint.

Poultry: Combine 2 tablespoons Tamari soy sauce, 1 tablespoon sake or dry sherry, 1 tablespoon chopped green onions, 1/4 teaspoon each finely minced garlic and ginger root and mild honey to taste.

Beef: Combine 3 tablespoons olive oil, 1 tablespoon red wine vinegar, 1/4 teaspoon salt, 1/8 teaspoon each pepper and paprika, 2 slices onion, 1 small garlic clove, sliced, 1 thyme sprig and 4 mint sprigs.

Pork: Combine 3 tablespoons Tamari soy sauce, 1-1/2 tablespoons sake or dry sherry, 1/2 teaspoon mild honey, 1/4 teaspoon each finely minced garlic and ginger root, 1/8 teaspoon Oriental sesame oil, and 1 to 2 tablespoons toasted sesame seeds.

Fish: Combine 2 tablespoons each olive oil and fresh lemon juice or white wine, 1 small garlic clove, bruised, 1/4 teaspoon minced fresh rosemary or thyme, dash salt and white pepper. Marinate only 15 minutes.

Breads

Breads

YEAST BREADS

Yeast is available in 3 forms: pre-packaged active dry yeast granules, compressed yeast cakes and natural active dry yeast granules sold in bulk. Packaged active dry yeast contains preservatives. Each package is dated and should last several months if stored in a cool place, longer if refrigerated. Both compressed yeast cakes and natural active dry yeast granules are perishable and should be refrigerated, the compressed yeast wrapped tightly to prevent it from drying out and the granular yeast in a small jar with a tight-fitting lid. Compressed yeast will keep up to 2 weeks refrigerated and up to 3 months frozen.

(Once defrosted, however, it should not be refrozen.) Natural active dry yeast keeps up to 2 months in the refrigerator. In the following yeast bread recipes amounts have been given in tablespoons of granular active dry yeast. One tablespoon natural active dry yeast equals one .6-ounce cake of compressed yeast or one package active dry yeast. We recommend using yeast without preservatives.

Liquids usually used alone or in combination when making bread are milk, water or potato water. Fluid milk should be scalded and cooled to lukewarm before use. (When using reconstituted dry milk this step is not necessary.) Milk adds to the nutritive value of the bread and gives it a soft crust and creamy texture, while water gives bread a crispy crust. Both milk and potato water increase the storage life of breads.

The optimal temperature range for growth of the yeast organism is from 105° to 115°. Bread-making liquids should always be within this range when the yeast is crumbled in or stirred in to dissolve. Liquid hotter than 115° will kill the yeast and prevent the bread from rising. Let yeast solution stand several minutes before adding to rest of ingredients. If bubbles begin to form and rise to the surface, the yeast is still alive and bread will rise properly.

Flour Types of flour vary greatly. Not only are there differences in cooking properties among white, wheat, rye and other flours, but each type of flour will differ from place to place due to the variety of grain and the processing method. To add to the confusion, flour and therefore bread making are affected by climate—temperature and humidity. These factors combine to make the capacity of flours to absorb moisture variable; therefore the amount of flour needed in recipes cannot be exactly specified. Follow the instructions below for mixing and kneading, adding only enough flour to make dough non-sticky, smooth and elastic. Too much flour will result in a dry, compact bread. The recipes in this chapter are designed for use with unsifted flour.

Salt stabilizes fermentation. By controlling the action of the yeast, it slows the rising process of the dough. Salt is also a necessary flavoring in breads.

Sweeteners are not necessary for fermentation, but the right amount does activate the yeast during rising. Too much sweetener or salt will inhibit the action of the yeast and the bread will not rise. Sweeteners also add flavor, improve the texture and increase the browning potential of the crust. We recommend using raw unfiltered honey or unsulphured sorghum molasses when making yeast breads.

Butter and oil help the dough expand and stretch. They produce a smooth texture, brown crust and a tender, moist loaf. We recommend using only butter or oils containing no preservatives.

To enrich bread naturally The flavor, texture and nutritional value of breads can be enhanced in many ways. Experiment with one or more of the following combinations, but not in greater quantity than 25% of the weight of the flour in the recipe.

- Replace 1/3 cup of each cup of flour with toasted wheat germ.
- Replace 2 tablespoons of each cup of flour with peanut, soy or garbanzo flour or with sunflower seed meal.
- Substitute 1/2 cup rice or potato flour for each cup of flour.
- Replace 1/3 cup of each cup of flour with steel-cut oatmeal. Add oatmeal and oil to heated liquid and cool to lukewarm before mixing in yeast and flour.
- If using water as bread-making liquid, add 1/2 cup non-instant powdered milk per loaf.
- Dried fruits, nuts and seeds may be substituted for flour but not in quantities greater than 25% of the weight of the flour.
- If adding eggs to a recipe, beat lightly, measure and replace equal volume of bread-making liquid with egg.

Breads

BASIC METHOD FOR MAKING YEAST BREADS

The yeast-bread recipes in this chapter should be made using the following procedure.

To mix and knead Combine ingredients as directed in recipe. Stir in flour until dough becomes thick, begins to leave the sides of bowl and can no longer be stirred. Work in remaining flour with hands. (You may want to flour hands lightly to keep dough from sticking.) Then turn dough out onto floured board and begin kneading. To knead, flatten dough and fold edge of dough farthest away toward you, then push down and away with the heels of your hands. Give dough a quarter turn and repeat. Continue kneading dough until it is smooth and elastic, at least 10 minutes, working in additional flour only as needed to prevent sticking. Doughs with little or no white flour take up to 20 minutes of kneading time.

To let rise Place dough in a large oiled bowl and brush top with oil or turn dough in bowl to oil top. Cover with tea towel and let rise in a warm place, free from drafts, for length of time specified in recipe. Dough should double in size during first rising. Allowed to rise too long, dough will not rise a second time. If imprint remains when finger has been pressed into dough, dough has risen sufficiently.

To shape Divide dough into parts as specified in recipe. To insure a smooth-surfaced loaf, flatten each half into a rectangular shape, approximately 12 by 5 inches. Fold narrow ends in to meet in center; work out seam with base of hand. Then fold in half along worked-out seam; gently work out creases along lengthwise edge and on ends of loaf using downward strokes with the bases of your hands. Repeat this process with each loaf. Place in greased 9 by 5 by 3-inch loaf

pans, or form into shape specified in recipe and place on prepared baking sheet. Cover with a tea towel and let rise again until doubled in size. Over-rising during the second rising will cause your bread to fall when it is baked.

To bake Bake as directed in recipe. When done, bread will pull away from sides of pan and will have a hollow sound when tapped. Top should be well browned.

To cool Place bread on cooling rack for 10 minutes before removing from pan; then turn out on rack and let cool. Wrap bread in tea towel if soft crust is desired. Allow air to circulate around bread for a hard crust.

To store Keep homemade breads fresh by wrapping them airtight and storing them in a cool place. Refrigerate if necessary to prevent molding. When freezing bread, slice before freezing.

BASIC WHOLE-WHEAT BREAD

Scald:
2 cups milk
Remove from heat and stir in to dissolve honey:
1/2 cup honey or molasses
3 tablespoons safflower or corn oil
1 tablespoon salt
Cool to lukewarm. In large mixing bowl, soften in:
1/3 cup lukewarm water
2 tablespoons active dry yeast, or
2 cakes yeast, crumbled
Add and combine well:
milk mixture
Gradually blend in:
1/2 cup wheat germ
5 cups whole-wheat flour
Following instructions in basic method, turn out onto floured board and knead 20 minutes and let rise until doubled. Punch down and form into 2 loaves. Place in 2 buttered loaf pans, let rise 1 hour or until doubled and bake in 350° oven 45 to 50 minutes, or until bread tests done. Cool and store.
Makes 2 loaves

FRENCH BREAD

Dissolve in:
1-1/4 cups lukewarm water
1 tablespoon active dry yeast, or
1 cake yeast, crumbled
Stir in:
1-1/2 teaspoons salt
1 tablespoon each melted butter and mild honey or raw natural sugar
3 cups unbleached white flour
Following instructions in basic method, turn out onto floured board and knead 10 minutes, using up to 1/2 cup additional flour. Dough will be light and tender. Let rise until doubled, punch down and let rise another 30 minutes. Punch down, form into 2 small loaves with tapered ends. Place on oiled baking sheet sprinkled with yellow cornmeal. Brush loaves with:
cornstarch or egg white glaze (following)

Let rise uncovered 1-1/2 hours or until doubled. Brush again with glaze and slash surface of loaves diagonally with razor blade or sharp knife. Bake in 400° oven 30 to 35 minutes. If dry crispy crust is desired, place a shallow baking pan filled with hot water on bottom shelf of oven while baking. Remove bread from oven and brush with any remaining glaze. Cool on wire rack. French bread does not keep well. Freeze one loaf if not needed within 24 to 48 hours. To recrisp, place in wet brown paper bag and heat in 300° oven, wetting bag as needed, until crust is crispy.
Makes 2 small loaves

Cornstarch glaze: Combine 1 teaspoon cornstarch, dissolved in 2 teaspoons cold water, and 1/3 cup boiling water. Cook and stir 3 minutes until thickened. Cool.

Egg white glaze: Combine and beat gently with fork 1 egg white and 2 tablespoons cold water.

Breads

MOIST WHITE BREAD

Boil, covered, until soft in
1-3/4 cups water:
1/4 pound potatoes
Drain, reserving cooking water, and mash or rice potatoes to make 1/2 cup. Set aside. Dissolve in:
1/2 cup lukewarm water
2 tablespoons active dry yeast, or
2 cakes yeast, crumbled
1/2 teaspoon mild honey
Add:
2 teaspoons salt
1-1/2 cups potato cooking
  water cooled to lukewarm
reserved mashed or riced potatoes
Gradually blend in:
5 cups unbleached white flour
Following instructions in basic method, turn dough out onto floured board and knead 10 minutes or until smooth and elastic, adding flour as needed to prevent sticking. Let rise 1 hour or until doubled in bulk. Turn out onto floured board and knead briefly. Shape into 2 long loaves with tapering ends and place on oiled cookie sheets sprinkled with yellow cornmeal. Let rise 45 minutes or until doubled. Make diagonal slashes on surface of loaves, brush with water and bake in 375° oven 30 minutes or until bread tests done. Remove from cookie sheets and cool on rack.
Makes 2 loaves

Note: Bread may also be shaped into loaves and baked in buttered loaf pans. If making rolls, after first rising break off pieces of dough and roll into balls 1 inch in diameter. Place in buttered cake pan about 1-1/4 inches apart, allowing about 12 balls to a 9-inch cake pan. Let rise until doubled and bake in 375° oven 20 minutes.

RYE BREAD

Boil, covered, until soft in 2-1/2 cups water:
1/2 pound potatoes
Drain, reserving cooking water, and peel and mash or rice potatoes. Set aside. Combine and cool to lukewarm:
2-1/4 cups potato water
1/4 cup safflower or corn oil
1/4 to 1/3 cup honey or molasses
1 tablespoon salt
Add and stir to dissolve:
2 tablespoons active dry yeast, or
2 cakes yeast, crumbled
Stir in, 2 cups at a time:
4 cups rye flour
1/2 cup nonfat dry milk
1 tablespoon caraway seeds
  (optional)
Then add:
1 cup firmly packed reserved
  mashed or riced potatoes
3/4 cup whole-wheat flour
Following instructions in basic method, turn out onto floured board and knead, using up to 1/4 cup additional whole-wheat flour as needed. Dough will take at least 20 minutes of kneading to become smooth and elastic. Let rise 1-1/2 hours or until doubled, punch down and form into 2 oval loaves. Place on oiled cookie sheet and slash top with razor blade or sharp knife. Let rise 45 minutes or until doubled and bake in 375° oven 50 minutes or until tests done. Cool and store.
Makes 2 loaves

CHIA BREAD

Dissolve in:
2 tablespoons lukewarm water
1 tablespoon dry active yeast, or
1 cake yeast, crumbled
Heat to lukewarm:
1 cup buttermilk
Stir in to dissolve molasses:
1/3 cup molasses
1 tablespoon chia seeds
1 teaspoon salt
2 tablespoons melted butter
dissolved yeast
Gradually add:
1 cup whole-wheat flour
Blend in:
2/3 cup grated raw carrot
1/4 cup pumpkin seeds
Gradually stir in to make stiff dough:
2 cups unbleached white flour
Following instructions in basic method, turn out onto floured board and knead 10 minutes, working in up to 1/4 cup additional flour as needed. Let rise 2 hours or until doubled. Punch down and shape into loaf. Place in buttered loaf pan and let rise 1 hour or until doubled. Bake in 350° oven 35 to 40 minutes or until bread tests done. Cool and store.
Makes 1 loaf

MOIST PUMPERNICKEL BREAD

Good buttered or with cheeses and ideal for brown-bag lunches because it stays so moist.

Boil, covered, until soft in 1-3/4 cups water:
1/2 pound potatoes
Drain, reserving cooking water, peel and mash or rice potatoes. Set aside. In heavy saucepan combine and cook until thickened:
1-1/2 cups potato water
6 tablespoons yellow cornmeal
Transfer to large bowl and combine with:
2 tablespoons corn oil
3/4 cup minus 2 tablespoons honey or molasses
1 tablespoon salt
1 tablespoon caraway seeds
1-1/2 tablespoons carob powder, dissolved in
1 tablespoon water
Cool to lukewarm.
Dissolve in:
1/4 cup lukewarm water
2 tablespoons active dry yeast, or
2 cakes yeast, crumbled

Add dissolved yeast to cornmeal mixture with:
1 cup firmly packed reserved mashed or riced potatoes
3 cups rye flour
1 cup whole-wheat flour
Following instructions in basic method, turn out onto well-floured board and knead, using up to 1 cup additional rye flour. Dough will take at least 20 minutes kneading to become smooth and elastic. Let rise 1 to 1-1/2 hours or until doubled. Punch down and form into 2 round or rectangular loaves. Place on oiled cookie sheet sprinkled with yellow cornmeal or in 2 well-buttered loaf pans. Let rise 1 to 1-1/4 hours or until doubled. For crispy crust, brush top of loaves with:
1 egg, beaten with
1 tablespoon water
Bake in 375° oven 45 to 50 minutes or until bread tests done. Cool and store refrigerated.
Makes 2 medium-size loaves

Basic Corn-Rye Bread: Omit carob powder and caraway seeds.

Breads

OATMEAL-RAISIN BREAD

Scald:
1 cup milk
Add, stirring to melt butter, and cool to lukewarm:
1/2 cup softened butter
1/3 cup mild honey
2 teaspoons salt
In large bowl dissolve in:
1/4 cup lukewarm water
2 tablespoons active dry yeast, or
2 cakes yeast, crumbled
Add, stirring with wooden spoon
1 to 2 minutes until smooth:
milk mixture
3 eggs, beaten
2 cups unbleached white flour, sifted with:
  1 teaspoon ground cinnamon
  1/2 teaspoon freshly grated nutmeg
Add and blend well:
1-1/2 cups each rolled oats and raisins
1-1/4 cups unbleached white flour
1/2 cup wheat germ
Following instructions in basic method, turn out onto floured board and knead 10 minutes, adding 1/2 to 2/3 cup additional flour as needed. Let rise 1 hour or until doubled. Shape into 2 loaves and place in 2 buttered loaf pans. Let rise 30 minutes and bake in 350° oven 40 to 45 minutes or until bread tests done.
Cool and store.
Makes 2 loaves

WHOLE WHEAT-OATMEAL BREAD

Scald:
1-1/2 cups each milk and water
Remove from heat and stir in to dissolve honey:
1/4 cup mild honey
3 tablespoons safflower or corn oil
Transfer to large bowl and cool to lukewarm. Add to dissolve:
2 tablespoons active dry yeast, or
2 cakes yeast, crumbled
Stir in with wooden spoon until smooth:
1 cup whole-wheat flour
1 cup unbleached white flour, sifted with
1/2 cup soy flour
1 tablespoon salt
Gradually add:
2 cups whole-wheat flour
2 cups rolled oats
1 cup unbleached white flour
1/2 cup wheat germ
Following instructions in basic method, turn out onto lightly floured board and knead 10 minutes, working in up to 3/4 cup additional white flour to make firm dough. Let rise approximately 50 minutes or until doubled. Punch down, divide in half and form into 2 loaves. Place in 2 buttered loaf pans and let rise 40 to 45 minutes or until doubled. Bake in 375° oven 35 minutes or until bread tests done.
Cool and store.
Makes 2 loaves

CORN-WHEAT BREAD

A bread of firm texture combining in perfect balance the flavors of corn and wheat. It stays moist and is good toasted or fresh.

In a large bowl combine and stir until smooth:
3/4 cup cold water
1 cup yellow cornmeal
3/4 cup boiling water
Let cool to lukewarm. Dissolve in:
1/2 cup lukewarm water
2 tablespoons active dry yeast, or
2 cakes yeast, crumbled
Add to cornmeal mixture with:
1/2 cup honey or molasses
1/4 cup corn oil
When liquid ingredients are evenly blended, add to make soft dough:
1/2 cup soy flour, sifted with
1 tablespoon salt
2-3/4 cups whole-wheat flour

Following instructions in basic method, turn out onto well-floured board and knead, using up to 1/4 cup additional whole-wheat flour as needed. Let rise 1-1/2 to 2 hours until doubled. Punch down and form into 2 small oval or round loaves. Place in small buttered loaf pans or on cookie sheet sprinkled with yellow cornmeal. Let rise 1 hour or until doubled and bake in 375° oven 40 to 50 minutes or until bread tests done. Brush surface of each loaf with butter and cool. Store refrigerated.
Makes 2 small loaves

ORANGE RIVER RYE

Dissolve in:
1-1/2 cups lukewarm water
2 tablespoons active dry yeast, or
2 cakes yeast, crumbled
Combine in large bowl with:
1/2 cup dark honey, or
1/4 cup each honey and molasses
2 tablespoons corn oil
2 tablespoons firmly packed freshly grated orange peel
1 tablespoon salt
1 teaspoon ground allspice or cardamom
Add, stirring with wooden spoon

2 to 3 minutes until smooth:
1 cup each rye and whole-wheat flour
Stir in:
1-1/2 cups each rye and whole-wheat flour
Following instructions in basic method, turn out onto floured board and knead; dough will take approximately 20 minutes to become smooth and elastic. Let rise 1-1/2 hours or until doubled. Punch down and form into 2 small oval loaves. Place on buttered cookie sheet sprinkled with yellow cornmeal. Slash surface of each loaf 3 times with razor blade or sharp knife. Let rise 45 minutes or until doubled. Bake in 375° oven 45 minutes or until bread tests done. Brush surface of each loaf with butter and cool. Store refrigerated.
Makes 2 small loaves

Breads

SPROUTED WHEAT BREAD

Scald:
1-1/2 cups each milk and water
Add to dissolve honey:
**1/3 cup each mild honey and
    corn oil**
Transfer to large bowl and cool to
lukewarm. Stir in to dissolve:
**2 tablespoons active dry yeast, or
2 cakes yeast, crumbled**
With wooden spoon blend in 1 to
2 minutes until smooth:
**2 cups whole-wheat flour
1/2 cup soy or garbanzo flour,
    sifted with
1 tablespoon salt**
Add to make stiff dough:
**2-1/2 cups sprouted wheat (see
    mung beans)
3 cups whole-wheat flour
1/2 cup each wheat germ and
    nonfat dry milk**

Following instructions in basic
method, turn out onto floured
board and knead 20 minutes,
using up to 1/4 cup additional
whole-wheat flour. Let rise 50
minutes or until doubled. Form
into 2 loaves and place in 2 buttered loaf pans. Let rise 30 minutes or until doubled. Bake in
350° oven 40 to 45 minutes or
until bread tests done. Cool
and store.
Makes 2 loaves

BROWN RICE-HERB BREAD

Dissolve in:
**1/4 cup lukewarm water
1 tablespoon active dry yeast, or
1 cake yeast, crumbled**
In large bowl combine:
**1 egg, beaten
1/4 teaspoon baking soda
1-1/4 teaspoons salt
1 teaspoon dried dill weed, or
3/4 teaspoon crumbled dried
    thyme
2 tablespoons corn oil
1/4 cup mild honey
3/4 cup lukewarm water
dissolved yeast**

Gradually stir in:
**1/2 cup white or yellow cornmeal
1 cup cooked brown rice
2 cups unbleached white flour**
Beat well and add:
1 cup unbleached white flour
Following instructions in basic
method, turn out onto floured
board and knead 10 minutes,
working in additional flour as
needed. Let rise 1 hour or until
doubled. Punch down and turn
out onto floured board. Cover
with tea towel and let rest 15
minutes. Form into a round loaf
8 inches in diameter and place
on buttered baking sheet. Let
rise 1 hour or until doubled and
brush lightly with water. Bake in
350° oven 35 minutes or until
bread tests done. Cool and store.
Serve cut into wedges.
Makes 1 loaf

Breads

QUICK BREADS

Quick breads do not require the same rising time before baking that yeast breads need. The leavening action of the baking powder and/or baking soda takes place while the quick breads bake. The top crust of a quick bread should crack during baking. To test for doneness, insert a toothpick in center. If it comes out clean, the bread is done.

• Whole-wheat pastry flour may be substituted for unbleached white flour in all of the quick bread recipes. One-half cup soy flour has been incorporated into nearly all of these recipes because it is very high in protein. Soy flour, however, may be replaced with unbleached white or whole-wheat pastry flour. When baking with soy flour, lower oven temperature 25 degrees after first 30 minutes of baking time.

• Amounts for both honey and sugar are included in quick bread recipes. Date sugar may also be used in the same proportion as cane sugar. Quick breads baked with honey will generally take 5 minutes more cooking time than those with sugar. Honey or date sugar will improve nutritional value and give a light texture and flavor.

• Stir quick breads only enough to moisten dry ingredients. Do not beat.

• Dust raisins and nuts with flour to prevent them from falling to bottom of loaf during baking.

• Always preheat oven.

• Cool breads on wire rack, wrap well and store in cool place or refrigerate.

APPLE SPICE BREAD

Cream together:
1 egg, beaten
1/3 cup safflower oil or softened
  butter
3/4 cup honey, or
1 cup raw natural sugar
1/4 teaspoon grated fresh vanilla
  bean
Add:
2 to 2-1/2 cups cored and thinly
  sliced tart apples (2 medium-
  size apples)
1/4 cup ground filberts
sifted mixture of:
  3/4 cup unbleached white
    flour
  1/4 cup soy flour
  1 teaspoon each baking soda
    and ground cinnamon
  1/4 teaspoon each salt, freshly
    grated nutmeg and ground
    cardamom or allspice
Pour into buttered loaf pan and bake in 350° oven 30 minutes. Lower heat to 325° and bake 20 minutes longer or until bread tests done.
Makes 1 loaf

MOIST PUMPKIN BREAD

Cream together with wire whisk:
2 eggs, beaten
1/2 cup safflower oil or softened
   butter
3/4 cup mild honey, or
1 cup raw natural sugar
1 cup Pumpkin Purée
1/4 cup milk
Add, stirring with wooden spoon
just to moisten dry ingredients:
1/2 cup whole-wheat flour
sifted mixture of:
   1 cup unbleached white flour
   1/2 cup soy flour
   1 teaspoon ground cinnamon
   1/2 teaspoon each salt, baking
      soda, and ground ginger
   1/4 teaspoon each ground cloves
      and allspice
Fold in:
3/4 cup broken walnuts or raisins
Spoon batter into buttered loaf
or Bundt pan. Smooth out surface. Bake in 350° oven 30 minutes. Lower heat to 325° and
bake 30 minutes or until bread
tests done.
Makes 1 loaf

ORANGE-GINGER BREAD

Cream together with wire whisk:
1/3 cup butter, at room temperature
3/4 cup mild honey, or
1 cup raw natural sugar
2 eggs, beaten
1 tablespoon firmly packed
   freshly grated orange peel
Add, stirring with wooden spoon
to just moisten dry ingredients:
1/2 cup each fresh orange juice
   and plain yoghurt, sour cream
   or buttermilk
sifted mixture of:
   2 cups unbleached white flour
   1/2 cup soy flour
   1 tablespoon baking powder
   2 teaspoons ground ginger
   1 teaspoon salt
   1/2 teaspoon baking soda
1/2 cup wheat germ
1/4 cup whole-wheat flour
2/3 cup broken pecans or walnuts, light raisins or pitted
   chopped dates
Spoon into buttered loaf pan and
bake in 350° oven 30 minutes.
Reduce heat to 325° and bake 20
to 25 minutes longer or until
tests done.
Makes 1 large loaf

MOIST BANANA NUT BREAD

Cream together with wire whisk:
2 eggs, beaten
1/2 cup safflower oil
3/4 cup mild honey, or
1 cup raw natural sugar
2 tablespoons buttermilk or
   plain yoghurt
1 tablespoon fresh lemon juice
1-1/2 cups mashed very ripe
   bananas (2 to 3 bananas)
Add, stirring only to moisten dry
ingredients, sifted mixture of:
1-1/2 cups unbleached white
   flour
1/2 cup soy flour
1-1/2 teaspoons baking powder
1/4 to 1/2 teaspoon freshly
   grated nutmeg
1/2 teaspoon each salt and
   baking soda
Fold in:
2/3 cup coarsely chopped nut
   meats
Spoon into buttered loaf pan and
bake in 350° oven 30 minutes.
Lower heat to 325° and bake 25
to 30 minutes longer or until
tests done.
Makes 1 loaf

Breads

CRANBERRY FRUIT BREAD

Sift together:
1-1/2 cups unbleached white
  flour*
1/2 cup soy flour
1-1/2 teaspoons baking powder
1 teaspoon salt
1/2 teaspoon baking soda
Combine and mix well:
1 egg, beaten
3/4 cup fresh orange juice
3/4 cup mild honey, or
1 cup raw natural sugar
3 tablespoons safflower oil
1 tablespoon freshly grated
  orange peel
Slowly blend in dry ingredients
and mix just to moisten. Fold in:
2 cups chopped or halved
  cranberries
1/2 cup chopped pecans or
  walnuts
1/4 cup wheat germ
Spoon into greased loaf pan and
bake in 350° oven 30 minutes.
Lower heat to 325° and bake 30
minutes longer or until bread
tests done.
Makes 1 loaf

*One-half cup whole-wheat flour
  may be substituted for 1/2 cup
  of the white flour. Gently stir
  whole-wheat flour into sifted
  flour mixture.

CARROT SESAME BREAD

Cream together with wire whisk:
2 eggs, beaten
1/2 cup safflower or corn oil
2/3 cup mild honey, or
3/4 cup raw natural sugar
Sift together:
1 cup unbleached white flour
1/2 cup soy flour
1 teaspoon each baking powder,
  baking soda and ground
  cinnamon
1/2 teaspoon salt
Add sifted ingredients to
creamed mixture, stirring just
enough to moisten dry ingredients. Fold in:
1 cup firmly packed grated
  carrots
1 cup light raisins or sultanas,
  plumped
1/4 cup unhulled sesame seeds
Spoon into buttered loaf pan and
bake in 350° oven for 30 minutes.
Lower heat to 325° and bake for
25 to 30 minutes or until bread
tests done.
Makes 1 loaf

Variation: Substitute 1/4 cup
toasted wheat germ for the
sesame seeds (this will result in
a somewhat drier bread). The
carrot bread also lends itself well
to improvisation with spices. Try
ground nutmeg or ginger, coriander, anise, allspice or cardamom.

POLENTA CARROT BREAD

In mixing bowl combine:
1 cup polenta
3/4 cup boiling water
Stir in:
1 cup firmly packed grated carrot
1-1/2 tablespoons corn oil
2 teaspoons mild honey
1/2 teaspoon salt
Beat together and add to polenta
mixture:
2 egg yolks
2 tablespoons fresh orange juice
  or cold water
Fold in:
2 egg whites, beaten stiff but
  not dry
Pour into buttered loaf pan and
bake in 400° oven 25 minutes or
until top is lightly browned and
toothpick inserted in center
comes out clean.
Makes 1 small loaf

HONEY POUND CAKE

Cream together with wire whisk:
1/2 cup butter, at room
  temperature
3/4 cup mild honey, or
1 cup raw natural sugar
3 egg yolks
1/2 cup half-and-half
1-1/2 tablespoons fresh lemon
  juice
1/4 teaspoon grated fresh vanilla
  bean
1 teaspoon each freshly grated
  lemon and orange peel
Stir in just to moisten dry ingredients:
1/2 cup whole-wheat flour
sifted mixture of:
  1 cup unbleached white flour
  1/2 cup soy flour
  2-1/2 teaspoons baking powder
  3/4 teaspoon salt
  1/4 teaspoon baking soda
Fold in:
3 egg whites, beaten stiff but not
  dry
Pour into buttered loaf pan and
bake in 350° oven 30 minutes.
Lower heat to 325° and bake 15
minutes longer or until cake tests
done.
Makes 1 loaf

POPPY SEED POUND CAKE

Cream together:
1/2 cup each cream cheese and
  butter, at room temperature
1/2 cup mild honey, or
3/4 cup raw natural sugar
1/4 teaspoon grated fresh
  vanilla bean
Beat in one at a time:
2 eggs
Add, stirring only to moisten,
sifted mixture of:
1 cup unbleached white flour
3 tablespoons soy flour
3/4 teaspoon baking powder
Stir in:
1/2 cup each light raisins or sultanas and broken walnuts
Spoon half of batter into buttered loaf pan sprinkled on
bottom and sides with:
3 tablespoons ground walnuts
Then spread evenly onto batter
layer mixture of:
1/3 cup poppy seeds
3 tablespoons mild honey
1-1/2 teaspoons firmly packed
  freshly grated lemon peel
1/8 teaspoon grated fresh vanilla
  bean
Top with:
remaining half of batter
Bake in 325° oven 60 to 65 minutes or until cake tests done.
Makes 1 loaf

APPLE MUFFINS

Mix together with wire whisk:
1 egg, beaten
1/4 cup each safflower or walnut
  oil and honey
3/4 cup milk
1/2 teaspoon freshly grated
  lemon or orange peel
Sift into egg mixture:
1-1/2 cups unbleached white
  flour or whole-wheat pastry
  flour, or
3/4 cup each unbleached white
  flour and whole-wheat pastry
  flour
1 tablespoon baking powder
1/2 teaspoon salt
1/2 teaspoon ground cinnamon
1/4 teaspoon ground allspice
few gratings of nutmeg
Stir only enough to moisten dry
ingredients. Fold in:
1/4 cup thinly sliced and cut-up
  apples
2 tablespoons chopped walnuts
  or pecans
Fill buttered muffin tins two-
thirds full. Bake in 375° oven 20
minutes or until toothpick inserted in center comes out clean.
Makes 12 muffins

Breads

BRAN MUFFINS

Combine:
2 eggs, beaten
2 tablespoons each molasses and
   safflower oil
1 cup 100 percent whole-wheat
   bran, softened in
1 cup buttermilk or plain yoghurt
Stir in mixture of:
1 cup whole-wheat flour
1 tablespoon baking powder
1/2 teaspoon each baking soda
   and salt
Fold in:
1/4 cup raisins or chopped nut
   meats (optional)
Spoon into buttered muffin pans,
filling each muffin form two-
thirds full. Bake in 375° oven 30 to
35 minutes or until toothpick inserted in center comes out clean.
Makes 12 muffins

WHOLE-WHEAT BISCUITS

Sift into mixing bowl:
1/2 cup each unbleached white
   flour and whole-wheat flour
1-1/2 teaspoons baking powder
Work in until crumbly:
2-1/2 tablespoons safflower or
   corn oil
With fork, stir in until smooth:
1/3 cup milk
Knead briefly and roll 1/2 inch
thick. Cut into 2-inch rounds and
place in cake pan. Bake in 400°
oven 12 to 15 minutes.
Makes 10 biscuits

FRENCH TOAST

Beat with wire whisk:
2 eggs
1/3 cup milk
1-1/2 tablespoons fresh orange
   juice
1/4 teaspoon freshly grated
   orange peel
1 teaspoon honey
1/8 teaspoon each ground cinnamon and grated fresh vanilla
   bean
pinch salt
Dip into batter:
2 slices bread
In skillet, heat:
1-1/2 teaspoons each butter and
   safflower oil
Fry bread slices over medium-
high heat 2 to 3 minutes per
side until golden brown. Repeat
with 2 more slices of dipped
bread, adding to skillet if needed:
1 teaspoon additional butter
Serve for breakfast with honey,
honey and wheat germ, or honey
and fresh fruit.
Makes 4 slices

BUTTERMILK GRIDDLE CAKES

Combine well:
1 egg, beaten
1/2 cup buttermilk
1 teaspoon mild honey
1/2 teaspoon corn oil
Gradually sift into egg mixture and stir until smooth:
3/4 cup unbleached white flour
1/4 teaspoon each salt and baking soda
In heavy skillet heat:
2 teaspoons each butter and corn oil
Stir pancake batter well and spoon into skillet, making 3 pancakes approximately 3-1/2 inches in diameter. Brown first side. When bubbles appear on top of pancake, turn and brown other side. Adding more butter and/or oil as needed, repeat with remaining batter. Be sure to stir well each time batter is spooned into skillet.
Makes approximately 8 3-1/2-inch pancakes

Cornmeal Griddle Cakes: Substitute for 6 tablespoons of the unbleached white flour 6 tablespoons yellow cornmeal.

PLAIN WAFFLES

Beat together with wire whisk:
1 egg yolk
2/3 cup milk
2 teaspoons honey
Add, stirring only to moisten, sifted mixture of:
2/3 cup unbleached white flour
1 teaspoon baking powder
1/4 teaspoon salt
Fold in:
1-1/2 to 2 tablespoons melted butter
1 egg white, beaten stiff but not dry
Refrigerate at least 10 minutes. Preheat waffle iron and when drop of water sizzles on lower grid, pour 1/2 batter in to cover 2/3 of lower grid. Close lid and cook 4 to 5 minutes or until waffle is golden. Repeat with remaining batter.
Makes 2 waffles

Whole-Wheat or Rye Waffles: Substitute for 2/3 cup unbleached white flour 1/2 cup whole wheat or rye flour and 3 tablespoons soy flour.
Nut or Wheat Germ Waffles: Increase baking powder to 1-1/2 teaspoons and milk by 2 tablespoons. Fold into batter with egg white 1/4 cup ground filberts or toasted wheat germ, 1/4 teaspoon cinnamon and pinch freshly grated nutmeg.
Cornmeal Waffles: Substitute for 1/3 cup of the flour 1/3 cup yellow cornmeal. Increase honey to 1 tablespoon, baking powder to 1-1/2 teaspoons and salt to 1/2 teaspoon.
Berry Waffles: Add to batter before folding in egg white 1/2 cup rinsed and well drained fresh berries, 1/4 to 1/2 teaspoon cinnamon and a pinch of grated fresh lemon peel.
Cheese Waffles: Add to batter before folding in egg white 1/3 cup grated mild cheddar or Edam cheese, 1 slice bacon, cooked and crumbled (optional) and 1/4 teaspoon dry mustard (optional).

Desserts

CHEESE AND FRUIT DESSERT SUGGESTIONS

Cheese and fruit, arranged attractively on a platter, should be at room temperature. Serve any of the following complementary combinations with nuts and mild crackers.

• Peaches and/or nectarines with double-crème or triple-crème, Teleme, Brie, Mel Fino
• Pears with Provolone, Camembert, Gouda, Crème de Gruyère, Jarlsberg
• Grapes with Camembert, triple-crème, Brillat-Savarin
• Apples with cheddar, Babybel, Gouda, Edam, Roquefort
• Melon with Edam, dry Monterey Jack, Münster, Samsoe
• Strawberries with triple-crème, Brie, Coeur à la Crème
• Plums with Petit-Suisse, Stilton, Fontina, Bel Paise
• Apricots with Banon, Brie
• Pineapple with Chantelle, Gervaise
• Cherries with Crème Danica, Brie

FRUIT DESSERT SUGGESTIONS

• Combine 1-1/2 cups halved seedless grapes with fresh lemon juice, mild honey and sherry or brandy to taste. Refrigerate 8 hours or more. Just before serving top with sour cream.
• Peel and halve 1 ripe pear. Brush with lemon juice and fill with mixture of 3 tablespoons crumbled Gervaise cheese and mild honey, brandy and all-spice to taste. Chill and just before serving sprinkle with sliced toasted blanched almonds.
• Marinate fresh pineapple chunks in Kirsch or white wine. Garnish with whole strawberries.
• Roll halved firm not overly ripe bananas in fresh lemon juice and mild honey. Sauté, turning once, in butter, approximately 5 minutes. Flame with brandy.
• Soak halved ripe pears in Kirsch. Top with raspberries and sprinkle with grated bitter-sweet chocolate.
• Soak papaya, mango and pineapple cubes and lichee nuts in Japanese plum wine several hours. Chill and garnish with mint sprigs.
• Serve fresh figs in sour cream sprinkled with raw natural sugar to taste.

• Combine 3 to 4 tablespoons sour cream and mild honey, lemon juice, orange-flavored liqueur and freshly grated orange peel to taste. Use as dip for large whole strawberries.
• Let raw natural sugar stand at room temperature to dry and then break up granules. Dip large strawberries in small glass of Cointreau and then in sugar.
• In tall glasses place alternate layers of 1-1/2 cups diced fruit or whole berries and ground mixture of 1/4 cup shelled fresh peanuts, 3 spice cookies or gingersnaps, ground cinnamon, anise and cloves, and grated fresh vanilla bean to taste. Top with whipped cream.
• Bring to boil 1/2 cup white wine vinegar, 1/3 cup water, 1/4 cup mild honey, 1 whole clove, 1 1-inch stick cinnamon, 1/4 teaspoon salt and 1/8 teaspoon ground cardamom. Remove from heat and pour sauce over 2 cups cantaloupe or casaba melon balls or cubes. Cool, cover and chill 4 hours or overnight. Garnish with mint sprigs.
• Halve 1 grapefruit and loosen sections. Drizzle with honey and broil until heated through.

Desserts

SPICED ORANGES

Combine and bring to gentle boil:
3 tablespoons water
1/4 cup red wine
1 slice lemon
1 whole clove
1 1-inch stick cinnamon
mild honey to taste
Reduce heat and simmer until syrupy. Place in crystal bowl:
2 oranges, sectioned
Pour sauce over and chill several hours. Garnish with:
mint sprigs

CAROB SOUR CREAM DESSERT DIP

Combine:
1 tablespoon each carob powder, milk and honey
1/4 cup sour cream
grated fresh vanilla bean to taste
Chill in small bowl. Serve with whole fresh fruits such as oranges, peaches or bananas. Each person should peel or slice his own fruit and use the carob mixture as a dip.

MELON FILLED WITH RICOTTA

Whip until smooth:
1/2 cup ricotta cheese
1/2 tablespoon mild honey or to taste
1/4 teaspoon each ground cinnamon and allspice
2 to 3 teaspoons cognac or fruit brandy
Adjust seasonings and chill.
Mound in:
2 melon halves
Sprinkle lightly with:
freshly grated nutmeg

Note: Ricotta mixture may also be served as a spread for fruits and crackers.

Variation: In place of honey, blend in puréed apricot or peach preserves to taste.

BAKED APPLES

Core and place in shallow buttered baking dish:
2 large apples
Sprinkle inside of each apple with:
1 teaspoon honey
ground cinnamon or freshly grated nutmeg to taste
Pour over apples:
juice of 1 large orange
Drizzle over apples:
2 to 3 teaspoons honey
Sprinkle with:
ground cinnamon or freshly grated nutmeg
Place any extra pulp from orange in cored center of apples and bake in 300° oven 45 minutes or until apples are tender. Place on serving plates and spoon hot sauce over.

Variation: Add to pan before baking 2 to 3 tablespoons Cointreau or other orange liqueur.

Note: If a very soft baked apple is desired, raise oven temperature to 325°.

PINEAPPLE CRÊPES

Prepare:
1 recipe Crêpes
Reserve 4 of the crêpes for
another use.
In a skillet or chafing dish, melt:
2 tablespoons butter
Add and heat:
1 tablespoon fresh orange juice
1/2 teaspoon fresh lemon juice
1/2 teaspoon raw natural sugar
One at a time, coat 4 crêpes in
the butter mixture and push to
side of pan. Add to juice and
heat:
1/2 cup finely cut fresh pineapple
Fill crêpes with pineapple and
fold. Add to pan:
**1 tablespoon warmed Grand
Marnier**
2 tablespoons warmed Kirsch
Turn crêpes in liqueur mixture
to coat well. Ignite and turn
crêpes several times while they
are flaming. Serve topped with:
whipped cream

CHEESE CRÊPES

Prepare:
1 recipe Crêpes
Reserve 4 of the crêpes for
another use.
Combine:
2/3 cup ricotta cheese
1 tablespoon honey
1/4 cup sultanas, plumped
2 tablespoons chopped almonds
**ground cinnamon or grated fresh
vanilla bean to taste**
Fill 4 crêpes with cheese mixture
and place in skillet with:
1 tablespoon melted butter
**1-1/2 teaspoons brandy
(optional)**
Turn to coat crêpes evenly and
heat gently. Serve plain or topped
with strawberries, blueberries or
other fresh fruit.

CAROB MOUSSE

Melt over low heat:
2 tablespoons butter
Combine and add to melted
butter:
**1 tablespoon unbleached white
flour**
**3 tablespoons finely sieved carob
powder**
Mixture will be a pasty consistency. Add, a little at a time and
stirring to blend after each
addition:
1/2 cup milk
Continue cooking, stirring constantly, until thick. Stir in:
**2 to 2-1/2 tablespoons mild
honey**
Beat lightly:
1 egg yolk
Add a little hot carob mixture to
yolk, stir to blend, then add to
pan, stirring briskly. Remove
from heat and cool.
Beat together until stiff peaks
form:
1/2 cup heavy cream
**1/8 teaspoon grated fresh vanilla
bean**
Fold cooled carob sauce into
whipped cream, blending until
texture is smooth and color is
evenly brown. Spoon into 2 custard cups and chill 8 hours or
overnight before serving.

Note: Recipe may be doubled.
Cover and refrigerate up to
4 days.

Desserts

DEEP DISH PEACH PIE

Prepare:
**1 recipe Whole-Wheat Pastry
(page 175)**
Peel and slice thinly to make
3 cups:
1-1/2 pounds peaches
Toss slices to coat evenly with:
**2-1/2 tablespoons raw natural
sugar**
1/2 teaspoon ground cinnamon
1 teaspoon fresh lemon juice
**1/4 teaspoon each freshly grated
nutmeg and ground cardamom**
dash of salt
Layer slices evenly in 2 well-
buttered, 1-cup deep dishes
(approximately 4-1/2 inches in
diameter). Mound to allow for
shrinkage when peaches cook.
Pour over slices in each dish:
2 to 3 teaspoons cognac
Dot each with:
1 teaspoon butter
Cover with pastry round, making a rim and fluting edges.
Make several small slashes in
crust and bake in 350° oven 40
to 50 minutes or until golden.
Cool slightly before serving,
or serve at room temperature.

Note: If less crust is desired,
cut pastry into strips, making
5 strips across top of peaches
and 5 crisscross strips.

Deep Dish Apple Pie Variation:
Substitute 1-1/2 pounds apples
for the peaches.

BAKED HONEY CUSTARD

Combine and cool to lukewarm:
1-1/3 cups scalded milk
3 tablespoons honey
Mix together:
3 eggs, beaten
**1/4 to 1/2 teaspoon grated fresh
lemon or orange peel**
pinch grated fresh vanilla bean
**1/8 teaspoon each salt and
ground allspice**
Slowly pour milk mixture into
egg mixture, blending thoroughly.
Ladle into 4 custard cups and
place in pan filled with 1 inch of
hot water. Bake in 350° oven
1 hour. Serve warm or cold.

OLD-FASHIONED SHORTCAKE

Sift together:
3/4 cup unbleached white flour
1-1/2 teaspoons baking powder
1/4 teaspoon salt
Cut into flour mixture:
2 teaspoons honey
2 tablespoons butter
Quickly stir in with fork:
1/4 cup half-and-half
Mix with hands until flour is
incorporated, adding 1 to 2 teaspoons additional half-and-half
if necessary. Knead lightly; then
divide dough in half and shape
into rounds on an ungreased
cookie sheet, about 2 inches
apart. Bake in 400° oven 12 to
15 minutes until golden brown.
Serve with fresh berries or fruit
sweetened with honey and top
with whipped cream.

Variation: To make scones, add
3 tablespoons currants with the
half-and-half. Shape dough into
one round about 3/4 inch thick
in center and tapering to about
1/2 inch thick at rim. Cut into
quarters and place 2 inches apart
on ungreased cookie sheet. Bake
as directed. Serve hot; split in
half and spread with butter and
jam.

ZABAGLIONE

In top of double boiler (not touching water), beat together over simmering water until pale yellow and fluffy:
4 egg yolks
3 to 4 tablespoons raw natural sugar
Add:
1/4 cup Marsala
1/4 teaspoon freshly grated orange or lemon peel
Continue beating until thickened and fluffy. Pour into parfait glasses and serve immediately.

ICE CREAM DESSERT SUGGESTIONS

• Marinate fresh pineapple chunks in green Crème de Menthe 4 to 5 hours. Spoon pineapple and juices over pineapple sherbet. Garnish with mint sprigs.

• Pour brandy or green Crème de Menthe over pineapple sherbet.

• Spoon light chocolate or coffee ice cream into parfait glasses. Carefully pour into each glass 1/4 cup hot espresso coffee and 2 teaspoons coffee-flavored liqueur. Top with whipped cream and sprinkle with grated bittersweet chocolate. Serve with a straw and a spoon.

• Soften 1 pint French vanilla ice cream and fold in 1/3 cup heavy cream, whipped, and 2 tablespoons Galliano or cognac. Freeze and when ready to serve spoon over 2 ripe peach halves. Garnish with bittersweet chocolate curls.

• Top vanilla ice cream with mixture of ripe persimmon pulp mashed with fresh lemon juice, grated fresh lemon peel and honey to taste. Sprinkle with toasted sliced almonds or chopped pine nuts.

• Soften 1 pint vanilla ice cream and blend in 1 tablespoon Tia Maria and 1-1/2 teaspoons cognac. Freeze in serving dishes. Just before serving sprinkle with powdered espresso coffee.

LEMON SQUARES

Cream thoroughly:
1/4 pound softened butter
Blend in:
1 cup unbleached white flour
1/4 cup raw natural sugar
Press into bottom of greased 9 by 9-inch pan. Bake in 350° oven 20 minutes. Let cool 10 minutes.
Combine and mix well:
2 eggs, beaten
1 cup raw natural sugar
3 tablespoons fresh lemon juice
1/4 teaspoon salt
mixture of:
 2 tablespoons flour
 1/2 teaspoon baking powder
Spread on cooled cake layer and bake in 350° oven 30 minutes. Cool completely before cutting into squares. Store in refrigerator or may be frozen.
Makes 2 dozen squares

Desserts

APRICOT BARS

Mix in bowl:
1 cup unbleached white flour
1/4 cup raw natural sugar
Cut in until crumbly:
1/4 pound butter, at room temperature
Press mixture evenly into bottom of 9 by 9-inch pan. Bake in 350° oven 25 minutes. Cool 10 minutes. Sift together and set aside:
1/3 cup unbleached white flour
1/2 teaspoon each salt and baking powder
Beat:
2 eggs
1/4 teaspoon grated fresh vanilla bean
Gradually add, beating until creamy:
1 cup raw natural sugar
Blend in:
1 teaspoon grated orange peel
flour mixture
1 cup chopped dried apricots
1/2 cup chopped pecans
Turn mixture onto cooled baked layer and spread evenly. Bake in 350° oven 30 minutes. Cool completely before cutting into bars. Store in refrigerator. Bars can be frozen.
Makes 2 dozen bars

LINZER COOKIES

Thoroughly combine:
1/2 cup butter, softened
1/2 cup raw natural sugar
Blend in:
1 egg yolk
1/2 teaspoon firmly packed freshly grated lemon peel
Mix in:
3/4 cup ground almonds
3/4 cup sifted unbleached flour, sifted with:
    1/2 teaspoon ground cinnamon
    1/4 teaspoon powdered cloves
Blend well and form into ball. Wrap well in waxed paper and place in plastic bag. Refrigerate at least 1 hour or overnight. Roll a portion at a time 1/8 inch thick between pieces of waxed paper, keeping remainder of dough refrigerated until needed. Cut into 2-inch rounds and place 2 inches apart on cookie sheet. Place on each round:
3/4 teaspoon cherry, plum, apricot, peach or other jam
Cover each cookie round in crisscross pattern with 6 small strips of rolled dough. Bake in 375° oven 10 to 12 minutes or until just starting to brown. Remove from cookie sheet immediately, cool and store in airtight tin. May be frozen.
Makes approximately 3-1/2 dozen

CAROB BROWNIES

Cream together with wire whisk:
4 eggs, beaten
2/3 cup safflower oil
1/2 cup honey
1/4 to 1/2 teaspoon grated fresh vanilla bean
Add sifted mixture of:
1 cup carob powder
1/2 cup whole wheat* or rye flour
1 teaspoon baking powder
1/2 teaspoon salt
Stir in:
3/4 cup nut flour (raw peanuts, filberts, walnuts or almonds ground to flour)
1/2 to 2/3 cup chopped nut meats (optional)
Place in buttered 9 by 9-inch cake pan and bake in 325° oven 25 to 30 minutes or until toothpick inserted in center comes out clean. Cut into 24 squares and cool on wire rack.

*When sifting whole-wheat flour, add any bran that remains in top of sifter to bowl.

Basics

Basics

HOMEMADE YOGHURT

Because most commercial yoghurts contain additives and preservatives, we recommend making your own. Homemade yoghurt is economical and easy to prepare. To make your own yoghurt, you will need milk and a yoghurt starter. The starter can be either plain unsweetened commercially prepared yoghurt without additives or preservatives, or a pure powdered culture that can be obtained in health and natural foods stores. Once you have made a batch of yoghurt, refrigerate some of homemade yoghurt to be used as the starter for the next batch. It is best to use the new starter within a week; older starter takes longer to incubate. The strength of the yoghurt culture also often weakens after several batches, so periodically use a commercial starter or powdered culture.

Basic Method

To make 1 quart of yoghurt you will need 1 quart of milk and 3 to 4 tablespoons of starter. Scald the milk but do not allow it to boil, as this kills the beneficial bacteria. Cool the milk to lukewarm (105° to 115°). At this point you may add 1/4 to 1/2 cup non-instant, nonfat dry milk to the lukewarm. This makes a thicker, more nutritious yoghurt. Then stir in the yoghurt starter or culture, and, if desired, blend in a blender to make a smoother, creamier yoghurt. Cover and incubate yoghurt, maintaining a temperature of between 90° and 115°, approximately 6 hours or until thick. Two foolproof devices for incubating yoghurt are commercial yoghurt makers and wide-mouthed thermos bottles. Yoghurt can also be incubated in warmed quart jars or earthenware bowls and set in a warm place such as over or near the pilot light on top of the stove or in a turned-off gas oven. You may also set the yoghurt container in a dish of warm water (about 120°), cover it with a towel or set it on a heating pad turned on to the lowest setting. The yoghurt should not be disturbed during the incubation period. Often the whey will separate from the yoghurt; it can be stirred back into the yoghurt or reserved for use in other recipes as a substitute for water. Store yoghurt refrigerated for up to 2 weeks.

Flavored Yoghurts:

- Stir into scalded milk before adding starter, honey, real maple syrup, molasses, carob powder or vanilla and/or other spices.
- Flavor prepared yoghurt with fresh or dried fruits, wheat germ and honey, nuts and/or seeds, homemade preserves.

HOMEMADE MAYONNAISE

To make mayonnaise, use room temperature ingredients, a wooden bowl and a wooden spoon. When adding the oil, beat gently in circular motion, always in the same direction. If the mayonnaise should curdle because the oil is added too fast, gradually stir curdled mayonnaise into a fresh egg yolk. Then add oil, vinegar and seasonings as if making a new batch. Store in covered jar up to 3 or 4 days. If using for sandwich spreads or in potato salads do not allow to stand out and do not keep more than 1 day.

Measure into a cup with a pouring spout:

1/2 cup olive, corn or safflower oil

In bowl, stir until creamy:

1 egg yolk

Gradually, drop by drop, stirring constantly, add:

1/4 cup of the oil

Then stir in:

1/4 teaspoon salt
1/8 teaspoon white pepper
1/2 teaspoon cider or tarragon vinegar

Gradually stir in:

2 tablespoons of remaining oil

When thick and smooth, gradually stir in:

1/2 teaspoon cider or tarragon vinegar
remaining oil

Adjust seasonings with:

salt, white pepper, cayenne pepper (optional) and paprika

Makes 1/2 cup

Variations:

• Substitute lemon or lime juice for vinegar.
• Add with salt 1/4 teaspoon dry mustard or to taste.
• Add with salt 1/8 teaspoon anchovy paste or to taste.
• Stir into mayonnaise made with lemon or lime juice 1 teaspoon minced fresh dill.
• Stir into mayonnaise 1/4 cup firmly packed watercress leaves, blanched, drained and crushed in mortar and pestle.
• To serve on fruit salad, add 1/4 cup heavy cream and finely chopped raisins, currants and almonds.
• Aioli Sauce: Add to mayonnaise made with lemon or lime juice 1 to 2 garlic cloves, very finely minced.

HOMEMADE MUSTARD

Combine in small saucepan and blend to dissolve over low heat:

1-1/2 tablespoons each dry mustard and white wine vinegar or cider vinegar
2 tablespoons dry white wine or champagne
1 teaspoon mild honey or raw natural sugar
1/8 teaspoon salt

Let stand uncovered at room temperature 1 to 2 hours. Return to low heat and beat in:

1 egg yolk

Stirring constantly, cook 5 minutes or until thickened. Pour into small jar and cool. Cover tightly and refrigerate up to 1 month.

Makes approximately 1/3 cup

Note: Recipe doubles well.

Variations:

• Tarragon or Herb: Add to mustard before cooling 1/4 to 1/2 teaspoon dried tarragon or herbs of choice.
• Spicy: Add to mustard mixture with egg yolk 1/8 teaspoon turmeric and dash each ground cloves and cayenne pepper.

Basics

CREAM SAUCE

Melt until bubbly:
2 tablespoons butter
Sprinkle with:
**2 tablespoons unbleached white
    flour**
Cook and stir this roux over low
heat 3 minutes and gradually
stir in:
**1 cup milk, half-and-half, or
    combination**
Season to taste with:
**salt, white pepper, sweet Hungarian
    paprika**
Makes 1 cup

BÉCHAMEL SAUCE

Follow directions for Cream
Sauce, substituting for half the
milk or half-and-half, 1/2 cup
meat, fowl or vegetable stock.

MORNAY SAUCE

Add to Cream Sauce 2 tablespoons each grated Parmesan
cheese and grated Gruyère.
Season with dash of cayenne
pepper and swirl in 1-1/2 tablespoons butter, cut in bits.

HOLLANDAISE SAUCE

In heavy teflon pan or top of
double boiler beat:
1 cold egg
**1-1/2 tablespoons cold fresh
    lemon juice, or**
**1 tablespoon cold lemon juice
    and 1/2 tablespoon ice water**
1/8 teaspoon salt
Add:
4 tablespoons hard butter
Cook and stir over low heat or
over hot, not boiling water, until
butter is melted and sauce is
thickened. Serve immediately, or
remove from heat and let stand
at room temperature for up to
10 minutes until ready to use.

BÉARNAISE VARIATION

Combine:
**1-1/2 tablespoons each wine vine-
    gar and dry white wine**
**1/2 teaspoon finely minced white
    of green onion or shallot**
1/8 teaspoon finely minced garlic
**1/2 teaspoon each finely minced
    parsley and tarragon**
dash of white pepper
Bring to boil and reduce liquid to
1-1/2 tablespoons. Cool and chill.
Substitute for the lemon juice in
Hollandaise Sauce.

CHILI SAUCE

Peel and chop to measure 5 cups:
2-1/2 pounds ripe tomatoes
In large saucepan combine tomatoes with:
1 cup chopped onion
1/2 cup cider vinegar
1 tablespoon mild honey
**1 teaspoon each salt and mus-
    tard seed**
**1/2 teaspoon seeded and crushed
    dried red chili pepper**
**1/2 teaspoon each minced garlic
    and ginger root**
**1/4 teaspoon each freshly grated
    nutmeg and ground coriander**
1 whole clove
Bring to boil, lower heat and simmer gently, stirring often, 2-1/2
hours until thickened. Increase
heat for final 10 minutes of cooking time.
Cool and store in covered jar in
refrigerator up to 5 days. Serve
hot or cold spooned onto pork
chops, kebabs, hamburgers or
steaks.
Makes 2 to 2-1/4 cups

TOMATO SAUCE

Sauté, covered, until soft in:
**1 tablespoon each butter and
    olive oil**
**1/2 cup each diced red or green
    bell pepper, onion, carrot, and
    celery and tender leaves**
2 to 3 garlic cloves, minced
1 teaspoon minced fresh thyme
**3 Italian parsley sprigs and tender
    stalks, minced**
Raise heat and stir in:
1 to 2 teaspoons mild honey, or
**2 to 3 teaspoons natural raw
    sugar**
Stirring, brown vegetables and
force through food mill or purée
in blender with:
2/3 to 1 cup chicken or veal stock
Transfer to large saucepan and
add:
**3 pounds ripe tomatoes, peeled
    and chopped (approximately
    6 cups)**
**1 teaspoon sweet Hungarian
    paprika**
2 teaspoons salt
1/2 teaspoon pepper
2 bay leaves
**1 dried red chili pepper, seeded
    and crushed (optional)**
2 whole cloves (optional)
Cover with tilted lid and cook
over medium-low heat, stirring
occasionally, 2 hours or until
thickened. Adjust seasonings and
jar. Cool and refrigerate up to 5
days. Tomato sauce may be
frozen but should not be kept
longer than 2 months.
Makes 3-1/2 to 4 cups

TOMATO PURÉE

Add to Tomato Sauce while
cooking bouquet garni of:
6 to 8 large fresh basil leaves
1 celery stalk and leaves, cut up
6 whole allspice, lightly crushed
Cook 3 to 4 hours, stirring occasionally until of purée consistency. Discard bouquet garni.
Sieve if desired. Put in jars and
refrigerate up to 5 days. May be
frozen up to 2 months.
Makes approximately 2 cups

TOMATO CATSUP

Add to bouquet garni of
Tomato Purée:
**1 to 3 dried red chili peppers,
    seeded and crushed**
1 1-inch stick cinnamon
**1 teaspoon each celery seed and
    mustard seed**
Cook and stir until reduced by
half. Then add:
1 tablespoon mild honey, or
2 tablespoons natural raw sugar
Cook and stir until very thick.
Discard bouquet garni and add:
2 tablespoons cider vinegar
Continue cooking, stirring often,
until of desired consistency.
Adjust with more honey and/or
vinegar and cook to blend flavors.
Put in jars and refrigerate up to
3 days. Freeze in ice cube trays
no longer than 1 month.
Makes approximately 3/4 cup

TOMATO PASTE

Add to:
1 recipe Tomato Sauce
bouquet garni of:
    **1 celery stalk and leaves,
        chopped**
    2 large oregano sprigs
    1 large bay leaf
    6 Italian parsley sprigs
Cook, stirring often, until very
thick (be patient). Discard
bouquet garni and adjust seasonings. Place in small jars, cover
and refrigerate up to 3 days.
Or freeze in jars or ice cube trays
up to 1 month.
Makes approximately 1/2 cup

Basics

VINAIGRETTE DRESSING

Combine:
1/2 cup garlic olive oil
3 tablespoons cider or tarragon
   vinegar
1 to 1-1/2 tablespoons each
   finely minced celery, carrot
   and fresh parsley
2 teaspoons each grated onion
   and minced fresh chervil and
   chives
1 to 1-1/2 teaspoons finely
   minced green bell pepper
1 tablespoon capers (optional)
1/4 teaspoon salt
1/4 teaspoon each dry mustard
   and pepper
Chill several hours. Just before
serving add:
1/2 hard-cooked egg, sieved or
   finely chopped (optional)
Good on hearts of palm, fish,
vegetable or cold meat salads.
Makes approximately 3/4 cup

Note: May be refrigerated up to
3 days. Add egg just before
serving.

TANDOORI MARINADE

Combine:
3/4 cup plain yoghurt
2 tablespoons peanut oil
1/4 cup finely minced onions
2 teaspoons each finely minced
   garlic and ginger root
3 to 4 tablespoons fresh lemon
   juice
3/4 to 1 teaspoon each freshly
   ground coriander and ground
   cinnamon
1/2 teaspoon each ground cardamom and turmeric
2 teaspoons crumbled bay leaves
1 tablespoon ground almonds
1/2 teaspoon salt
1/4 teaspoon freshly ground
   black pepper
1/2 to 1 teaspoon crumbled
   seeded and dried red chili
   pepper
Makes approximately 1 cup

GRAVIES

In many cases, the juices from
cooked meats or poultry may be
served as they are. The drippings
that remain in a roasting pan may
be thickened by the addition of
flour. Pour off all but 1-1/2
tablespoons of the fat, sprinkle
fat in pan with 1 tablespoon of
flour or enough to absorb the fat,
cook and stir to brown lightly.
Gradually add 3/4 cup water,
stock, or a combination of stock
and half-and-half. Cook and stir
until thickened and smooth.
Adjust consistency with more
liquid or flour. Season to taste.

If thickening juices, several
kinds of binders can be used;
however, the proportion of binding agent to liquid will vary. The
liquid should complement the
dish—wine, stock, milk, cream,
etc. The binding agent and liquid
should be mixed together and
added to the pan juices slowly
over medium-low heat, stirring
until thickened. If the gravy does
not thicken enough, add more
binder; if too thick, add more
liquid. The following proportions
are recommended for 1 cup of
pan juices.
• 1-1/2 teaspoons flour and
3 tablespoons liquid
• 1/2 teaspoon cornstarch,
arrowroot, rice flour, potato
flour or tapioca flour and 1-1/2
teaspoons liquid
• 1 teaspoon ground walnuts
and 2 tablespoons liquid

LEMON-GARLIC BUTTER SAUCE

Sauté gently 3 to 4 minutes in:
1 tablespoon butter
1 small garlic clove, finely
    minced
Blend in:
2 teaspoons fresh lemon juice
1 to 2 tablespoons minced fresh
    parsley
1/4 teaspoon Herb Salt
Spoon over broiled liver or fish, cracked crab, fried squid, cooked green vegetables. Allow 1 tablespoon sauce per serving.
Makes 2 tablespoons

HERB BUTTER SAUCE

Omit garlic in above butter sauce and increase lemon juice to 1 tablespoon. Substitute for the parsley 2 to 3 tablespoons minced mixed fresh herbs of choice.

BROWNED BUTTER

Melt:
2 tablespoons butter
1 teaspoon grated onion
    (optional)
Cook over medium-high heat until butter is well browned. If desired, stir in:
1 teaspoon fresh lemon juice
2 teaspoons to 1 tablespoon
    sliced toasted almonds
Serve on cooked vegetables such as broccoli, cauliflower, beans, on pasta, etc.

HONEY BUTTER

Cream together 2 parts softened butter and 1 part honey. Add grated peel and fresh juice of lemon, lime or orange to taste. Store covered in refrigerator. Serve on toast, French toast, pancakes, waffles.

HERB BUTTER

Cream together 2 tablespoons softened butter and crumbled dried or minced mixed fresh herbs to taste. Amount depends on herbs used. Lemon juice to taste may be added. Serve on steamed vegetables, pastas, grains, toast.

GARLIC BUTTER

Cream together 2 to 3 tablespoons softened butter, 1 small garlic clove, minced, 1 tablespoon Parmesan cheese (optional), 2 teaspoons minced fresh parsley, 1/4 to 1/2 teaspoon Herb Salt and 1/4 teaspoon crumbled dried oregano leaves. Spread generously on French or Italian white bread, wrap in foil and bake in 350° oven 15 to 20 minutes. Also good spread on toast, mixed into hot cooked pasta, rice, steamed vegetables.

SESAME BUTTER

Cream together 3 parts softened butter and 1 part Sesame Salt or toasted sesame seeds. Store covered in refrigerator. Serve sesame salt butter on unsalted, cooked vegetables. Serve sesame seed butter on toast, cooked grains or pasta.

Basics

HERB SALT

Herb salt mixtures are a matter of taste and can be made from crumbled dried herbs ground in a mortar and pestle and used for cooking, or from powdered dried herbs for use in a salt shaker at table. Powdered herb flavors are more concentrated, so reduce proportions accordingly. There are a number of herb salts available in health and natural food stores that cannot be duplicated at home. One we highly recommend is Vege-Sal.

Combine:
2 tablespoons sea salt
2 teaspoons each crumbled dried
    oregano and celery leaves
1 teaspoon dried crumbled thyme
1 teaspoon onion powder
1/4 to 1/2 teaspoon each garlic
    powder and sweet Hungarian
    paprika

Note: Vary herbs with basil, parsley, summer savory and/or dry mustard. If using paprika in recipes, reduce amount in herb salt mixture.

SESAME SALT

In heavy skillet heat gently, stirring constantly, until seeds begin to brown:
6 to 8 tablespoons sesame seeds
Remove from skillet and grind in mortar and pestle until powdery and well blended with:
1 tablespoon sea salt
Some of the seeds will remain whole. Good combined with toasted brown rice as a crunchy snack. At table, sprinkle on soups, salads, entrées, omelets, reducing salt measurement in recipe.

SEASONED SESAME COATING

Combine:
1/2 cup toasted wheat germ
2 tablespoons sifted soy flour
2 tablespoons whole-wheat flour
    or bread crumbs
1 teaspoon Herb Salt
1 teaspoon sweet Hungarian
    paprika
1/2 teaspoon pepper
1/4 to 1/3 cup sesame seeds
Use as coating for chicken, fish or vegetable such as sliced celeriac. Store in covered jar in refrigerator.
Makes approximately 1 cup

AROMATIC CURRY MIXTURE

Whole seeds should be freshly ground with mortar and pestle. Character and flavor of curry can be varied by adding other spices such as nutmeg, ginger, bay leaf or cinnamon. Curry can be made hotter by increasing amount of cayenne or by adding seeded and crushed dried red chili pepper. Store in covered jar.

Combine:
2 teaspoons freshly ground
    coriander
1 teaspoon each ground turmeric
    and fenugreek
1/4 teaspoon each freshly ground
    cumin and cardamom
1 whole clove, ground
1/8 teaspoon ground mace
1/16 teaspoon cayenne pepper
Makes approximately 2
tablespoons

BREAD CRUMBS

Break bread into small pieces and dry in 200° oven on cookie sheet. Crush with rolling pin. For fine crumbs, whirl in blender. May be frozen.

SEASONED BREAD CRUMBS

Season bread crumbs to taste with Herb Salt.

BREAD CRUMB TOPPING

Melt 2 tablespoons butter and stir in 5 to 6 tablespoons Seasoned Bread Crumbs. Toss in 2 to 3 tablespoons grated Parmesan cheese or 1 teaspoon freshly grated lemon peel.

CROUTONS

Cut bread into 1/2-inch cubes to make 1 cup. Dry on cookie sheet in 200° oven. Toss with 1-1/2 to 2 tablespoons melted butter and any one of the following seasonings. Place in shallow pan and, turning often, brown lightly in 350° oven. Cool and store in airtight container in refrigerator or freezer.

Seasonings:
- 1-1/2 to 2 tablespoons grated Parmesan cheese, 1/4 teaspoon paprika, dash cayenne pepper
- 1 teaspoon fresh lemon juice or 1/2 teaspoon freshly grated lemon peel and 1/4 teaspoon paprika
- 1 small garlic clove, grated, 1/8 teaspoon crumbled dried oregano, salt and pepper to taste

TOASTING AND BROWNING NUTS AND SEEDS

Do not use a seasoned cast-iron skillet as it will smoke when heated hot enough to brown rice or seeds. Toast brown rice and sesame seeds in hot dry skillet, stirring, until just browned. Whole nuts such as blanched raw almonds or cashews are best browned in a small amount of hot oil in a wok. With the hot oil concentrated in one area, the nuts brown quickly on all sides. A heavy skillet may also be used. Pine nuts may be toasted in oil or in a dry pan. Spread wheat germ, grated coconut or ground nuts on cookie sheet, place in 300° oven and, stirring occasionally, toast until golden. (Coconut should be barely golden.)

Basics

MIXED FRUIT CHUTNEY

In heavy saucepan combine and mix well:
1-1/2 cups chopped, peeled and cored apples
1 cup chopped, peeled and cored pears
1/2 cup chopped, peeled and cored quince
1/2 cup each chopped onion and raisins
1 teaspoon minced garlic
1 teaspoon minced ginger root
1-1/4 cups firmly packed raw natural sugar
1 cup cider vinegar
1/2 to 1 dried red chili pepper, seeded and crushed
1 2-inch stick cinnamon, broken
1 tablespoon mustard seed
Cook, stirring occasionally, 1 hour or until fruits are soft and liquid has thickened. Last 10 minutes of cooking time, add:
3/4 cup coarsely chopped walnuts
Immediately pack into hot sterilized jars, filling within 1/4 inch from top, and seal according to directions on lid box. Store in dark place.
Makes approximately 4 half pints

FRUIT COMPOTE

Combine and simmer 2 to 3 minutes just to soften:
2 cups chopped or sliced fresh fruit or whole berries
2 tablespoons mild honey, or to taste
1 to 1-1/2 tablespoons fresh lemon or orange juice
1 1-inch stick cinnamon
2 whole cloves
1/8 to 1/4 teaspoon grated fresh vanilla bean
Fruit or berries should retain their shape, so do not overcook.
Makes approximately 2 cups

FRUIT SAUCE

Cook fruit as above 5 to 7 minutes; for smooth consistency mash with fork or back of wooden spoon. Serve warm on griddle cakes, waffles or French toast.

ONCE-A-WEEK JAM

Omit lemon or orange juice in Fruit Compote. When fruits are soft add:
1 teaspoon unflavored gelatin, soaked to soften in
1 tablespoon fresh lemon or orange juice
Cool and refrigerate.

HONEY-FRUIT JUICE SYRUPS

Combine in saucepan and simmer gently uncovered 20 minutes or until reduced to 1 cup:
1/2 cup heated honey
1-1/2 cups unsweetened fruit juice (orange, grape, apple, apricot)
1 to 2 tablespoons fresh lemon juice
Serve warm on pancakes, waffles or French toast. Or cool and refrigerate up to 1 week.
Makes 1 cup

CARROT COCONUT RELISH

Sprinkle with:
pinch sweet Hungarian paprika
1/3 cup grated fresh or unsweetened coconut
Combine coconut with:
1/2 carrot, grated
1 small apple, grated
1-1/2 teaspoons fresh lemon juice
1/4 teaspoon ground ginger or cinnamon (optional)
1/3 cup plain yoghurt
Serve chilled as accompaniment to rice meals.
Makes approximately 1 cup

GARNISHES

For color, eye appeal and flavor, choose garnishes that complement hot or cold dishes.

- parsley, chervil, mint, watercress, rosemary sprigs
- fennel or dill feathers
- minced herbs, celery leaves
- chicory or other curly-leaf lettuce
- chopped or sieved hard-cooked eggs
- sliced olives
- croutons
- carrot or celery curls
- lemon, lime or orange slices
- lemon, lime or orange peel curls
- sliced radishes or radish flowers
- finely grated carrot, citrus peel
- grated or shredded cheese
- paprika, freshly ground nutmeg, freshly ground pepper

BASIC METHOD FOR STEAMED DISHES

Steaming foods in the dish in which they are served is an ideal way to prepare an easy meal which can be ready ahead of time and simply removed from the refrigerator and steamed while preparing the vegetable or salad accompaniment. An Oriental bamboo steamer placed in a wok with water is not necessary; nor is a special aluminum steamer. Use a rack, an inverted Pyrex dish or a tuna fish can with both ends removed.

The kettle must be large enough to hold the dish and to allow room for easy removal of the dish from the kettle. Fill the kettle with water to 1 inch above rack, but not more than halfway up the sides of the dish; wrap kettle lid in tea towel to prevent condensation drops from accumulating and place lid on kettle. Bring to boil, lower heat and keep water boiling gently amount of time specified in recipe. Start timing after water has come to steam and add water, if necessary, to keep original amount.

WHOLE-WHEAT PASTRY

For quiches, pot pies, fruit pies.

Blend together:
1/3 cup each whole wheat and unbleached white flour
1/4 teaspoon salt
Cut in with pastry cutter or 2 knives until the size of small peas:
4 tablespoons cold butter, cut into bits
Add:
2-1/2 tablespoons ice water
Work mixture with one hand on side of bowl until water is incorporated and dough forms into ball, kneading lightly to distribute butter evenly. Dust with whole-wheat flour and wrap in waxed paper. Chill for at least 1 hour. Roll out dough on lightly floured board into 10-inch diameter round. Fit into buttered 7-1/2-inch pie pan (preferably Pyrex). Turn uneven edges under and flute.

Basics

PLANNING AND SHOPPING

The major problem with shopping for two is buying too much food rather than too little. It is important to plan and shop carefully to eliminate an excess of leftovers which could result in waste and food spoilage. This will save both time and money. Plan a weekly menu and accordingly a weekly shopping list. It is important to note that appetites do vary and the amounts you buy will depend on your personal needs.

Some staples should always be kept on hand. Other ingredients should be bought as you need them for your weekly menu.

Plan 2 or 3 meals each week that can be partially prepared ahead, and perhaps an omelet or soup meal to use cooked or fresh foods left in the refrigerator at the end of the week. When planning menus, choose only one dish per meal that requires constant attention while cooking. Consider complementary flavor, color and texture combinations within a meal, keeping in mind that presentation is important to the enjoyment of a meal.

STORING AND FREEZING

• Always cool foods to room temperature before covering and refrigerating. Use within 3 to 4 days.
• Do not keep uncooked fish longer than 1 day, meat longer than 3 days. Do not wrap tightly; allow air circulation.
• Store cheese well wrapped in plastic in refrigerator. If mold spots develop, cut them out; rest of cheese is edible. Cheeses such as cream and cottage cheese do not keep well after opening. Use within 1 week.
• If keeping for long periods, store wheat germ, millet, health cereals, whole-grain flours and flours such as soy and garbanzo in airtight containers under refrigeration.
• If buying brown rice in bulk, store in cool place or refrigerator.

• Fresh herbs such as parsley and basil keep up to 3 days if stalks are immersed in water; change water each day. They may also be washed, dried and wrapped in a towel and refrigerated in plastic bag up to 1 week.
• Do not wash vegetables until ready to use. Store in plastic bags in crisper of refrigerator.
• Do not freeze seafood.
• Do not freeze ham more than 1 week. Meat and poultry, if well wrapped, may be kept frozen up to 1 month.
• Store onions and potatoes in cool, dark place. Wrap and refrigerate partially used onions.
• Underripe fruits, especially avocados, should be allowed to ripen at room temperature before refrigerating. Do not refrigerate bananas.
• Store dried herbs in dark place away from heat of stove. Dried herbs lose flavor if kept too long, so do not buy in large quantities.
• Store dried fruits such as prunes, apricots, peaches and apples in plastic bag at room temperature; figs and dates in refrigerator.
• Store nuts in refrigerator if not using within 1 week.

UTENSILS

Basic Utensils
1 large cast-iron skillet (12-inch)
1 large stainless-steel skillet
   with tight lid
1 6- or 7-inch pan for crêpes,
   omelets, etc.
1 large heavy pot (Dutch oven)
   for soup, pasta (6 quart)
2 medium-size saucepans with
   tight lids for vegetables
1 small saucepan for melting
   butter
1 roasting pan
1 1- or 1-1/2-quart ceramic
   casserole dish with lid
4 individual 4-inch soufflé dishes
   or custard cups
1 shallow baking dish
1 shallow heatproof ceramic
   serving bowl for steamed dishes

2 loaf pans
2 cookie sheets
1 muffin tin
1 small pie, quiche or flan pan
1 colander
1 strainer
1 rack for roasting pan, steaming,
   cooling bread, etc.
1 collapsible steaming rack
wire whisk
asbestos pad
set of wooden spoons of
   various sizes
spatula
slotted spatula and/or spoon
large fork
chopsticks and/or tongs
skewers
knives for cutting vegetables,
   meat, paring, tomatoes
   (serrated), bread, carving, etc.
soup ladle
3 mixing bowls
mortar and pestle (wood is best)
French Mouli grater with 3 blades
   or comparable flat grater
rolling pin
pastry brush
2 sets measuring cups and spoons
hand juicer for lemon, orange
   juice
flour sifter
large cutting board
nutmeg grater

Optional Utensils
cake pans
wok
8- or 9-inch cast-iron skillet
double boiler
1 1- or 1-1/2 quart soufflé dish
2 5- or 6-inch ramekins
waffle iron
blender
old-fashioned meat grinder
meat pounder
extra cutting board
oven thermometer and cooking
   thermometer
funnel
ricer or food mill
citrus peel grater
nut grinder or equivalent chopper
vegetable brush

Glossary
and Index

GLOSSARY OF TERMS AND GENERAL HINTS

Al dente: Cooked until tender but still firm.

Bean curd: Made from puréed soybeans, then formed into 2-inch squares, 1 inch thick. Available in soft or firm cakes in Oriental stores and many supermarkets.

Bind: Thicken gravy juices; see Gravies.

Blanch: Place nuts in boiling water until skins loosen. Drop vegetables into boiling water for specified time, drain and rinse in cold water to prevent further cooking.

Bruise: Lightly smash garlic clove with blade of large knife. Peel will come off easily and essence of garlic will be released.

Carob: The carob bean is the fruit of the honey locust. Carob powder can be used in cooking and/or baking as a substitute for chocolate. Three tablespoons carob powder plus 2 tablespoons milk or water are equivalent to a 1-ounce square of chocolate. Carob is also available in chunks, bits, granules for carob drink, and syrup.

Cheese: To avoid chemical additives and preservatives, buy only natural cheeses. These are available in cheese stores, delicatessens and some supermarkets. Grate dry cheeses or grate or shred semi-dry cheese just before using. Freeze grated cheese in airtight container up to 1 week.

Chili oil: Oil used in place of Tabasco sauce or as a condiment for those who like spicy, hot food. Heat 1/4 cup peanut oil and add 1/2 teaspoon crumbled dried red chili pepper. Cool and jar. Chili oil is available in Oriental stores and some supermarkets.

Coconut, grated: To grate coconut, break open ripe coconut, pour off liquid and bake in 375° oven for about 15 minutes. Cut meat away from shell, pare off brown outer skin with small sharp knife and grate the coconut meat with a hand grater. Unsweetened grated coconut is available at health and natural foods stores and some supermarkets.

Coconut milk: Combine equal amounts of unsweetened grated coconut and milk (or water) and bring just to boil. Cool and sieve, pressing out as much liquid as possible. Repeat process with pulp for less concentrated milk.

Curry powder: May consist of a combination of as few as 5 or as many as 50 spices. The strength of the curry depends upon the amount of red chili or cayenne pepper used. The principal ingredients of curry powder are turmeric, coriander, fenugreek, cumin, cardamom, cloves, allspice, mace, bay leaf, ginger, cayenne pepper or crumbled dried red chili peppers, nutmeg, anise, cinnamon, garlic and mustard seed. For Aromatic Curry Mixture, see page 172.

Date sugar: Made from dried dates and used for sweetening uncooked and baked dishes. Pit dried dates and let harden uncovered in cool place until completely dried. Grind in blender or grain mill and use to sweeten cooked cereals, muesli, plain yoghurt or fruit salads.

Glossary

Deglaze: Pour water, stock or wine into skillet juices over high heat and scrape up bits left in skillet after sautéing.

Eggs: All recipes call for grade A large eggs.

Garlic olive oil: Add 1 bruised garlic clove to 1 cup olive oil. Let stand at least 2 days. If not using within 10 days, discard garlic clove. Use oil when subtle garlic flavor is desired.

Herb salt: A blend of salt and herbs (see page 172). Vege-Sal available in health or natural food stores, is an excellent substitute.

Herbs: Fresh are preferred. When using dried, cut measurement for fresh down by one-third.

Honey: When possible, use raw unfiltered honey. Some honeys have a distinct flavor (orange, eucalyptus, wild flower); when mild honey is specified, it is best to use clover. When a recipe calls for both oil and honey, measure the oil first so that the cup or spoon is coated and the honey will flow easily from it.

Julienne-cut: Vegetables and meats cut in matchstick pieces.

Marinate: To let stand in seasoned liquid to tenderize and add flavor. Never use a metal container when marinating.

Miso: Highly nutritious soybean paste made from soybeans, barley water, sea salt and fermented rice. Used mainly in salad dressings and soups.

Mushrooms, dried forest: Available in Oriental stores and some supermarkets. Cepes or other dried mushrooms may be substituted, but flavor is not as strong. Soften in warm water to cover; reserve soaking water for recipe or for soups or gravies.

Nuts, ground: Use hand nut grinder. Do not use blender, as the oil will be lost and the nuts will turn to paste.

Oils: With the exception of Planter's peanut oil and olive oil, most oils commercially available in supermarkets contain preservatives. Pure oils can be purchased unrefined and cold pressed in health and natural food stores and some supermarkets. Corn, peanut, safflower, walnut and olive oils are the ones most often used in this book.

Oriental sesame oil: Sesame oil extract available in Oriental stores and some supermarkets.

Paprika: Sweet Hungarian paprika is used in most recipes calling for paprika in this book. Available in bulk in specialty stores. For garnishing, domestic paprika may be used.

Peppercorns: White or black peppercorns have more flavor if freshly ground into cooked dishes or at table.

Plump: To plump raisins or other dried fruits, soak in warm water to cover for 10 minutes or until soft.

Pyrex baking dishes: When using Pyrex dishes, lower oven heat 25 degrees.

Render fat: Chicken, ham, pork or beef fat may be minced and cooked over medium heat to melt. Cool, pour into container and refrigerate or freeze. Use rendered fat for sautéing. Pure pork lard may be made by boiling minced pork fat back in water until soft. Push softened fat through strainer, return to water and jar. Refrigerate; the pure lard will rise to surface. Use for baking or sautéing.

Scald: To scald milk, heat slowly to just below boiling point until skin starts to form on surface of milk. Do not boil.

Sea salt: An unrefined salt that is solar evaporated and then briefly kiln dried. It is high in trace minerals, not just sodium chloride and synthetic iodine, the major ingredients of common table salt.

Sesame oil, Oriental: See Oriental sesame oil.

Sesame seeds, unhulled: Superior to hulled variety because of the high mineral content in hulls. Available in health and natural food stores.

Soy sauce: See Tamari soy sauce.

Spices: Whenever possible grind spice seeds such as cardamom, coriander, anise and cloves in mortar and pestle just before using.

Sugar, raw natural: The raw sugar sold in this country is actually "partially refined" sugar. It does, however, retain more of the natural nutrients of sugarcane than white or brown sugar (white sugar with molasses added for color), and for that reason is preferred over them. It is also free of chemicals designed to make it free-flowing. Use raw unfiltered honey in place of sugar when possible.

Tamari soy sauce: Soy sauce is made from a naturally fermented mixture of soybeans, wheat, sea salt and water. Tamari soy sauce and some Japanese brands contain no chemical additives and/or preservatives and are slightly saltier than other brands. Store in cool place.

Toasting and browning: See page 173.

Vanilla bean, fresh: Granules scraped from inside of bean can be used in cooking and baking; the flavor is far superior to that of vanilla extract. The bean pod can be used whole for flavor in cooking. For 1/16 teaspoon grated fresh vanilla bean, substitute 1/4 to 1/2 teaspoon vanilla extract. Wrap bean well in foil and store in cool dry place.

Wheat germ: Toasted wheat germ is preferred in cooked and baked dishes for its crunchy texture and toasty flavor. In uncooked dishes, use raw wheat germ for the added B and E vitamins.

Index

Index

184

Index

Index

Index

BIOGRAPHICAL DATA

Coralie Castle and Astrid Newton both base their culinary backgrounds on a European heritage and extensive travel abroad. Ms. Newton was born in Germany, raised in Canada and the United States, and presently teaches English in West Berlin while working towards a masters' degree at the Free University there. Ms. Castle, though raised in Illinois, learned to cook in the continental kitchen of her German-born parents; widened her knowledge of ethnic cuisines through many years of dining-out in the cosmopolitan San Francisco Bay Area where she now lives; and broadens her recipe file through annual trips to Europe. Coralie Castle is also the author or co-author of four other 101 Productions cookbooks: *Soup; Country Cookery of Many Lands; The Edible, Ornamental Garden;* and *Hors d'Oeuvre, Etc.*

Sara Raffetto, whose drawings grace these pages, studied art at the University of California at Berkeley, later in Los Angeles with Rico LeBrun, and spent two years in Florence, Italy, on a Fulbright fellowship to study painting. She also has illustrated three other 101 books: *The Wine Bibber's Bible; Vegetarian Gourmet Cookery;* and *The Food Conspiracy Cookbook.*